10/04

$25.00

Family Matters

Robert Evans

· ·

Family Matters

· ·

How Schools Can Cope with the Crisis in Childrearing

JOSSEY-BASS
A Wiley Company
www.josseybass.com

Published by Jossey-Bass
A Wiley Imprint
989 Market Street, San Francisco, CA 94103–1741   www.josseybass.com

Jossey-Bass books and products are available through most bookstores. To contact
Jossey-Bass directly call our Customer Care Department within the U.S. at 800-956-7739,
outside the U.S. at 317-572-3986, or fax 317-572-4002.

Jossey-Bass also publishes its books in a variety of electronic formats. Some content that
appears in print may not be available in electronic books.

Library of Congress Cataloging-in-Publication Data
Evans, Robert, 1944-
  Family matters : how schools can cope with the crisis in childrearing /
Robert Evans.—1st ed.
      p. cm. — (The Jossey-Bass education series)
  Includes bibliographical references and index.
  ISBN 0-7879-6656-8 (alk. paper)
  1. Child rearing—United States. 2. Home and school—United States.
  3. Children—United States—Social conditions. I. Title. II. Series.
  LC225.3.E83 2004
  649'.1—dc22   2004000406

Printed in the United States of America
FIRST EDITION
HB Printing   10 9 8 7 6 5 4 3

The Jossey-Bass Education Series

· ·

Contents

• •

Introduction   xi

About the Author   xxi

Part One. The Changing Context of Child Development

1. "Something's Gone Way Wrong"   3
2. The Building Blocks of Healthy Growth   17
3. Back to Basics: A Parenting Primer   39
4. Fast Forward: The Fragile Family   57
5. Losing Connection   67
6. Abandoning Authority   81
7. Building Résumés   97
8. The New Insecurity   113
9. The New Individualism   127

Part Two. Limits and Leverage: Real-Life Coping for Schools

10. Rethinking Accountability   143
11. What Makes Us, Us: Clarifying Purpose and Conduct   159

12. Redefining the Home-School Partnership   177

13. Resistance and Leadership: Building
     Faculty Will   191

14. Parenting Parents: Building Faculty Skill   207

15. Paradox, Realism, and Hope   223

     Appendix: Practical Parent Education   231

     Notes   249

     References   263

     Acknowledgments   279

     Index   281

Introduction

Contrary to most of what you could have read about education over the past twenty-five years, we do not have a crisis in schooling. We have something much worse: a crisis in childrearing. At a time when the requirements for successful adulthood have risen steeply, the supports vital to child development are in sharp decline. The symptoms of this crisis—an accelerating deterioration in the civility, values, work ethic, and academic achievement of many youth—appear most vividly at school, and so the crisis is often seen as educational, but it begins well before school and extends well beyond it. Schools, even those that serve their students poorly, are much more its victims than its perpetrators. Its immediate cause lies at home with parents, who are suffering a widespread loss of confidence and competence. Its deeper causes are economic and cultural—changes in the way we work and in our national values that undermine the developmental mission of families and schools alike.

For educators, the widespread misinterpretation of the crisis as caused by schools is doubly difficult—factors beyond their control make their work more and more challenging, yet at almost every turn they are told the fault is theirs; if only they worked harder and better, it would all go away. But it won't go away. Teachers, administrators, policymakers—indeed, all who are involved in the enterprise of schooling—need to understand the crisis in its broad context and rethink its implications. This book offers a diagnosis of its most troubling symptoms, argues that these call for redefining our notions of school accountability, and proposes new ways for schools to cope and to help their families cope.

The perspective I apply is not new, but it is increasingly rare. In the lengthy debate about school improvement, most combatants, despite their sharp differences, have long shared a single lens, one that focusses on the school as an institution, asking how it can better serve students. This viewpoint is vital—we can't improve schooling without it—but used alone, it distorts. It exaggerates the school's influence. It leads conservative and liberal reformers alike to treat a child's education as though it consists almost entirely of formal schooling and to minimize the enormous impact on students of the living and learning they do outside of school.

In this book I adopt an older lens, one that focusses on students as they present themselves at school, asking what conditions at home and elsewhere are necessary to permit the school to serve them better. To see schools right we need both perspectives, but this one deserves primacy. It is crucial to situating schooling in its true context in a child's growing up and understanding the actualities of school life, and thus to establishing realistic expectations for educators' performance and designing realistic strategies for them as they respond to their students and parents.

The key problems I explore are also not new—and they don't encourage easy optimism. Most are widely discussed. But though they cause much head shaking, they are rarely taken seriously enough—rarely acted upon in a sustained way, rarely factored into the expectations of educators or the mandates of legislators and policymakers. To take their full measure is to see that the obstacles to children's development—and the challenges facing their teachers—are deep and complex, so embedded in psychological, economic, and cultural realities that they have no easy answers. There is simply no avoiding the fact that far too many children are growing up with too few of the essentials that nourish healthy psychosocial growth. Although the deficits occur widely, my focus in this book is on the broad swath of middle-class American youth. (The urban poor, especially those who are black and Hispanic, face some unique issues. Much of what I have to say applies to young people from these groups, but not all, and some of the issues that are significant in their lives I do not address—not because they are unimportant but because they have rightly been a focus of concern and attention by a number of writers.) The evidence is that too few parents now feel a primary responsibility for meeting their children's emotional needs and teaching them the habits and values vital to successful adulthood; their abdication is often startling and disturbing. And too many parents who do still accept this responsibility have lost confidence in their ability to fulfill it as rapid social, technological, and economic changes have combined to disempower them.[1]

Like parents, educators also contend with the impact on children of these changes, but they suffer doubly. In their direct work with students they face the same external challenges as parents but they also confront an additional dilemma: the decline of the supports parents themselves have traditionally provided to students and to the school. This decline is perhaps the most complex of all the many issues confronting schools today, because it affects their ability to cope with all the others; it intrudes on virtually everything they try to do. Even as they are pressed to innovate, to accelerate academic performance, and to prepare students for the demands of a high-tech, globalized, multicultural world, they find themselves struggling to fill more gaps of the most basic kind. More and more children arrive at school less ready to learn—not less intelligent; less ready to be students.

Teachers in all sorts of schools face a decline in fundamentals they used to take for granted: attendance, attention, courtesy, industry, motivation, responsibility. At the ordinary, everyday end of today's spectrum, students are more difficult to reach and teach, their concentration and perseverance more fragile, their language and behavior more provocative. At the catastrophic end lie student killing sprees like the infamous one at Columbine High School in 1999. And in their relationships with parents schools find themselves unable to take for granted the shared understandings and mutual responsibility on which they have long counted. Indeed, shifts in the attitudes and behavior of parents often cause more concern among teachers than those of students. Struggling to cope, schools have chosen and have been forced to undertake developmental tasks that have always been the province of families, tasks that lie on the fringes of—and, often, beyond—their capacity. The toll on morale is high; anyone who travels widely among teachers and administrators across the country can easily find a growing sense of frustration and futility, even in the best of schools.

To be sure, schools contribute problems of their own. Too many are doing badly by their students. The worst have dilapidated buildings, ancient textbooks, teachers and administrators who are unqualified or burnt-out (or both), and a resistant union. Even the best, say many critics, offer much mediocre teaching. Reformers have long argued about what's gone wrong and how to fix it, but their arguments have focussed almost exclusively on the educational system, seeing the school as both cause and cure. Educators have been widely blamed for their legitimate shortcomings and for others well beyond their reach. There is no doubt that many of our schools need significant improvement, but most of a child's learning occurs outside of school and what has deteriorated most is not the skills of teachers but the lives of children. School improvement, alone, will never be enough.

This doesn't mean schools are helpless or without influence or that they should be absolved of responsibility. Far from it. It means they need to rethink the ways they have been addressing the changing nature of students and parents. This will not be a matter of simply improving their traditional efforts—better communication, stricter rules, more preventive programs for students, more evening lectures for parents—but of fundamentally reshaping the experience of membership in the school community and the relationship between the school and the family.

Plan of The Book

To make this case the book is divided into two parts. Part One examines the remarkable changing context of child development that has so affected students' school- readiness. It spends much time outside of schools, because so many of the problems that challenge educators are rooted there, but it notes throughout the direct and indirect ways these problems manifest themselves at school. It begins with an overview of the crisis in childrearing as seen from the schoolhouse, a sampling of its symptoms among students and parents (Chapter One). Then, to provide a framework for understanding these and responding to them, it outlines the essentials of healthy child development and effective parenting and traces the evidence, impact, and key sources of their decline. To thrive in our society, children must grow up with adequate levels of nurture, structure, and latitude (Chapter Two), which are best provided by authoritative parents whose childrearing is sufficiently strong on all three of these dimensions (Chapter Three). Unfortunately, the family is increasingly fragile, and, as a context for childrearing and school-readiness, functions much less developmentally than in the past (Chapter Four). Many parents are now less inclined and less able to provide nurture, structure, and latitude (Chapters Five, Six, and Seven). This is not because they have willfully chosen to deprive their children but in part because longstanding economic and cultural trends have accelerated in ways that intensify their insecurity and self-concern, putting unprecedented pressure on family life and parenting (Chapters Eight and Nine).

Part Two focusses on what schools can do in response. It begins by looking at what they *can't* do—at the inherent limits on their influence on students and parents—and then concentrates on ways they can maximize the leverage they do have. The immediate implication of the evidence reviewed in Part One is that we must modify our notion of educational accountability, acknowledging a smaller role for the school and a larger role for the family than we currently do (Chapter Ten). Such a change in perspective counters both conventional wisdom and current policy; schools cannot simply wait for it to be widely embraced, since this is unlikely to happen any time soon. To cope, they must start by thinking strategically and restructuring their relationships with families. This begins with a systematic effort to build and sustain consensus throughout the school community about two key facets of school life: purpose and conduct—the core values that truly animate the school and the basic responsibilities expected of all its participants (Chapter Eleven). Educators must see the home-school partnership less as one of equally informed parties and more as one in which schools need to parent both students and parents (Chapter Twelve). These measures promise to reduce problem behavior and improve the climate for learning, but they represent new challenges for teachers and are likely to raise anxiety and resistance. To help build faculty will to undertake them and skill at implementing them requires effective leadership (Chapter Thirteen) and realistic, useful training (Chapter Fourteen). The book closes with a reflection on ways to sustain hope and commitment in the face of unprecedented challenge.

For most readers, it will be most productive to read the book from front to back. Those who find they are already familiar enough with the themes in Part One or who are impatient to know how schools can respond to changing families may prefer to go straight to Part Two. It refers back to the chapters in Part One whenever this would be particularly relevant, allowing readers to return to these as necessary to supplement understanding and to find the basis for the arguments and proposals I advance in Part Two.

A Special Caveat

A book like this runs a risk of scapegoating parents, of wallowing in nostalgia for the past and exaggerating concerns about the present. I have much to say about contemporary parenting that is critical, but I have no illusions about returning to the supposedly good old days. This is not just impossible, it would prove intolerable. And the problems I address, though ominous and intensifying, are not yet entrenched norms. In many families, child development still unfolds in a healthy, constructive way. In most schools, it is the trends that are worrisome; the majority—often a large majority—of students and parents are still positive participants and the general tenor of the home-school relationship is still cooperative and respectful. Most importantly, we cannot grasp the crisis in childrearing or think clearly about how schools can respond if we simply blame parents without considering the challenges they face raising children.

There is no harder job. No paid work taxes more of a person in more diverse, intense, surprising ways than parenting does. Many jobs share some of its requirements—sensitivity and patience, long hours and repetitive drudgery, emotional drain. Only parenting demands all of these. Only parenting touches so much of a person's deep self. And with such immediacy. Though it stretches over many years and stirs the most powerful and primitive feelings, it occurs in interactions that are spontaneous, instinctive, improvised. Experts can catalog its key skills, but none of us, when we are with our children, can be such a catalog. We can think about it planfully when we read an expert's book, but we can rarely *do it planfully in the moment*. Then we must deal whole person to whole person. We react, and so do our children, and these reactions are affected by a host of factors, from personality and family dynamics to cultural customs and economic conditions.

Most of this has always been true, and yet parents managed for thousands of years even though they had much less control over their own life circumstances than we do today and no professionals to advise them. But in the twenty-first century, despite all our advances and expertise—indeed, *because* of some of our advances and expertise—raising children is more complex than it is has ever been. Parents are finding it more difficult than ever to provide the basics of healthy child development. They are overwhelmed and undermined, caught between rising expectations and rising fears about the future, weakened by economic and social changes. Life at all levels has been transformed around families and within them. The ever-escalating pace of change that brings unprecedented opportunities also invalidates traditional certainties, the continuity on which childrearing has always depended.

Few human tasks are more conservative, more traditional than raising the young. For almost all of human history growing up has been marked by relatively low opportunity and relatively high predictability. A young person's occupational, marital, and lifestyle options have typically been quite limited, which, in turn, has helped adults to know how to prepare him or her. But in the developed world, especially in the United States, we have hugely expanded children's life options. This has made it much harder to know what they will need to know and how they'll need to function if they are to make both a living and a life. At the same time, the demands of the workplace and our obsession with wealth and individual fulfillment have drawn parents, by necessity and choice, away from home and children, and helped to sever generational and community connections. In such a context, how are parents to foster caring, character, and competence in the young? To ready them for a nearly-impossible-to-predict future? To counter the media influences that undermine their values? To balance their own lives so as to spend enough time with the kids? How *would* one feel confident and competent about childrearing?

In thirty-five years of working with parents and educators I have never seen such anxiety and uncertainty among the former or such concern and frustration among the latter, much of it about the fundamentals of child development. And although the symptoms and issues I explore are not yet the norm, they are not just isolated outliers, either. They are the leading edge of a spreading shift among students and parents. There are among parents many more problems of being overwhelmed than of being unconcerned, and of bad judgment than of bad faith, but this is not to say that, collectively, we are doing right by our children. On the contrary, we are abandoning the essentials of sound maturation and in the process creating enormous problems for our schools—to our peril. The noted psychiatrist James Comer contends that our society is unlikely to thrive for long in "conditions that require exceptional performance from large numbers of people who have not had reasonably adequate developmental experiences."[2] A full failure to thrive may not be imminent, but the evidence is unmistakable that the number of children lacking adequate development is growing rapidly.

The Commission on Children at Risk, a group of eminent physicians, neuroscientists, social scientists, and mental health professionals, recently concluded that "basic foundations of childhood in America [are] at best anemic. . .and at worst toxic."[3] The long-term implications are truly dangerous, not just for our schools but for our society. To respond successfully, we must think anew about what our children need and what our schools can do. I hope the pages that follow will help us do both.

About the Author

Robert Evans is a clinical and organizational psychologist and the executive director of The Human Relations Service, in Wellesley, Massachusetts. A former high school and preschool teacher, and a former child and family therapist, he has consulted in hundreds of public and private schools throughout the United States and internationally, working with teachers, administrators, boards, and parents. His interests have focused on school change and resistance to it, on leadership, and on changes in families and their effect on schools. He is the author of many articles and a book, *The Human Side of School Change*. He lives in suburban Boston with his wife, Paula; they have two sons.

To my family

Part One

. . . .

The Changing Context
of Child Development

1

"Something's Gone Way Wrong"

By the time high school students cross the stage to receive their diplomas, they have spent barely 10 percent of their lives in school. School may have been their activity center—the place where they have gathered, made friends, worked, and played. And as the commencement speaker suggests, school may have developed skills and awakened interests that prove lifelong—perhaps even life-shaping—for some graduates; we should never underestimate the potential of a teacher to affect a student. But nine-hundred-plus hours of schooling per year, spread over thirteen of a graduate's eighteen years of life, offer a relatively small window for influence. Indeed, by the time they finish school, typical seniors have been spending three hours in front of the television for every two in class. For quite a while, it has been clear that the impact on students of their many thousands of nonschool hours are complicating and undermining the efforts of teachers. I thought I knew this, but I rediscovered it vividly when I had to go back to dance duty.

For the entire thirty years after I left teaching I didn't have to chaperone a high school dance; I never missed it once. Then my wife became a high school principal, and I found myself on dance duty again. My first event was the "Semi-formal." It was breathtaking. It could have been the *Semi-nude*, given the tiny, tight tops and tiny, tight skirts the girls wore—two postage stamps connected by a kite string, a matching shiny loincloth. It could have been the

Semi-safe sex, given the dancing the students did—safe only because they were not actually naked and not actually having intercourse; they just looked like they were. They were freak dancing. If you haven't seen this, you ought to. It's just what the Baptists have always said dancing would lead to. Here's how one reporter described it:

> It looks like sex, but it's dancing. . . . A girl might be on all fours, with one boy's pelvis pressed into her face and another's pressed into her bottom. [School officials] see boys on their backs with girls spread-eagled over them; girls bent forward with boys' hips thrust into their backsides. Students know it by different names in different towns: freaking, grinding, jacking, booty dancing, the nasty. . . . Articles of clothing sometimes come off.[1]

I felt like a dinosaur.

I wasn't alone. A teacher, surveying the dance floor, said, "Every time I see this, I can't help thinking that something's gone way wrong." As we talked, I remembered myself as a new teacher in the late 1960s. Back then, I had dismissed the dinosaurs of that era who thought miniskirts and long hair and the way teenagers (and we young adults) danced were signs of decadence; I had been sure I'd never become one. Watching the dancers, I reminded myself that the waltz was scandalously sexual when it was introduced in the early nineteenth century; so was Elvis Presley wiggling his hips in the 1950s. Today, of course, the waltz is a relic and Elvis is easy listening. The new and dangerous inevitably become old and quaint; radicals inevitably become dinosaurs. And yet, something really does seem different about many aspects of child and adolescent behavior today. It is hard to imagine a world in which freak dancing turns out to be as comparatively staid as Elvis now is, let alone the waltz. I haven't met an adult who can watch it without feeling that something has gone way wrong.

Freak dancing, by itself, is not a perfect symbol for America's youth—the top students in most schools perform at levels far higher than anyone could have predicted back when Elvis was the rage— but it's an accurate one. To the professionals who teach and treat children, the idea that something has gone way wrong isn't just an occasional observation to be made at school dances; it's a constant, gnawing certainty, visible in a host of symptoms, not all as vivid as freak dancing but many more important and more worrisome. Teachers, child care workers, pediatricians, and human service providers are, as John D'Auria, principal of the middle school in Wellesley, Massachusetts, notes, our nation's seismographs; they register the tremors of social trouble early and keenly.[2] For some time now, there has been broad agreement among them that far too many of America's young people are showing steep declines in their performance, behavior, and values. In 1990, a special commission cosponsored by the American Medical Association concluded that for the first time in American history children were "less healthy, less cared for, [and] less prepared for life than their parents were at the same age."[3] In 2003, the Commission on Children at Risk confirmed this trend, pointing to "high and rising rates of depression, anxiety, attention deficit, conduct disorders," as well as suicide.[4] The public at large shares the professionals' concern, though from a different perspective. In survey after survey, two-thirds of Americans, when asked what comes to mind when they think about teenagers, choose adjectives like *rude, irresponsible,* and *wild*; for younger children they choose *lacking discipline* and *spoiled*. Forty-one percent complain that teenagers have poor work habits; nearly 90 percent feel that it is rare for youth to treat people with respect.[5]

To most child development professionals and to much of the general public, the immediate cause of these declines lies with parents. Large proportions of those surveyed say it is very common for parents to have children before they are ready to take responsibility for them, that they are far too permissive and have let standards slip, and that they no longer teach children good moral values.

Interestingly, parents themselves agree with these critiques. Fewer than 20 percent of them think it's very common for their fellow parents to be good role models and teach children right from wrong. Half feel it is routine for their peers to equate buying things for children with caring for them, and most say that couples divorce too easily, without regard for their offspring, and fail to discipline them sufficiently. It is easy to engage almost anyone in discussions that move in these directions. Of course, public opinion surveys are suggestive but not conclusive. They often tell us what the conventional wisdom is, not more. In this case, however, we have reason for real worry; the conventional wisdom is on target. Virtually anyone can confirm in the course of ordinary daily living the evidence of deterioration in the behavior and attitudes of young people and their parents. The clearest proof is found at school.

Over the past ten years I have spoken with educators from several thousand schools across the country—public and private, elementary and secondary, urban and suburban, large and small, rich and poor—and have visited nearly six hundred schools myself. Without exception, teachers and principals report that students are harder to reach and teach, their attention and motivation harder to sustain, their language and behavior more provocative—and at ever earlier ages. They also note that parents are increasingly anxious about their children's success, yet increasingly unavailable to support and guide them, and increasingly distrustful and critical of the school.

"It's an utterly different world," a high school headmaster recently said. "We're seeing more performance and conduct problems than ever before, and more of the exceptionally serious kind. We can't keep up with parents' relentless expectations and we can't get used to their inability to engage with their kids and to set clear limits on them." When asked why he and his teachers didn't set clearer limits on behavior themselves—he had been complaining not just about students freak dancing but about them making out in the corridors and trashing the cafeteria—he shook his head. "We do try," he said, "though in all honesty, not as hard as we used to, largely because the parents almost never back us up."

From the schoolhouse, the crisis looms as two pyramids: the first of children, the second of parents. At the very top of each the problems are the most dramatic but rarest; lower down they become less intense and more common. We begin with children.

Pyramids of Problems: Children

The peak of the child pyramid is occupied by acts of violence that, although truly exceptional, are the extreme examples of a much broader pattern of problem behavior. When I first began this chapter, four consecutive years had been marked by eruptions of school murders that at first stunned the nation—episodes in Alaska, Arkansas, California, Colorado, Florida, Kentucky, Mississippi, Oregon, and Pennsylvania in which students, some of them not yet teenagers, shot and killed teachers and schoolmates, sometimes in large numbers. The preceding decade had seen much publicity and concern about acts of lethal violence by urban youth, such as drive-by shootings and gang assaults. Although the nation's crime rates have dropped noticeably, episodes of school violence continue. As I was revising the chapter, students in Arizona, California, Maryland, Minnesota, and Washington killed or seriously wounded fellow students at school. By some estimates more than 135,000 students bring a gun to school each day. More than 125,000 teachers are attacked physically by students each year. Some urban high schools now start very early in the morning and dismiss early in the afternoon without serving lunch because students are too unruly in the cafeteria to be controlled. And many high schools I visit report more outbreaks of fighting both among competing teams and among spectators (notably parents) in sports from boys' football to girls' volleyball—fighting that sometimes results in serious injury and even, occasionally, in death.

Less extreme but far more extensive is an accelerating trend toward behavior that, though not violent, is antisocial. Here are a few episodes cited by educators at schools I've recently visited:

- Third graders scrawl graffiti on the walls of the school's main hallway.

- Sixth graders break into the school office, photocopy classmates' report cards, and distribute them at a party.

- Ninth graders pursue a year-long, organized, carefully planned scheme of cheating on tests and exams.

- Tenth graders create a Web site devoted to attacks on a teacher, accusing her, among other things, of having sex with various colleagues; later they attack individual students in the same way, inviting visitors to post their own derogatory remarks about the victims.

- Eleventh-grade boys download hundreds of pornographic pictures from the Internet onto computers in the school library.

- Seniors at one school publish a "scum sheet" accusing some classmates of drug abuse and ridiculing the appearance, race, and religion of others; seniors at another school use a new technology lab to produce sophisticated counterfeit $20 bills.

- Students at a boarding school secretly videotape a boy and a girl having sex in a dorm room, use their computers to copy the tape onto compact discs, and distribute these throughout the campus.

Events like these cause no physical harm, but they threaten a school's "psychosocial safety," its sense of community, and its norms of fairness. They damage the confidence and trust of all students, not just those who are slandered, and threaten all students' freedom to express themselves. But the larger concern they raise is about fundamental issues of character, responsibility, and values. When officials at the boarding school disciplined not only the students who made the videotape but those who watched it, many of the latter insisted they had done nothing wrong. "What kind of young people are we raising in this country?" asks an administrator there. "How have we managed to produce such insensitivity, such thoughtless cruelty—and so little sense of responsibility?"

Finally, at the base of the student problem pyramid, at the least extreme but broadest level, teachers and administrators see a growing crisis of readiness, one that involves the fundamentals of learning, working, and being part of a group. It is reflected in symptoms like these:

- More children, beginning with the very young, start school lacking the basics of organization and cooperation on which schooling depends—how to follow directions, form a line, listen while someone else speaks, share toys, and engage in age-appropriate cooperative play. Preschool and elementary teachers now encounter more children who literally can't tolerate not being the center of attention.

- More students also show a lack of basic social awareness. For example, elementary teachers complain that, at dismissal, with no sign of malice but also no apparent concern, students awaiting carpool pickups routinely step all over one another's book bags, knapsacks, and sports equipment, even on the hands and feet of those who are sitting on the floor, and can't fathom what they've done wrong when teachers correct them.

- More students at all grade levels show a pronounced unevenness in their functioning, such as strong, sophisticated verbal skills accompanied by bursts of remarkably immature social behavior, notably selfishness and aggression.

- More students at all grade levels show difficulty in paying attention to their work and sustaining their concentration—this refers not just to an increase in those formally diagnosed with Attention Deficit Disorder, but more broadly to a decline of the attention span and of the ability to delay gratification.

- More students, including the very young, are presenting serious symptoms of mental illness and behavior disorder. Though still few in number they are increasing rapidly and are extremely difficult—and costly—to treat, teach, and manage.

- More students are uninvested in the educational process (a trend that becomes more apparent among older students), unmotivated to be active learners, and unconvinced that there is a serious price to be paid for tuning out and turning off.

The key word in this list is *more*. None of these problems at the base of the pyramid are new. Teachers have always had to work with students who are not school-ready, who lack social awareness, who function unevenly, who have trouble paying attention, and who are hard to interest and motivate. But they have never had to work with such large numbers of them and never with so many who present these problems in kindergarten and chronically throughout their school careers. It is nearly impossible to spend a day in a school, let alone a week, without seeing forceful evidence of the negative impact of these behavioral issues on teaching and learning (although current school improvement mandates virtually ignore it). The only problems that draw more comment from educators are the changes in parent behavior.

Pyramids of Problems: Parents

Surveying the dancers at the Semi-formal, one of the teachers shook her head. "Whenever I see this," she said, "I wonder how their parents could let them out looking like this and raise them so they could act this way." As worried as they are about the trends among students, many educators are even more concerned about parallel trends in parents' own performance, behavior, and values, which they see as fostering the problems presented by students and as a new and distinct area of difficulty in their own right. At the top of the parent pyramid are examples like these:

- When a school decides that a second grader is not ready, academically or socially, for third grade, her parents demand that she be promoted, sue the school, and write an open letter to all the school's families detailing their complaints and demands. Then they contact local news media and make the child available for interviews.

- When a science teacher discovers that students have used a Web site to plagiarize on a major project and gives them zeroes, their parents object and convince the school board to order that the assignment be given a reduced weight in the semester's overall grade— this despite the fact that both the students and their parents had signed an agreement acknowledging the importance of the project and the penalty for cheating.

- Learning that a sophomore has planned a wild party (with beer kegs already ordered) for a weekend when his parents will be away, an administrator calls the

boy's mother to alert her and is subjected to a tirade
of denial and accusation that begins, "How dare you
accuse my son of such a thing!" and escalates into
enraged profanity.

- For an after-graduation party, parents of seniors rent a
  hotel suite where alcohol will be served. When school
  officials express concern, parents explain that this will
  keep their children from driving drunk and that no
  students would come if the party were alcohol-free.

- The parents of serious offenders, including those
  described at the top of the student pyramid—the ones
  who cheated, counterfeited money, downloaded pornography, and published the scum sheet—hire lawyers to
  contest the discipline meted out by the school. Neither
  apologetic nor apparently concerned by the nature and
  impact of their children's behavior, they concentrate
  on the fine points of school discipline procedures. The
  father of one shouts at the principal, "You didn't read
  my son his rights when you questioned him!"

To many noneducators these items—especially the last—might
seem unbelievable or an occasional silly nuisance, fodder for Jay
Leno and David Letterman jokes on late-night television, but school
people know better. Parents now sue schools not only over discipline
imposed on their children for major infractions but for a student
being cut from a sports team, or just not getting enough playing time
(in a Nebraska case, parents brought stopwatches to games to measure their children's playing time). They also sue over a student's
being dismissed from the marching band, or receiving a D, or not
being chosen valedictorian. In my favorite incident, parents sued
when a boy injured himself by tripping over his own pant leg.[6]
Administrators everywhere spend much more time in legal training and in consultation with school attorneys and in actual court

proceedings than ever before. As one superintendent says, "We used to see serious behavior problems as potential 'teachable moments,' where the student could learn an important lesson. No longer. Now they are potential legal confrontations where the parent downplays the student's misbehavior and attacks our policies and procedures."

Further down the pyramid lie episodes that are more common and less confrontational, though hardly friendly. These often involve parents' worries and challenges about performance in academics and sports, but they also include parents' refusals to support school efforts to structure a good learning environment:

- In a topnotch school in a wealthy suburb, fourth-grade teachers report that if they give a student an A-minus they now receive calls from parents asking two questions: "What could he do to get an A?" and "How come you only gave her an A-minus?"

- Despite their concern about their children receiving good grades, more and more parents take them out of school for family vacations that do not coincide with scheduled school breaks, and think nothing of asking teachers for a full week's worth of special lesson plans and assignments—work that, in most cases, the students do not complete.

- When an elementary principal, concerned about fifth- and sixth-grade girls wearing the same provocative clothes as their high school counterparts and eager not to encourage premature sexuality, invites parents to consider a voluntary, minimal set of limits for school attire, she is roundly criticized by mothers, who accuse her of being antifeminist and of violating their daughters' constitutional rights.

- After athletic contests coaches everywhere now receive calls and faxes and e-mail messages from parents offering advice on strategy and especially about which students should be playing the most.

- More and more parents take their children's complaints and stories about incidents at school literally; they don't hesitate to call the principal or write accusatory letters about teachers and demand prompt corrective action based only on their child's account of an event.

- Anxiously—and aggressively—seeking the absolute best teacher for their elementary children in the coming year, mothers lobby principals intensely to put their child into a particular classroom; if next year's potential teachers include young married women, mothers accost them to make sure they have no plans to get pregnant (thus requiring a maternity leave and a substitute teacher).

These kinds of events leave school staff shaking their heads in dismay and frustration and feeling that parents do not respect their professional judgment or the school's authority—or their own children's resilience.

At the bottom of the parent pyramid, schools face an epidemic of anxiety—and sometimes, it seems, of helplessness. Educators now field many more requests from parents to intervene in the most basic parental and family matters. I recall sitting with a principal who received two urgent phone calls the morning I visited, the first from a mother begging him, "Please tell my ninth-grade daughter to stop dating those senior boys," the second from a father asking him to make a rule forbidding kids to drink at home on weekends. When I told this to a middle school principal, he replied that the parents of a student had just asked him to tell their daughter they were going to divorce. I have since met many principals who have faced such a request. And parents now routinely seek elementary teach-ers' advice about fundamental matters of child care and family living, such as bedtime (the mother of a first-grader recently asked her child's teacher, "Is it all right if I insist that my son go to bed at ten o'clock, even if he really doesn't want to?"). Preschool teachers report that many fewer parents seem to be comfortable just playing with their children. "They have to instruct or tell their kids how to do things," says a day-care director. "They can't just sit with a child at the dollhouse for a while and play some make-believe. Lots of our kids are hungry for just plain *play with me, be with me* time with their parents."

What *Has* Gone Wrong?

These lists of behaviors merely skim the troubled surface of deeply troubled waters. The evidence is abundant: schools are facing a cohort of students that is harder to interest, motivate, and engage, and a cohort of parents that is less effective, supportive, and trusting than any in recent generations. Of course, anecdotes and empirical facts, by themselves, are one thing; it is how we understand them that determines how we respond to them. If, for example, we concentrate simply on the needs of children it is easy to blame parents for failing to fulfill their responsibilities. From a pure child development perspective the evidence of growing parental irresponsibility and incompetence is unmistakable. Thus, many teachers I meet, whose primary devotion is to students, see the shortcomings of parents as essentially a matter of "won't" rather than "can't." To many of them, parents are focussed on entitlement, aggressive, and selfish, ignoring their children's needs to gratify their own. If, however, we look at the dilemmas of being a parent today, we often find people struggling to do the best they can in conditions of high demand and high uncertainty. Many of the same troubling facts look much more like "can't" than "won't." Responsibility shifts to larger trends in America's social, economic, political, and cultural life that leave even the most caring, devoted parents anxious, confused, and isolated.

There is truth in both of these perspectives, and the following chapters explore each of them, addressing the question asked by so many worried teachers, psychologists, pediatricians, clergy, and dance chaperones: What *has* gone wrong? I want to ask this question quite literally, however, not in the exasperated tone that conveys accusation or the dismissive tone that sniffs about things' not being what they used to be. A crisis presents not just a real threat but a rare chance. To understand the challenges confronting our schools and our nation, we need a template, a framework for understanding the changes in children and parents. This requires a pause to step back and reflect, to seek perspective on the larger enterprise of childrearing, to review its fundamentals and to see how current practices accord with those fundamentals. That means beginning where education does, in the home, examining the basics of successful parenting that should be in place long before children reach school and should sustain them throughout their school careers.

The Building Blocks
of Healthy Growth

To grow up healthy and successful, to become people of competence, caring, and character, what do children need from their parents and caregivers? By the time they graduate from high school they have spent, as I have said, barely a tenth of their lives in school. As important as schooling is, almost all students learn their most essential life-shaping lessons outside the formal curriculum-and-instruction context. If they are to become first good learners, then good earners, and ultimately good citizens, spouses, and parents, what must the adults who raise them know and do? A comprehensive answer would take volumes.

It is hard to imagine a subject that has stimulated more theory and research, or been more vulnerable to speculation and fads, than the raising of the young and the role of parents. Written advice on the matter dates back several thousand years. It multiplied exponentially in the second half of the twentieth century, when the field of child development saw remarkable growth: literally thousands of scholarly studies have now been published, and these have in turn spawned several thousand advice manuals for parents and been factored into teacher preparation courses nationwide.

Although in recent years research has taught us much about how children's growth unfolds in the family, we still have far to go. For one thing, even a casual review of the history of the research itself and especially of its distillation into advice books suggests that both have often reflected the prevailing prejudices and priorities of the period. For another, child development professionals remain sharply divided about how to interpret some of the facts that are widely accepted. Caution, then, is always in order in any generalization about parenting. But if one doesn't seek to be comprehensive, if one asks instead what are the core essentials that have so far stood the test of time and that recur over and over in the research, these themes immediately emerge:

- All children need roots and wings.

- These are significantly influenced by three dimensions of their parents' behavior—nurture, structure, and latitude.

- These in turn are successfully provided in a wide variety of ways in the normal course of childrearing.

- One particular pattern of nurture, structure, and latitude seems to lead to the most successful outcomes for children growing up in America.

This chapter takes up the first three, and I turn to the fourth in the next chapter.

Roots and Wings

Every theory of child development must, like every parent, come to grips with two fundamental tendencies that lie at the source of behavior, indeed of life itself: the impulse to be connected to others and the impulse to master the world separately on one's own. Variously called attachment and agency, affiliation and autonomy, dependence and independence, the two are seen in different theories as needs that must be met or as drives that assert themselves. Almost every living organism needs to connect to others—for sustenance at first, for procreation later, and for protection throughout. And almost every living organism also needs to master its environment enough to achieve self-sufficiency—to be able to feed itself, fend for itself, find a mate, and so on.[1]

Among humans these twin drives exist not just at the biological level but at the psychological level. Born much earlier in embryonic development than many other creatures, we need an extended period of dependence on our primary caregivers if we are even to survive, let alone thrive. As infants we arrive preadapted for lengthy dependence. The obvious aspects of this dependence are physical and behavioral, but the psychological dimensions begin early and last long. We remain connected to, engaged with, and psychologically dependent upon our parents far beyond childhood and adolescence. And when we move out of our family and into the world we take with us predispositions and ways of treating others that we learned at home, often dealing with coworkers as we did with siblings, and with bosses as we did with parents. Then we start families of our own, on whom we also come to depend. From birth to death, in myriad ways both direct and indirect, we remain linked to a nexus of relationships with kin at its core.

At the same time, all infants are also born as exploring, learning, constructing beings. We do not enter the world as mere passive recipients, even if we are at first nearly helpless. From our earliest hours outside the womb we begin sensing, looking, touching, testing, tasting, holding, feeling. We have a primary tendency to reach out, to try out, to experience and master objects and events. It is now known that the most basic biological processes, including our senses—sight, smell, hearing, touch—are not just fixtures that appear fully formed at birth; they develop in the course of experience. This propensity, too, has a psychological corollary: an impulse to be self-sufficient, to separate from others and to control our world. In endeavors of all kinds—schooling, business, art, athletics—we show a will to impose ourselves on the world, to order it, organize it, shape it, and master it.

Attachment and agency are lifelong and reciprocal. Both kinds of behavior begin at birth and last throughout life. Although infants are more attached than adolescents, they are not purely dependent; and although adults are more autonomous than infants, they never outgrow their dependent needs, which are fulfilled in romantic relationships, family kinship, friendships, and workplace colleagueship. And although affiliation and autonomy point in opposite directions, they are in fact complementary tendencies; each enables the other. Most toddlers, for example, venture and explore more confidently when they feel sure of the whereabouts and availability of a parent or other familiar caregiver. And most adults feel freer to assert their true opinions when they are in the presence of those they trust.

Children differ, of course, in their dependent and independent tendencies. Temperament plays a role here. Just as some infants are more reactive to intrusion from birth and others much less so, some are more placid and pliant, and some are more inclined to cuddle, while others start and stay more active right from birth, or are harder to hold and contain, or seem to need less in the way of human contact and interaction. These general tendencies usually endure throughout life. Gender, too, plays a role. Females tend to show stronger affiliative and expressive tendencies; males, stronger independent and instrumental inclinations. These are visible quite early on and constitute much of what we see as the typical differences between men and women. They are the stuff of both high tragedy and low comedy.

Though these predispositions toward and needs for affiliation and autonomy are innate in humans, their actual expression and fulfillment are affected by all sorts of factors in the environment in which the child lives and grows up, most notably by family and society. For example, it has long been axiomatic among American psychiatrists and psychologists that healthy development requires individuation, a clear psychic separation from parents and family of origin, that full independence is crucial to true mental health as an adult. This reflects in part our nation's longstanding norms of independence and individualism and a way of life that has promoted high mobility. In many cultures around the world this kind of individuation seems odd, even bizarre, because the accepted way of life keeps adults far more directly linked to their families of origin or to extended kinship groups. In most of these cultures the collective group, not the individual member, is accorded primacy and the individual is expected to submerge personal interests and priorities to those of the group. Nonetheless, in close-kinship societies people still need to achieve significant levels of individual competence, and in individualistic societies people still depend on each other. Human infants cannot survive and grow to successful adulthood without both the security that is engendered by strong social ties and a push away from the group to be able to fend for themselves.[2] Children need to grow up in an environment that offers them care, connection, and protection, yet also urges them to explore, strive, and become self-sufficient.

So what fosters the growth of roots and wings? A complete catalogue would be very long, but at its core lie three quintessential necessities—nurture, structure, and latitude: love and acceptance, expectations and limits, support for autonomy and the freedom to learn from experience. Over the past fifty years a substantial body of research on parent-child interaction has repeatedly confirmed the importance of these dimensions.[3] Other factors are also important to children, but these three are absolutely indispensable.

Nurture

We all know what nurture is. Most of us associate it immediately with the mothering of infants. It is the earliest and most obvious component of child development. It begins as the affection and attention, the holding and ministering, the care and comfort an infant receives. It is acceptance, not reward; given, not earned. It flows like mother's milk not because a child achieves a goal or demonstrates a skill, but because we share flesh and blood and we belong to each other. It provides what psychologists used to call "unconditional positive regard" and what a veteran preschool teacher I know calls "your basic warmth."

When I think of nurture I think not first of mothers but of Mr. Rogers. As a generation of small children watching *Mr. Rogers' Neighborhood* on public television heard Fred Rogers tell them, "I like you just the way you are." He is dead now, present, as I write this, only in reruns, but he still likes you just the way you are. You never had to be smart for Mr. Rogers to like you, nor did you have to be good-looking, athletic, or even nice. You could be unintelligent, unattractive, uncoordinated, and unpleasant; it could be 5:30 in the afternoon when even your mother couldn't stand you; you were still fine to him. This is nurture, the primary building block of healthy growth. Every child needs to start life with a good dose of it. In fact, we never outgrow our need for it, although as we get older we come to receive it in less overt and direct ways. But any adult who has cared for a dying parent knows how important the fundamentals of caring, comforting, and ministering are. And when adults express love and affection to each other, their behavior often involves nurturance and dependence.

Nurture is initially the vehicle through which we survive, but it is also the vehicle through which we become uniquely human. It is crucial not only to the development of a positive sense of self but to the ability to function as a member of a community. Through nurture we first begin to be aware of others, first learn about give-and-take, and eventually come to appreciate that others are separate beings with powers and intentions of their own. Gradually, our experience with caregivers teaches us how fully we can trust the world and how confidently we can count on other people to meet our needs—when to be open and when to be cautious. Over time, it helps us learn how safely we can express our feelings and how fairly we can expect others to behave. In all these ways it fosters an essential confidence: the basic belief that we are lovable and can expect our relationships to be governed by reciprocity, that if we moderate our own needs to meet the needs of others, they will do so for us. This confidence is fundamental to psychosocial development.

This much may be obvious. Not always so obvious is that the lessons about reciprocity taught through nurture are important not only to self-esteem but to socialization and the development of conscience and character. In families with close social bonds, where parents foster reciprocity as a behavioral norm, their children typically show greater compliance and adherence to their values.[4] Children who become securely attached to their parents are reluctant to lose parental support and approval and are more likely to adopt their parents' standards for conduct and to control their own behavior accordingly. This will, in turn, earn them more praise and positive response from those outside the family, further buttressing self-esteem.[5] It will make them easier to teach and to manage in school. And it will make them better participants in the communities to which they belong, first at school and later in the larger world. Nurture, in short, is "the seedbed of trusting and socially responsible personal relationships [and] civic virtues."[6]

Nurture begins in early parent-child interaction, especially early mother-infant interaction. The establishment of a close, nurturing mother-child relationship, a critical first task of growth, typically unfolds quite naturally. It is a task for which infant and mother are both preadapted. The infant begins life largely under the control of built-in instinctual mechanisms that both trigger basic physical needs (crying when hungry) and that provide an almost immediate inclination to relate to others. As these automatic behaviors express themselves, they trigger reactions in the mother, some of which are also basic physical "built-in's" (milk letting down in response to the infant's cry), others of which are purely social. As she begins to respond to the child's emerging behaviors in certain repeated ways (during feeding, for example), the infant begins to expect these responses, anticipate them, and to behave in ways designed to produce or avoid them.[7] In addition, growing evidence from animal studies suggests that, as Michael Meaney, a leading researcher in the field, puts it, "maternal behavior regulates the activity of certain genes in certain areas of the brain, which in turn influences an animal's response to stress, which in turn regulates [its] vulnerability to stress-related disease." Good early nurturing, it seems, improves an animal's ability to respond to stress without elevated levels of so-called stress hormones. It also appears to increase nerve cell growth in the hippocampus, which is vital to memory and learning.

Infants, in other words, arrive already wired to relate. They have biologically based start-up software that enables them to form primitive internal representations of the world around them—representations then modified by experience (with parents at first, then with others), which in turn lead to new representations, and so on. In the first few hours after birth, infants lock in on the eyes of adults who hold them, and turn toward their mother's voice. Very quickly, they can imitate adults' facial expression and reciprocate their emotions. Mothers, too, are wired to relate. When they look at their children, register an expression, and the children reciprocate, the same areas of the brain are stimulated in both.[8] The preadapted-ness of parent and child are vital both to early nurturance and to creating the ability to relate to others, which is what truly makes us human.[9]

This preadapted system depends on and fosters what Daniel Stern, a psychiatrist who studies infant development, calls "attunement": an empathic connectedness of parent and child that is rooted in biology and built up during the recurring events of daily life, events that establish for children the fundamentals of social and emotional growth and development.[10] It is in the empathic mother-child connection in the course of ordinary living that nurture happens, not only in the feeding, comforting, and other obvious nurturing activities. From this matching of mother's reaction to child, repeated naturally and unthinkingly scores of times per day, infants develop an expectation of parental response, of having their feelings shared and reciprocated. Here, as in so much of childrearing, it is the song that matters, not just the notes that compose it. The exact way a parent feeds an infant or cautions an adolescent is not as crucial, observes developmental psychologist Jerome Kagan, as the melody those actions, repeated over time, construct.[11] Here, as also in so much of childrearing, influences are bidirectional. It is not just a matter of an adult imposing a melody that the child must learn; the parental melody itself begins partly as a response to the child's behavior and cues, and just as the child responds to the parent, the parent responds to the child. The very notion of attunement involves reading and matching a child's impulses and temperament even as one's responses in turn help to shape and structure the child's expectations and behavior. Here is where we can see biology and environment interacting. The capacity to connect, cooperate, and share emotions, which is present and operating at birth, is "the route by which interactions with caregivers regulate the child's brain development" and also on which later sophisticated social learning depends.[12]

There is an alternative view about nurture. Developmental psychologists, who study children in laboratory settings and in formal experiments, often argue that the importance of infant experience is exaggerated. Taking a broad, comparative perspective, looking at development not just in the context of early parent-child patterns and not just in our culture, they acknowledge the value of a nurturant relationship between child and caretaker, but dispute the direct, linear linking of early mothering to later adult behavior and the notion that the first years largely determine a child's eventual psychological makeup. For one thing, they point to strong evidence that children do not require a particular kind of attachment childrearing to develop healthily. Rather, "all children have built-in capacities to attain developmental goals in multiple ways and under varying conditions."[13] Thus, developmentalists agree that early experiences may create expectations of nurture or neglect for a child, but not that these are decisive. To be sure, says Kagan, "infants who are tickled, played with, talked to, and smiled at are more alert, more vocal, and laugh more fully and frequently than infants who missed these pleasurable experiences," but their brains, especially the frontal lobes, which process information about the environment, are too immature to form the sorts of perceptions and memories assumed by attachment theory.[14] And later experiences can transform or overcome their early expectations, as shown by studies of children orphaned during World War II and the Korean War whose early lives were marked by trauma but who, in the care of good foster parents, went on to develop well.[15] In this view, it is not just the beginning years of life that matter in forming character, values, and behavior patterns, but a whole childhood.

It is possible to embrace the best of both approaches. Development requires both stability and flexibility; it is not an either-or contest that pits the early years against the later years. The key issue is not which matters more, but how the early years influence the later years. They are vitally important not because they determine adult well-being, but because they set a foundation—sturdy or fragile—for later development. What children learn in their youngest years "establishes a set of capabilities, orientations to the world, and expectations about how things and people will behave," and this in turn affects how they process new experiences—beginning with school.[16] Although we want our schools, especially our elementary schools, to be nurturing places that will contribute positively to children's capabilities, orientations, and expectations, there is no way a school can ever overcome fundamental deficits in nurture. The laboratory for nurture and reciprocity lies at home in, as we say, the bosom of the family.

Structure

The second essential developmental ingredient is structure, by which I mean a framework for conduct, expectations for behavior and performance. There is virtually no controversy among experts about the importance to children of growing up in a setting that provides clear norms for how one should behave, treat others, and achieve. Nearly every school of thought in child development sees structure as both normal (in the sense that it has been ubiquitous in all human societies) and necessary to healthy growth.

I think of structure as a box. Inside the box is what we do and what is expected of us; outside is what we don't do and what is not expected. Every culture has a box. Within this broad framework each subculture may have its own modified version and within this version each family may have its own variant. Around the world, boxes differ in their contents—growing up is quite different in Kenya, Finland, and Japan—but each box prescribes and proscribes. Each encourages and rewards certain achievements and behaviors, forbids and punishes others.

In most families and cultures the box expands and contracts. It starts out large, gradually grows more restrictive, and then enlarges again. As infants and toddlers, children are often allowed considerable freedom and not held accountable for their actions. As they reach school age, they become subject to greater expectations and limitations, and then, as they approach adulthood, they begin to acquire more prerogatives. Throughout, structure involves a dynamic between freedom and responsibility. Children and adolescents typically focus on the former, parents and teachers on the latter. Much of the friction between adults and teenagers constitutes a kind of extended negotiation about this trade-off: teens want more freedom (money, the car, no curfew); adults want greater proof that teens can behave responsibly.

Like nurture, structure is a key contributor to social competence and confidence. Its importance is most easily illustrated by remembering when you last found yourself in a social setting where you didn't know what was expected of you or how you were supposed to act. These situations make most of us acutely uncomfortable and self-conscious. Knowing where we stand, how to behave, what goes and what doesn't go, is a great comfort. Behavioral guidelines and expectations make life and alternatives clearer. In addition, they give continuity and predictability to relationships, which makes it easier to be trusting of others—we know that we share basic assumptions in common. Growing up in a clear framework with boundaries also helps children learn to become more considerate of others; it makes them less likely to act out, to be inappropriately aggressive. Consequently, they tend to receive more positive, esteem-enhancing responses from others. Over time, they come to internalize their parents' regulations and thus develop their own ability to self-regulate.

This internalized structure is vital to the ability to resist external pressures, such as the temptations of dangerous peer influences in adolescence. And as children come to grasp and fulfill parental, social, and cultural expectations, their sense of competence is enhanced. Perhaps more important, children who grow up in families with clear boxes tend to take clear boxes into their own adulthood and childrearing. The exact content of their boxes is not necessarily the same as their parents', but what is repeated is the presence of a clear box, a defined set of standards and expectations for children.

Another benefit of structure, implicit in the very notion of boundaries and limits, guidelines and expectations, is the delay of gratification, the learning to defer, at least temporarily, one's own impulses. In *Emotional Intelligence* Daniel Goleman emphasizes how vital this capacity is to success in life. Considerable evidence confirms that children who don't develop this ability end up performing much worse academically and socially than those who do.[17] Some researchers would argue that the ability to delay gratification is genetically influenced, at least in those children who are, almost literally from birth, truly uninhibited, spontaneous, and fearless (research by Kagan and his colleagues at Harvard suggests that this group comprises roughly 15 percent of children). Even if this were conclusively proved, however, it would only argue for parents to provide firmer structure for these children. There is certainly no doubt that parents who provide too little structure help children grow up more self-centered and "entitled," less considerate of others, and more impulsive and prone to seeking instant gratification.

Structure is also, to the surprise of many parents and teachers, a key contributor to self-esteem. Since the 1970s, the importance of self-esteem to healthy growth has been an article of faith among many writers in child development, education, mental health—especially among those who offer advice to parents. Conventional wisdom sees it as crucial to personal, social, and intellectual maturation. Strong self-esteem, it is said, not only makes children feel good about themselves but strengthens their perseverance and resilience and improves their performance. When a student, especially an elementary student, falls into academic or social difficulty at school, low self-esteem is almost sure to be on the list of potential causes to be considered by the staff. For their part, parents now routinely worry to teachers that getting a low grade on a test will hurt their child's self-esteem. All told, an astonishing amount of energy has gone into promoting self-esteem, including a commission once created by the state of California to raise citizens' self-esteem statewide!

The case for the conventional view of self-esteem may be summarized simply: first, successful people have lots of it, so it must be a foundation, a beginning precondition of good development; second, it can be fostered by the right kind of upbringing. Assertions like this have long been common in the parent guidance literature. But little hard evidence of any kind suggests a causal link between a child's overall sense of self-worth and the development of important social, emotional, or intellectual skills. Indeed, self-esteem can easily correlate with undesirable traits. Boys with conduct disorders, for example, who regularly misbehave and disobey, who do poorly in school and in peer relationships, and whose behavior is characterized by macho excess, tend to score quite high on tests of self-esteem.[18]

The assumption that self-esteem is a foundation, a beginning precondition of healthy growth that ultimately leads to success, is accompanied by the parallel assumption that it can be fostered by the right kind of upbringing—one that does not emphasize structure. The parent advice industry has advised liberal doses of praise, frequent assurances of love, and a steady diet of successful experiences. Parents and teachers are encouraged to seek out opportunities of all kinds, no matter how small, to congratulate and reward the child. Whether undertaken by a parent or a teacher, this kind of effort, though well-meaning, is at best ineffectual. Self-esteem cannot be artificially implanted or boosted. It results primarily from trying one's best to address a challenge or achieve a meaningful goal. Meeting regular, appropriate demands that one work hard, be responsible, and follow through is the chief source of a sense of self-confidence and self-esteem.[19]

Self-esteem, in fact, is like happiness—pursuing it directly is impossible and self-defeating. Neither can be artificially manufactured or given to someone else; both can be earned and emerge in the course of living with others and fulfilling the responsibilities of doing so. Parents who have appropriate expectations for their children and hold them accountable for meeting these expectations will not only have natural reasons to praise their children, they will give their children the chance to earn a sense of accomplishment.

They will also confirm for their children that they love them. Contrary to what many parents think, raising children with a structure, even when it involves discipline, sends a positive message, as Fred Rogers confirmed. Although most people associate his television message with nurture, as I have, his show was full of messages about structure, too, because, as he told an interviewer, "Discipline is a kind of love. If children didn't have limits from those who cared about them they would never feel that they were loved. If a child ran out into the street, for instance, and nobody screamed and says [sic] come back or nobody ran after that child, that child would think that nobody loved him. So, healthy limits, which children understand, are a marvelous way of saying, 'I care about you.'"[20]

Latitude

The third key building block of healthy growth is latitude, by which I mean support for a child's autonomy—support that expresses itself in the freedom to learn from experience and to express oneself. From infancy onward, as noted earlier, children constantly explore the world around them and test their influence upon things and people. Some are more adventuresome than others, but all explore. Each culture has its own guidelines, implicit and explicit, about exploration: how much, what kind, when, and so on. (Again, within each society communities and families will have their own variants of these understandings.) The key to this aspect of development for a child is having enough latitude to learn the lessons necessary to each stage of life. Not so much as to become lost or to be allowed to get into serious danger, not so little that autonomy, curiosity, and mastery are stunted.

The learning this kind of latitude produces is vast and vital, and though much of it involves drawing upon the success of one's actions, some of the most important learning stems from disappointment and loss. To thrive in the world of work, first at school and later in a career (and, for that matter, to thrive in the world of interpersonal relations), everyone must become a problem solver. Everyone must be able to act on the world, draw conclusions and inferences from the results, and then apply this knowledge. This includes learning from accomplishments, but it also means facing up to errors and misjudgments, failures and shortcomings, trying to overcome these and, where this proves impossible, learning to compensate for—or accept—them.

Think for a minute about the most important lessons you have learned in your life. If you are like most people, you experienced these in a context of disappointment and loss. They are the roots of maturity. It is not whether we encounter such setbacks but how we cope with them that defines what we're made of and that determines our own well-being. Self-esteem is too often misunderstood as being produced by the outcome of an activity—whether the child wins the game—rather than by the effort the child puts into it. But it is when we confront issues and respond to challenges, regardless of their outcome, that we experience positive, self-affirming thoughts and feelings.[21] Over the course of a lifetime, what builds a feeling of self-worth is choosing to face meaningful problems rather than avoiding them.

Sometimes coping involves acceptance. There may be no remedy for losing a championship game or failing a crucial exam. Losing is, in this respect, a great builder of character. Though no parent I've ever known wants a child to encounter a particular disappointment, most of us know that disappointments are a necessary part of growing up and that, as an adult, a child will be stronger for being able to face them. Disappointment has another benefit: it is a great leveler, a teacher of humility and respect, an opportunity to walk in the shoes of others, and hence an important contributor to the capacity for empathy and to the skills of community membership and democracy. "Every society," as Kagan points out, "needs a small number of chiefs but a great many warriors."[22] Most of us will be warriors and we must learn how to accept this status and to get along with our competitors.

Latitude is not all about resignation, however; it can help foster resilience. Often, the lesson to be learned from acting upon the world is that we can do better, that we need to develop a new skill, or persist patiently, or try harder. Perseverance can be one of the most powerful outcomes of falling short. If you are like most people, the chances are that your proudest moments occurred when you mastered something that was difficult, something that had previously troubled or frustrated you or made you feel inadequate in some way. Without the freedom to fail, to struggle against difficulties, those moments wouldn't have been possible. Latitude, in short, helps make possible the development of resilience and persistence, which are vital to children's achievement.

What distinguishes top performers from peers who have similar abilities is often, as Goleman notes, "the degree to which, beginning early in life, they can pursue an arduous practice routine for years and years. And that doggedness depends on emotional traits—enthusiasm and persistence in the face of setbacks—above all else."[23] Here again, some children may seem to have more innate enthusiasm or persistence than others, but parents can make a real difference by giving children support for their autonomy.

Imagine four eleven-year-old girls who want larger allowances. They are becoming more interested in clothes and are spending more time at the local shopping mall. None of their parents like this growing interest; if asked, all would say they wish the girls would not grow up so fast, would spend their time more fruitfully, and would be less materialistic. The first girl's parents, however, despite their views, simply agree to their daughter's request. The second girl's parents criticize her harshly for even asking and threaten to ground her for a week if she asks again. The parents of the third and fourth girls engage their daughters in conversation. They acknowledge the girls' interests, ask how much they want and what they want to spend it on. They also express their own reservations. Ultimately, the parents of the third girl agree to an increase, but the parents of the fourth do not. They promise to revisit the matter in four months at her upcoming birthday. Although the last two couples reach different decisions, both do so in a way that offers a kind of psychological autonomy, that doesn't disengage from their daughter or dampen her sense that she can advocate for herself.

Managing latitude, letting and helping children learn from experience, requires us to respect children's different strengths and styles and to let them do their own problem solving where possible in developmentally appropriate ways. We need to balance our intervention so that it is neither too limiting nor too lax, neither too much too soon nor too little too late. The problems that develop in the area of latitude stem from overcontrol, overprotection, and underinvolvement. Parents who are overcontrolling value obedience over independence. They tend to be arbitrary and absolutist and to stifle the child's risk taking, autonomy, and expressiveness. Parents who are overprotective also don't give children sufficient room to grow. Instead of being punitive they hover, intrude, fix, correct, warn, and, often, do for the child tasks the child could manage independently. The child's life may be smoother, but the sense of competence, the confidence that success is possible through effort, simply won't develop.

Ironically, what overprotective parents often say they want most is for children to be confident and have strong self-esteem; they intervene because they want the child to succeed. Of course, when they do this to excess, their intervention itself helps teach children to doubt their own competence.

Meanwhile, parents who are underinvolved give their children lots of leeway but not lots of support for their autonomy. These are the parents who are often otherwise engaged or unavailable when their child is having trouble of a kind that does need adult help, or who don't attend the child's plays or performances at school even though their work schedule would permit them to, or who go off on weekends or vacations leaving their adolescent children at home unsupervised. Their children may occasionally revel in the freedom they are given, but they know they are not being supported in a caring way. This is not latitude but disengagement.

Enough Is Enough

There is a crucial truth about nurture, structure, and latitude: they occur in the course of ordinary parenting naturally and sufficiently and with tremendous variety. This truth runs directly counter to the perfectionistic fallacy that pervades the popular advice books for parents and early childhood educators. These volumes, full of watered-down, jazzed-up oversimplifications of the research, have seeded a steady succession of childrearing fads and a mistaken belief that successful development requires earlier and earlier applications of ever more complex patterns of stimulation. They share the assumption that if we can identify factors that compromise children's development, parents can avoid these factors, and if we can identify factors that foster development, parents can maximize those factors. It is astonishing how many parents, especially in middle-class and upper-middle-class homes, now see the task of raising happy, productive children as "walking a tightrope and passing through the eye of a needle—yet never mixing a metaphor," as a psychologist colleague of mine says.

Later I will address the rising tide of parental anxiety the advice industry fuels, along with its exaggeration of the importance of early stimulation. For now, I want to emphasize that, vital as they are, nurture, structure, and latitude need not be maximized and are not rarified features of childrearing that require exceptional skill.

It is not true that if nurture is good for children, extreme nurture is extremely good for them. Adequate nurture is all that is required for the normal human competencies to emerge. This point has been made repeatedly by the most authoritative students of development, beginning with Donald Winnicott, the British pediatrician and child psychiatrist who coined the phrase "good-enough mother,"[24] only to be obscured by waves of raise-perfect-children books. And adequate nurture—along with adequate structure and adequate latitude—have, for most of human history, occurred naturally among parents, without advice manuals or professional training. They have also occurred—and continue to do so—with enormous variety. No single, universal pattern of nurture, structure, and latitude is ideal for all children around the world. Even a cursory reading of anthropology confirms that, while the vast majority of the world's children are raised by "moderately predictable and reasonably nurturant adults," there is an enormous diversity "in the duration, continuity, and affective quality of the interaction between parents and infants."[25] Any number of dramatic examples from around the world describe practices we would find bizarre, sexist, and cruel that are nevertheless meaningful parts of the local culture and do not result in psychological scarring or stunted adulthood. Through all these variations of nurture, structure, and latitude, children not only survive, they thrive.

To developmental psychologists this confirms a key fact about children: their remarkable adaptability. They flourish in all sorts of childrearing contexts. And just as young Kenyans, Finns, and Japanese readily acquire their local language, they as readily adopt their local customs and practices. They are born preadapted for an average expectable environment, and so long as their caretakers' parenting practices fall within the broad limits of this framework, they prosper. Even when this is not the case, when challenges in early childhood exceed the limits of what children can manage, they can show a remarkable resilience; they are often able to use the experience of later childhood and adolescence to rebound from early deficits.

What makes children so adaptable is that the impact of any particular event is not fixed but contextual: it depends, as noted, on its meaningfulness to the child, that is, on the child's interpretation of the event. This interpretation in turn depends on the child's maturity, personality, beliefs, and feelings, and especially on the predictability and the social sanction of the parent's behavior. What matters is not so much a particular kind of caretaking or discipline but its consistency and cultural validation. Though the Puritans believed children needed strictness more than affection and punished in ways that might get them arrested for child abuse today, they produced generations of successful offspring. They surely had their special neuroses (as we have ours), but they were hardly dysfunctional, diminished people—indeed, they built the foundations of our nation. What some of us might see as deprivation may be unwelcome to children when it occurs, but if it is consistent enough to be expected and if it is generally accepted as appropriate in their social world, they can make sense out of it. They are neither being taken by surprise nor treated unfairly. In this view, it is the sense a child makes out of any particular event—even a punishment—that truly influences psychological development, not the pure event by itself.

In sum, the evidence is that raising children calls for common sense, not rocket science; attunement, not acceleration; that it depends upon fundamentals that have occurred naturally among parents and children throughout history, and that what is best for a child depends in good part on what that child is to become and where. What is best for children growing up in contemporary America?[26] What will best prepare them to be successful students and, ultimately, successful people? Surprisingly, there is a straightforward answer. I turn to it next.

3

. . . .

Back to Basics

A Parenting Primer

Theoretically, American parents might raise their children with many different combinations of nurture, structure, and latitude; in practice, they don't. Beginning in the late 1960s, scholars—led notably by Diana Baumrind, a research psychologist at Berkeley—began to study patterns of childrearing. Looking at the dimensions I have called nurture, structure, and latitude, they discovered that most American parents sort themselves into three predominant styles, typically called *authoritarian, permissive,* and *authoritative.* More than three decades and several hundred studies later, the evidence is clear that what is best for most American children is the third: children who turn out to be successful at school and later in their personal and professional lives tend to come from families led by authoritative parents. It is also clear that, *other things being equal,* this kind of childrearing is best provided by a mother and father.

In this chapter, I first review the concept of authoritative parenting, then turn to the respective contributions of mothers and fathers, with particular attention to the latter, then look briefly at social influences on childrearing and child development. Some of this does not bear immediately on what educators can do—except with their own offspring—but it provides a bedrock understanding of what children need to be able to bring to school and of deficiencies that can arise at home and then affect students' behavior and performance in school. And its core concept, authoritative parenting, has very practical relevance for ways teachers and administrators can redesign their relationship with parents.

Authoritative Parents

Parenting styles are fairly easily differentiated along three continua: acceptance and rejection (in my terms, nurture), firmness and leniency (structure), and autonomy and control (latitude). As they raise their children, parents may be more accepting or rejecting, firmer or more lenient, and more supportive of autonomy or more insistent on control. Although the exact balance along each continuum varies from parent to parent, and although the particular customs and practices of those who share similar approaches can include substantial variety, parents generally divide into the authoritarian, authoritative, permissive styles illustrated in Table 3.1.

Table 3.1.   Three Styles of Parenting

	Authoritarian	Authoritative	Permissive
Nurture	Low	High	High
Structure	High	High	Low
Latitude	Low	High	High

Source: Adapted from Baumrind.[1]

At one extreme, authoritarian parents are low on nurture and acceptance, high on structure and firmness, and low on latitude and support for autonomy. They are not just firm but controlling, often harsh. Their style tends toward the autocratic and simplistic: things are right or wrong. These parents may be consistent in their discipline, though in my experience they often are arbitrary and capricious, but they also tend to be very rigid, and to concentrate heavily on controlling both children's behavior and their expression of feeling. This cows more timid children; it also invites subterfuge and, in bolder children, outright sabotage and opposition. It is conceivable that this kind of parenting might prepare children for adult roles in societies that are themselves autocratic and emphasize obedience to authority. It is not nearly as good a fit in a diverse democracy that requires of adults both initiative and tolerance.

At the other extreme, permissive parents are, by contrast, easygoing. They tend to be high on acceptance and nurturance of their children and low on control, and to tolerate and encourage lots of autonomy. They are often seen as soft or indulgent, and are likely to concentrate on keeping children happy. They can permit their offspring considerable expressive freedom and may be quite accepting of idiosyncrasies. This kind of parenting can minimize friction, and in these families relationships between adults and children may be warm and almost peerlike. All this risks producing children who are self-centered and relatively unattuned to the needs and wishes of others, who often lack a sense of duty and conscience, and who expect things to go their way without having to work hard.

A separate subset of permissive parents are lenient in a different way; they are disengaged. They are not just nontraditional, they are disconnected from their children's lives. These parents might superficially seem permissive in that they don't set firm limits, but they lack the warm connection that permissive parents seek with their children. They are low on both nurture and structure and high on uninvolvement—not on latitude, which consists of providing real support for children's autonomy. These parents' uninvolved posture does not represent a principled stance; it is a kind of default. They are fundamentally detached from their children. Some research estimates the proportion of these parents at around a quarter to a third of the population (in one study, 25 percent let their children choose their own school courses, 30 percent did not know how well their children were doing at school, and 33 percent did not know how the children spent their spare time). Adolescents from these homes were much more likely to show immaturity and adjustment difficulties, along with lower self-esteem, self-reliance, and social competence.[2]

Authoritative parents are centrists. They lie between the authoritarians and the permissives, but not because they are paler versions of either. What distinguishes them is that they are relatively high on all three dimensions: nurture, structure, and latitude. Their approach to their children is very accepting but also firm (though not narrowly rigid), and it also encourages the child's autonomy. These parents tend to emphasize both caring *and* responsibility, not one or the other. They want their children to be happy, but also to be considerate, hard working, and self-governing, and they will tolerate friction to foster these outcomes, but without stifling exploration and expressiveness. In this kind of childrearing the whole turns out to be greater than the sum of its parts: high levels of nurture, structure, and latitude amplify each other. Acceptance, as noted earlier, enhances firmness. When children are unhesitatingly sure of a parent's love, they can more readily stand being disciplined—indeed, accepting parental limits helps them feel valued and virtuous. At the same time, firmness supplements acceptance. For example, temperamentally shy infants are more likely to overcome their anxiety and avoidance if they grow up with nurturing mothers who set clear and direct limits and demand age-appropriate levels of conformity and responsibility than if they are raised by equally nurturing mothers who are very protective and less firm. The latter actually exacerbate their children's uncertainty and hesitancy—precisely the opposite of the result they intend.[3]

Over the past thirty years the hundreds of research studies that have examined, in one form or another, the impact of these dimensions of childrearing have shown, almost unanimously, that children develop in healthier ways (by American standards) and do better in school when their parents are authoritative. And no studies have ever found better results for American children when their parents are authoritarian or permissive. No kind of parenting is a panacea, of course, and parents (and educators) must now compete with an unprecedented array of external influences that affect children—challenges to be explored in later chapters. Here, it is enough to emphasize that authoritative parenting fosters academic and social competence, empathy and considerateness toward others, self-esteem and the ability to self-regulate, and optimism and perseverance.[4]

Mothers and Fathers

Although authoritative parenting might potentially be offered by anyone, it is ideally provided by a child's mother and father, working together and fulfilling complementary but different roles. Without doubt, the behavior of parents includes large areas of actual and potential overlap. Apart from giving birth and breastfeeding, most of the child-related tasks they perform are technically interchangeable. Not every mother is highly nurturant and some fathers are. Many factors combine to shape one's childrearing role, including personality, identification with one's own parents, and values. Most people, for example, choose a partner whose personality differs from their own; these differences create a childrearing dynamic to which children must adapt. One parent may dominate the household while the other serves as a kind of assistant, or a couple may practice a division of labor in which each controls certain areas of parenting, or they may share leadership and tasks equally. Assumption of these roles often depends in good part on the example set in one's family of origin. We parent much as we were parented, and usually more in the manner of our same-sex parent, though not always and by no means exclusively. And our raising of children is also affected by our values and our beliefs about the nature of human nature.

These and other factors play out in each family in myriad complex ways that defy simple generalization. Since children can grow up healthily in a wide variety of settings, it is worth emphasizing that any childrearing arrangement that offers sufficient levels of nurture, structure, and latitude is good for children. But the norm throughout the world is sex-differentiated parenting. In all cultures, fathers and mothers engage with children differently; few parents

adopt, even for a short time, the behaviors and attitudes characteristic of the other sex—and virtually none do so with ease and effectiveness. And the evidence is very strong that these differences
benefit children, that sex-typed parenting enhances their competence as they grow up. The distinct styles and strengths of men and
women that lead a father and mother to be different as parents suit
them wonderfully to provide jointly the nurture, structure, and latitude that help children develop strong roots and wings.

To the dismay of some, the differences between mothers and
fathers conform, in the main, to traditional stereotypes. The characteristic differences in the natural way males and females think,
feel, and act clearly express themselves in parenting. On key dimensions of childrearing men and women diverge in style—not hugely,
but in important ways. The short form is that evolution prepared
women to be nurturers and relaters, men to be hunters and aggres-
sors. At the most fundamental level, biology predisposes women to
be more parental than men through the hormones activated during
pregnancy and childbirth, the physiology and psychology of lactation, and so on. Research into stress has shed new light on fundamental gender differences in neurobiology. When faced with
a threat, both men and women experience the so-called fight-or-
flight response, in which heartbeat, blood pressure, and levels of
epinephrine and norepinephrine all rise and the hypothalamic-
pituitary-adrenocortical system kicks into gear. These responses all
prepare us to flee danger or, if necessary, turn and resist it. However, testosterone and other male hormones seem to accelerate
these biological reactions. For women, meanwhile, stress also stimulates production of the hormone oxytocin, which is primarily
known for helping to induce labor in pregnant women, lactation
in newly delivered mothers, and sexual receptivity. It typically
induces a state of calm—and also stimulates nurturing and caretaking behavior. Oxytocin's effect is magnified by estrogen. Although men, too, produce oxytocin, its impact appears to be
weakened by male hormones.[5]

Active participation in childrearing, especially of infants, is not a primary role for fathers around the world; providing for (and protecting) wives and children is. Men do have parental instincts, but they have no hormonal priming, and in most cultures active, direct paternal involvement is discretionary. Provisioning and protecting, however, are almost universally mandatory. Even in twenty-first-century America, these requirements apply. Fathers no longer need to hunt, but they are still the primary breadwinners in most families. Women have always shared the task of provisioning, and in America over the past fifty years they have entered the workforce en masse and made enormous breakthroughs in corporate, medical, legal, and other professional fields, enabling many to be highly successful wage-earners. Still, providing financially remains chiefly the man's role in families and both husbands and wives see a man's failure to do so (but not a woman's) as a serious, fundamental shortcoming.

As for protection, men are physically stronger than women, more likely to be aggressive and to take risks. Today the need for actual physical defense and safekeeping is nothing like what it was in past centuries, but it is not unimportant. It is still the man who is expected to go downstairs at night and investigate a strange noise. And mothers and children in families without fathers are at measurably greater risk of assault and abuse.[6] Cultures, it seems, "respond to the universal biological role of women [in birth and nursing] by setting up universal cultural arrangements that place women and children together, not just in infancy but beyond." In this way they supplement biological predisposition "with a heavy overlay of cultural expectations and demands."[7]

In those societies, including our own, where the father's role goes beyond providing and protecting and the norm is for both parents to participate in parenting, the evidence is that they do so differently, particularly with respect to communication, discipline, and play. For the most part, these differences are matters of degree or emphasis. Communication styles are a good example. In conversation, fathers tend to be briefer, more directive and concrete; mothers, more discursive, less directive, more focussed on feelings. Fathers tend to use more imperatives and more assertion of power with children, to see them as potential adults and to focus on their progress toward productive maturity. Mothers tend to be much more attuned, receptive, and reciprocal, to read cues better, and to engage in conversation about feelings and ideas for its own sake rather than for instruction. However, the overall differences, though clear, are not large; most parents communicate in all these ways with their children.[8]

Similar but greater differences appear when it comes to play and discipline. Much research confirms that fathers and mothers play with their children differently. A mother generally does so in a more caretaking manner, often following the child's initiatives sensitively and adapting herself to the child's style. A father more typically adopts a rough-and-tumble, physical approach, one that moves from the lifting of infants to physical games and sports for older children, often with a teaching component. Fathers' play with children seems to be much more arousing than mothers'. In this kind of play, as in other ways they deal with children, they generally emphasize "competition, challenge, initiative, risk taking, and independence," whereas mothers are more likely to emphasize caretaking, safety, and emotional security.[9]

In matters of discipline both parents make important contributions. Mothers typically do much more of the daily training about the rights and wrongs of behavior, because they spend much more time with the children, but fathers also do lots of teaching, especially as children get older. Mothers are more likely to be responsive to a child's temperament and the situation, and to explain and negotiate; fathers, to be firmer, more matter-of-fact, and to emphasize rules and principles. Research studies have found that mothers are more hesitant to impose discipline and punishment and children are more willing to challenge them. Having to integrate firmness and direction with nurturance is by no means easy, and many mothers take more readily to the role of confidante than that of disciplinarian. Fathers may be uncertain about whether and when to engage actively with children, but not in the content or style of what they do. Accustomed in their work lives to hierarchical relationships, they are ready for a paternal role that often calls for them to assume authority. They are more willing to confront and limit their children and to enforce punishment. Children everywhere naturally see them as the more powerful, stern, even threatening parent.[10]

It is important to add a note here about the special importance of fathers. A substantial body of data now links paternal involvement and nurturance with children's academic, psychological, and social competence. For example, children of involved fathers are more likely to show higher quantitative and verbal skills and better problem solving and overall school achievement than children of disengaged fathers. Daughters who have a father present are more likely to do well in mathematics; this is even more true for sons. Paternal nurturance appears also to contribute to boys' verbal intelligence.[11] In this regard, a key function for fathers is as a role model for sons—and, in a different way, for daughters, too.

Boys learn what it means to be a father primarily from the example set by their own. They learn about responsibility and achievement, about being assertive and independent, about self-control, and about dealing appropriately with females. During their teenage years especially, boys need a male presence that projects authority and discipline and models the control of impulses, or else they are much more likely to engage in risky and antisocial peer behavior.[12] Among boys who have infrequent contact with their fathers, whether resulting from divorce or other reasons, the likelihood of exaggerated macho behavior is notably greater. Much of the most negative teen behavior occurs among adolescents from fatherless, single-mother homes; these youth are especially prone to negative peer influences.[13]

Fathers are also important to daughters. They provide girls' earliest and primary learning about heterosexual difference and also about heterosexual trust. They often treat daughters in ways that would once have been called chivalrous, and they are likely to express approval of a girl's femininity, even when she is young. A loving, respectful relationship between father and daughter helps teach a girl that she is worthy of love and also begins to introduce her to the complexities of getting along in a male-dominated world.[14] As a statistical matter, the active presence of a father is a significant factor in helping girls avoid premature sex and pregnancy and develop a sense of independence and self-assertion.[15]

Research that links good fathering to limit setting, safety, and children's instrumental accomplishments may not be surprising. However, evidence also shows that good fathering contributes to the development of empathy, something usually seen as a female preserve, and to adult happiness. A twenty-six-year longitudinal study of the relationship between parenting in early childhood and the capacity of children to experience sympathy and compassion for others as adults astonished the researchers. They found that the most important factor of all the ones they surveyed was paternal involvement in child care. Not maternal, *paternal*.[16] A fascinating study of young adults found that those who were emotionally close to their fathers lived, on the whole, happier and more satisfied lives, *regardless* of their feelings toward their mothers.[17]

As outlined here, mothers and fathers both play important—but generally different—roles in all three areas of nurture, structure, and latitude. Nurture is predominantly a mother's realm, rooted in the biological predispositions that come with pregnancy, birth, and nursing, and the attuned engagement, the sensitivity to feelings, and interest in emotionality that characterizes women much more than men. But if the father's role is secondary here, it is not unimportant. A mother's more empathic, reciprocal style is not the only way to develop parent-child intimacy; a father's playful style of interaction creates an important connection of its own. And as just noted, having an involved, engaged father contributes significantly to the capacity for empathy and compassion.

Structure is more typically a father's domain than a mother's. Fathers' greater willingness to confront and limit children, their tendency to see things more in matter-of-fact terms, to emphasize responsibility, and to focus on children as future adults all tend to give them a primary role in structure, particularly with respect to limit setting and discipline, but also in terms of expectations for achievement. As noted, the presence of a father in a household typically exerts a significant influence against adolescent acting out, both for boys and girls. However, mothers are also important to the structuring of children's behavior. As noted earlier, they usually provide much of the daily education and guidelines about what is right and wrong and do much of the frontline limit setting. Their expectations for achievement are important to their children. And a strong nurturing connection, in which mothers play a key role, contributes to children's ability and willingness to accept structure.

Latitude may be the area with the most parity in the natural contributions of parents, and therefore the area that offers the most visible value of having both a father and a mother. In general, men are more likely to be bolder with children in physical ways, to give them more freedom, even to encourage them to explore, try, take a risk. Women are not insensitive to these initiatives—many encourage their children in similar ways—but on the whole they are more likely to emphasize safety, harmony, and mutuality. However, when it comes to the expression of feeling and the maintenance and improvement of relationships, mothers are often more likely to tolerate and foster greater autonomy and latitude for children to voice feelings, wishes, and needs, while fathers are, as a rule, less interested in and tolerant of this kind of expression. In this respect, mothers, too, help children learn to explore, try, and take a risk. The key point in all this is that children need what both fathers and mothers naturally tend to provide. No wonder an extensive review of studies of parenting found children raised by traditionally sex-typed parents to be more competent than others.[18]

To reflect back on the summary of nurture, structure, and latitude is to see that any parent alone would be hard-pressed to be a
sufficient and continuous source of all three over time. I have already emphasized that the areas of overlap between mothers and
fathers can be quite high, but the natural stylistic differences
between them make a mother and father ideally suited to provide
what children need. This definitely does *not* mean that single parents, stepparents, or adoptive parents can't do well by children, and
it certainly doesn't mean that biological pairs always do so. It means
that two caregivers are almost always likely to be better than one,
and that however they are mated, it is ideal for them to combine
the advantages that good natural mothering and good natural
fathering provide.

The Social Context

Children aren't just raised by a family, of course, but by a family in
a social context. We live in nested social spheres that begin in the
home and extend out through the neighborhood to the larger society. Key to growing up, therefore, is the goodness of fit between a
family and the community in which it is embedded. No matter how
well parents nurture children, if they prepare them for a way of life
that differs markedly from the society's prevailing norms, their children may encounter difficulty adapting as adults. For all but the last
eyeblink of human history this was not an issue. Life was local. People lived in relatively small, homogeneous communities, sharing a
common culture, language, religion, and outlook. Rates of change
in norms and customs, in technology and communications, were
generally low and incremental. If this left little room for choice,
it also left little room for doubt; it maximized the likelihood that
parents would hold their children to similar expectations and incul-
cate similar values, that other adults in the community would reinforce these expectations and values, and that children would
reach adulthood well adapted for community membership.

In the twenty-first century we live amid accelerating change and unprecedented diversity. Life is no longer local. For all the richness and opportunity this creates it complicates the raising of children, both because of the range of varied influences that reach children directly, even at early ages, and because of the fragmentation of social norms and expectations, which decrease community cohesion and make it difficult to ensure a good fit between family and society. As children grow up and engage more with the world beyond the family, their individual identities are affected by the spheres in which they move and the groups (gender, kinship, peer, racial, ethnic, religious) to which they belong. Parents can influence these additions to a child's identity but cannot control them.

Even in our increasingly diverse and fragmented society, the evidence is impressive that children develop better when they grow up in families rooted in strong communities. The evidence comes primarily from scholars who have been studying the effects of "social capital," their term for what most of us would call "community." (Technically, *social capital* refers to the "connections among individuals—social networks and the norms of reciprocity and trustworthiness that arise from them."[19]) The functioning of families is enhanced in a neighborhood where people share similar values, trust each other, and can count on one another to keep an eye on children and to support public order. Urban neighborhoods with high levels of social capital have been shown to have significantly less violence and homicide than similar neighborhoods with lower levels of social capital.[20]

The effects of this kind of social capital are extensive. For example, schools in strong communities experience greater support from parents and less misbehavior and disruption by students. In an extensive review of the research on social capital, Robert Putnam, a professor of public policy at Harvard, shows that when it comes to minimizing student violence, two factors stand out as being most effective—two-parent families and community-based social capital—and together they stand way out, dwarfing the significance of poverty, among other social conditions. Socioeconomic status clearly plays a significant role in children's overall health and well-being, but social capital ranks right behind—and ahead of racial composition. Poverty is a powerful contributor to premature pregnancy, mortality, and idleness, but community engagement has precisely the opposite effect. Moreover, other factors being equal, higher neighborhood cohesion is associated with lower rates of child abuse, and in similar communities with similar income levels and similar rates of working women and single-parent households, social capital is the chief characteristic making one safer for children than another.[21] Unhappily, social capital is declining. I will return to this important challenge to children and parents in later chapters.

For many parents, particularly those whose children are adolescent, the beyond-the-family influence of greatest concern is that of their children's friends—peer pressure, as we have come to call it. No doubt peers are important throughout life—civilization would be impossible without certain kinds of peer pressure—and particularly as children grow into adolescence. The rise of what is sometimes seen as a separate youth culture in America has left many parents feeling powerless to shape the social behavior and foster the school performance of their teenagers. The short form of this worry is, in essence, that other people's children will corrupt our own, undermining our impact as parents.[22] In fact, research suggests that peer influence is broader than it is deep; that it involves similarity much more than influence; that individuals shape peer response more than we think; and most important, that parents can affect peer selection and susceptibility, though not necessarily in direct ways.

Perhaps the first thing to emphasize about peer influence among teenagers and preteens is that although it seems omnipresent and omnipotent, it does not operate at fundamental levels of personality. It acts strongly upon everyday behavior—dress and language, tastes in music, fads and crazes, attitudes—but not nearly as strongly upon underlying character traits. For one thing, peers do not begin to have a significant effect on a child until the age of seven or eight, by which time most basic traits, such as sociability, introversion, perseverance, and responsiveness to authority, have already been well established. Attitudes and tastes can have a significant influence on a person's life; I do not dismiss them lightly. But they change with time in ways that personality does not. For another, the evidence is that by the time they reach adolescence, if not before, children seek like-minded peers; we need to be careful not to mistake peer *similarity* for peer *influence*. Antisocially inclined children tend to link up with other antisocials; high-achieving students tend to connect with other high achievers. It is much less common for teenagers to be seduced by delinquents who change their personality than for teens to pick friends and gravitate toward certain peers *because of* their personality.

This selection effect may stem from the fact that children and adolescents, far from being just the product of peer influences, also act in ways that shape the responses of peers. This has been confirmed in fascinating studies of children who were aggressive and disruptive at school and rejected by classmates. Researchers had them participate in two kinds of playgroups, one consisting of peers from school, the other of strangers. When playing with school peers who already knew them, they were clearly rejected during the first session, as might be expected. However, in the groups where all the participants were initially strangers, these children, by only the third or fourth meeting, were also being rejected by the others. This offers a sharp challenge to the notion that rejected children are simply victims of negative perceptions by peers and strongly suggests that their own behavior helps provoke the rebuffs they receive.[23]

Although parents may feel helpless to influence a teenager's social contacts, they do, in fact, shape them. This can't be done directly by, say, trying to forbid one friendship and foster another— such efforts are generally futile. Instead, parents exert influence in part by the neighborhood they choose to live in. In communities characterized by high levels of social capital, teens not only encounter higher levels of parental oversight and structure in their own homes, they also meet more peers who are raised by authoritative parents and are themselves better at self-regulation. Many poor families, of course, have few options about where they can live, and the only housing they can afford is often in areas that have low levels of social capital, which means that there will be less collective adult support and supervision of children.

None of this is to deny that peers affect each other, particularly in adolescence. During the teen years peers can have a great impact on one another's alcohol and drug use and sexual experimentation. They can also affect school performance. For example, the much-discussed lag in academic achievement by African American high school students appears to reflect in part an attitude that being smart and working hard constitutes a kind of sellout—being "too white." This attitude is by no means the only contributor to the problem, but where it prevails, it can discourage black students, even those whose parents are upper-middle-class, college-educated professionals, from enrolling in challenging courses and investing in their work. (By contrast, Asian American students, even those whose parents are disengaged and underinvolved, generally have a peer group that values effort and worries about the consequences of not doing well in school.)[24] On a broader scale, it is certainly true that America is more peer-oriented and age-stratified than most societies—often far more. As far back as the 1830s Alexis de Tocqueville, the great French observer of post-Revolutionary America, noted this, reporting that little remained of the traditional family in America except a few vestiges during early childhood.[25] Since the 1970s, psychologists and other observers have pointed to the amount of time American children spend with peers, suggesting America was becoming a society segregated by age.[26]

Despite all this, parents remain, as David Elkind, author of *The Hurried Child* and one of the nation's leading psychologists, says, "the single most powerful, nonbiological influence on their children's lives."[27] And the most significant thing that parents can do about peer pressure—it is truly significant—is to be authoritative throughout childhood, to provide sufficient levels of nurture, structure, and latitude and so help children establish a strong internal compass. This does not make children immune to peer pressure, but it does affect their behavior with their friends and classmates in positive ways. Authoritative parents who are both responsive and demanding raise children who tend to be less susceptible to dangerous peer influence (drugs and alcohol, for example) and to perform better in school than the children of parents who are permissive or authoritarian. Their children internalize the box within which they have been raised. They are more inclined to pause, to think twice before engaging in risky behavior, to reflect on the consequences of their actions, to learn from their mistakes, and to connect with peers whose priorities include academic success. What this means is that much of what we call peer influence is in critical ways the outcome of earlier family influence, and that the best time to be influential with adolescents is well before adolescence.[28]

It also means that the spread of adolescent peer influence, which is just one aspect of the general deterioration in behavior, values, readiness, and performance that prompted this book, reflects a decline in authoritative parenting. In fact, it reflects an abandonment by many parents of fundamental developmental function. This abandonment is unplanned and often involves factors beyond their control, but it risks profound consequences for our children, our schools, and our nation. We need to understand it, its causes and context, as a basis for knowing how best to help schools respond.

4

Fast Forward

The Fragile Family

The family has never been static; it has always been changing, but probably never so radically as in recent decades. In barely half a century it has undergone a transformation that could never have been predicted, a transformation without precedent in recorded human history that has altered our entire social and educational landscape. The essence of this change is that marriage, family, and childrearing have suffered sharp and sustained declines. Americans marry less and later, break up sooner and more often, and are raising children in different configurations and in different ways than they used to. Parents spend more time at work, less time with their offspring, and are caught up in a rising tide of anxious expectation and developmental uncertainty. These changes are understood very differently by cultural conservatives and religious fundamentalists on one hand, and by liberals and feminists on the other. But from the perspective of child development it is increasingly clear that the changes in the family have disrupted parents' inclination and ability to be authoritative, to provide nurture, structure, and latitude. In so doing, they have created a childrearing deficit that makes it steadily more difficult for children to thrive, to grow into people of competence, caring, and character—and for their schools to help them do so.

The Nostalgia Trap

Some scholars argue that we often fall into what Stephanie Coontz, who studies the history of the family, has called a "nostalgia trap," unfairly comparing the contemporary family to a utopian notion of the family of the past, specifically that of the 1950s.[1] The idealized family of that era—a breadwinner, a homemaker, and several children, living in the suburbs—is often known by one of its exemplars on old television sitcoms—the "Ozzie and Harriet" family, the "Donna Reed" family, and so on. Labeling it this way acknowledges that this image of the family was not altogether real, that domestic life was not as simple and straightforward as these programs pretended or memory suggests. Yet in retrospect, the '50s do appear to many as a decade of peace and prosperity, of domestic contentment and stability. It was part of the most sustained period of economic growth in American history, a time when life expectancy, buying power, personal net worth, and government-sponsored security all improved markedly. The postwar economy was growing at a pace unseen before. Marriage was widely viewed as the foundation of social life and civic virtue. The rate of divorce was half what it is today, as was the rate of out-of-wedlock births. Gender roles were clearly demarcated: men were providers, women generally kept house and raised children. The Baby Boom was in full flower. Social and community life was orderly; respect for institutions was strong. Religious attendance was high, violent crime was relatively low, and serious school discipline problems were, by today's standards, rare. In retrospect, the '50s stand out, for many Americans and certainly for many veteran faculty, as a decade marked by clarity, consensus, and innocence.

The reality, of course, was much more complex. Many teachers are surprised to learn that the '50s were unusual, to put it mildly. For one thing, the breadwinner-homemaker family actually predominated in America only from the 1920s into the 1960s. (Prior to 1920 most children lived with two parents, but in farm families; by 1970, most lived in dual-earner or single-parent households.) And in its pure form—an intact family, parents in their first and only marriage, all children born after that marriage, father employed year-round, mother not in the labor force—it has never been the context in which most American children grew up. The 1950s were the first decade in a century when the average age of marriage and motherhood fell, birth rates increased, and divorce declined. Until then, the trends had been quite the opposite, and in the 1960s each resumed its previous course.

The image of the '50s family, comfortably middle-class, suburban, and white, also fails to capture America's diversity. In 1950 25 percent of Americans—nearly fifty million people, including more than half of intact, two-parent black families—lived below the poverty line and without a safety net. And by no means every mother was at home full time. Women's participation in the labor force had been increasing since at least the 1940s, as had non-parental child care for young children. Forty percent of black women with small children worked outside the home. As for those families who did fit the stereotype, the picture there was not so uniformly bright, either. Some of the tranquility of the suburban family required women to repress their own needs and interests. Meanwhile, many social problems were not absent, just camouflaged. Incest and illegitimacy, for example. The former went virtually unreported. The latter was actually more frequent than today but better hidden (a birth was often not identified as illegitimate if the mother lived with her parents).[2] And there were moral and political blights, as well, including, among others, segregation, which was still legal in many states and practiced in others, and McCarthyism, which ran rampant in the fear and fervor of the cold war.

There is no question, then, that some of our current family trends actually began long ago, and that the 1950s were in many ways unusual and by no means perfect. But even though some critics portray those years as notable for "crushing social conformity, stifling domesticity, egregious hypocrisy, and distressing female and racial oppression," they were in fact marked by high levels of optimism, of confidence in social institutions, and by a "remarkable familism." By the 1950s, the United States had become the world's most marrying society.[3] Most people wed at a relatively young age, most of the rest did so eventually (nearly 95 percent of those born between 1935 and 1945 married), and most marriages lasted a lifetime. The typical child was born to married parents and lived with them continuously until at least late adolescence. By 1960, a greater proportion of children (nearly 80 percent) lived with both natural parents than ever before—or ever again. This familism may have been an exception, but it couldn't have been better for children. For child development, the '50s in some key ways marked a peak, the culmination of a century of improvement during which children had been removed from factories and sent to school and through a range of legal and social changes protected from premature exposure to the dangers of adult life.[4]

The New Fragility

Even if the family was never as idyllic or stable as some imagine, this hardly means there is no cause for concern about the changes it has undergone. On the contrary, these have been wide and deep, and even if some are resumptions of longer-term trends, they have materially weakened the family as a setting for intimate relationships and child development. Our concept of family long took for granted some essential characteristics: families were created by married couples who had children and helped them grow into adulthood; their members were committed to one another for life; they spent a lot of time together; and they supported one another financially and with caring attention. These traits now define families much less fully, and each is in decline: couples are marrying less often and later in life, having fewer children, and splitting up more; connections are less obligatory and more fleeting; family members are with one another much less; and child care is increasingly provided by paid outsiders.[5] Tracing this transformation, David Elkind summarizes it as a movement from "nuclear" to "permeable." The breadwinner-homemaker couple with several children has yielded to today's postmodern family: single-parent, remarried, and two-career households. Where the nuclear family had a comparatively strong center and a comparatively distinct boundary separating it from the outside world, today's family is more fluid, less stable, and far more susceptible to external influences. For this reason, I think of it as the *fragile family*. The new fragility is both structural and behavioral, reflected in the ways families are configured and parents raise children.[6]

Everyone knows in a rough-and-ready way that family structure has changed, but to study the full extent of the changes is sobering. Unprecedented numbers of people now delay marriage until their late twenties or their thirties or cohabit without marrying. When they do wed, the chances of their first marriage breaking up are between 40 percent and 50 percent; of their second marriage, between 50 percent and 60 percent (barely more than half of American adults are currently married); when they cohabit, their chances of breaking up are even higher. More than one-quarter of all families with children are headed by single parents, overwhelmingly mothers. More than 40 percent of American children do not currently live with their biological fathers. At this writing, of the roughly seventy-three million children under the age of eighteen, about twenty million live in single-parent families, and perhaps as many as nine million in stepfamilies.[7] Each year, an additional one million children experience their parents' divorce and another million-plus are born out of wedlock. If current patterns prevail, the typical child may soon be likely to live apart from at least one biological parent at least part of the time while growing up, and fewer than half of all children may be living with both biological parents by the time they finish high school. Adding changes in adult employment to family disruption means that at least 80 percent of all American children now live in two-career or single-parent families.[8] In the 1950s, 75 percent of school-age children had a parent at home full time; as late as 1970, 57 percent still did. Today, barely 25 percent do.

The problem with the contemporary family as a context for growing up is not just that it takes more varied forms, is more fragile, and has fewer full-time parents, but that *it functions less developmentally* than it used to. As sociologist Arlie Russell Hochschild notes, love and care—the essential core of not only family but social life—have become a source of great confusion.[9] The evidence is clearest in single-parent and stepparent households. More and more research confirms that children of divorced and never-married parents are, as a group, at measurably greater risk for a variety of educational and social-emotional problems that pose real challenges to the children themselves and their teachers. For example, they are much more likely to present serious academic and behavioral problems at school: their grades are likely to be lower, their motivation weaker, their attendance poorer; they are more likely to form friendships with peers who misbehave, to repeat a grade, and to be suspended or expelled.[10] In terms of general health and well-being, they experience more problems with asthma, headaches, and speech defects, are four times more likely to smoke, and 20 percent to 30 percent more likely to experience accidents, injuries, and poisonings, and to be diagnosed with attention deficit disorder. Their mental health is also more vulnerable: among other risks, they are three to four times as likely to suffer emotional problems, notably anxiety and depression.[11] It is important to note that these risks do not just apply to children living with a single parent. When divorced parents remarry and children grow up in stepfamilies, there is no measurable improvement in their outcomes.[12] In the risk categories listed here, stepchildren, as a group, do no better than children of single parents. (Stepparenthood actually contributes some new perils of its own: stepchildren are at measurably greater risk of being abused.)[13]

These facts should not be exaggerated—as we all know, most children of single parents grow up successfully. I cite them because they illustrate in a vivid way the ultimate risks of family fragility. They are in this sense the leading indicators of profound shifts in parenting that are complicating the prospects for children and the work of teachers.

The shifts, as identified by Elkind, occur along five major dimensions of family life: emotional bonds, core values, authority relationships, views of child development, and views of childrearing (Table 4.1). At the heart of the nuclear family was togetherness: family was placed before self; spouses were to sacrifice for each other and parents, for their children's future. Marriage was to be a lifelong commitment; family, a haven from the pressures of a demanding world; parenting, the province of parents, especially of a warm, nurturing mother. Parental authority was largely unilateral. Children were seen as innocent and adolescents as immature, and they needed parental protection, guidance, and discipline. Parenting itself was seen largely as a matter of intuition informed by experience.

Table 4.1. The Changing Family: From Nuclear to Fragile

	Modern, Nuclear Family	Postmodern, Fragile Family
Bonds	Romantic love	Consensual love
	Maternal love	Shared parenting
	Domesticity (haven)	Urbanity (hub)
Values	Togetherness	Autonomy
Authority	Unilateral	Mutual, negotiated
Development	Childhood innocence	Childhood competence
	Adolescent immaturity	Adolescent sophistication
Parenting	Intuition	Technique

Source: Adapted from Elkind.[14]

By contrast, the fragile family is based on a core value of autonomy: individual family members pursue their own fulfillment. Marriage is seen neither as essential to becoming a parent nor as a permanent commitment but more as a current consensus that respects each party's individuality, a consensus that leaves both parents freer to focus on jobs and careers—and to leave the marriage if it is unrewarding. Reflecting this shift toward individual autonomy, the family has become, as Elkind says, a hub, a railway station for over-scheduled parents and children who all lead ever-busier outside lives. Childrearing is now a task shared heavily with hired caregivers. Parental authority has become much more mutual, a matter of negotiation with children, even the very young. We now emphasize children's competence and adolescents' sophistication. Accordingly, parenting is now treated much more as a matter of applying effective techniques that will cause children to respond in appropriate ways.

Looking Ahead

The next three chapters, using Elkind's framework as a primary lens, will examine the fate of nurture, structure, and latitude in the contemporary family. All three are under growing pressure. Children in all kinds of families, including the wealthiest, are having to grow up with declining levels of each. Though many children are, fortunately, able to cope, this shift is not ideal for any, and goes a long way toward explaining the kinds of behavior and performance problems they present at school and elsewhere.

Indeed, evidence is now accumulating that its negative impact is broader and deeper than previously thought. UCLA psychologist Shelley Taylor and her colleagues have been studying what they call "risky families." A risky family, though not pathological, fails to provide for children the good early tending, "the warmth and nurturance that help them form the biological and emotional repertoire" necessary to good stress management in life. Being left to fend for themselves and simply not receiving a lot of warmth and physical affection makes children more prone to depression and anxiety, and actually weakens the biological mechanisms that help them cope with stress. Taylor's team was surprised to find that on every stress indicator they measured, normal college students from risky families looked worse than their peers from non-risky families. They were, for example, more anxious, depressed, and hostile—not enough to require treatment, but clearly more than students from more supportive families. And biologically, their heart, blood pressure, and cortisol (stress hormone) responses were also noticeably less healthy. Though their families' general functioning and their own were in the normal range, their growing up had clearly left them with psychological and physical weaknesses.[15] "Permeable" and "fragile" are not synonyms for "risky," but permeability and fragility surely increase risk.

When they talk about changes in the family, many teachers express anger toward parents for letting their children down, for failing to provide the support, continuity, and structure their children need to function well in school. But the trend toward fragility is not the result of planned shifts in priority by parents. A principal reason the family has never been static is that it has always had to adapt to the economic and social realities around it. The nuclear family, for example, was made possible in part by America's enormous post–World War II economic strength and the social cohesion brought about by the war effort. Its structures and values were adapted to then-current economic patterns and priorities—patterns and priorities that are being superseded by new realities, such as the decline of manufacturing and the rise of service industries, new modes of production and distribution, new concepts of career and loyalty, and so on. Today's family mirrors in many ways our rapidly innovating, individualistic, entrepreneurial economy and our spreading social fragmentation—topics explored in more detail in Chapters Eight and Nine.

The nuclear family was by no means perfect, but it was strongly child-centered. It favored the well-being of the young because it was comparatively high on nurture, structure, and latitude, all of which required, in one way or another, self-sacrifice by parents. The contemporary family, as Elkind has noted, reverses the burden, favoring the well-being of adults and requiring adaptation and sacrifice by children. And although the children of the 1950s were not so innocent nor the adolescents so immature as parents and the larger society then supposed, today's children are not nearly so competent nor today's teenagers so sophisticated as we would like to believe.[16] Today's parents are able to devote ever more time to their jobs and careers, working harder and longer, by necessity and preference, but growing numbers of youth are denied the basics of healthy growth on which psychological health, learning, and civility and cooperation depend.

5

· ·

Losing Connection

S ome years ago, Hallmark began marketing cards that busy fathers and mothers could leave for their children—cards with messages like "Have a super day at school" (from the parent who will be gone before the child awakens) or "I wish I were there to tuck you in" (from the parent who will return after the child is asleep). When parental absence at breakfast and bedtime is common enough to become a marketing opportunity, it suggests something ominous about how children are growing up. In fact, the nurture of children has been reduced in both quantity and quality by the shift away from togetherness and toward autonomy as the family's core value, a shift reflected in the weakening of the marital bond between spouses and the parental bond with children. Families are less close and connected than they used to be, the relationships within them less structured, predictable, and caregiving. The ties that link family members are much less fixed and absolute, and have grown more complex and vulnerable. They make it harder for parents to attune themselves to children and thus to nurture them. This in turn requires children to make sacrifices—sacrifices that many can manage but that a growing number cannot, and that are far from ideal for most.

Weakening Ties

Not too long ago, marriage was seen as a matter of falling in love forever with a special person for whom one was destined. This love was to last a lifetime, and even if it didn't, the marriage was supposed to. Matrimony was the necessary path to sex and parenthood and it entailed an expectation of mutual sacrifice for each other's happiness and for the well-being of the couple's joint offspring. Romantic love led to the creation of a domestic haven, a comforting refuge from the pressures of a demanding world, a place for collective relationship, relaxation, and recreation. A place, too, where family members, parent and child alike, felt not just a primary allegiance, but a greater connection than they did with peers, friends, and colleagues outside the family.[1] Maintenance of this haven entailed collective sacrifice. It required that individuals' interests yield to the larger family good—notably that parents sacrifice for their children. Bound up in this ideal were many constraints, chief among them a definite gender-based role differentiation that today looks sexist and unequal—a woman having to wait for "Mr. Right," then becoming a homemaker, and so on. A strong commitment to the ideal of romantic love and of domesticity also helped to keep parents in marriages, even unhappy ones. Children might see through their parents' efforts to pretend that all was well, but they could also see their parents' willingness to sacrifice for them, to limit the pursuit of their own individual happiness so as to preserve a haven at home.[2] Taken together, these are the norms that created such a strong familism.

Over the past several decades in America the prevailing bonds and values of family life have shifted markedly. Romantic love hasn't vanished, but it is no longer as central. Love has become more consensual. Marriage is now seen more as a current agreement that respects each partner's individuality. "We no longer believe," notes Ann Swidler, "that an adult's life can be meaningfully defined by the sacrifice he or she makes for spouse or children." The primary duty is, rather, to respect one another's "need for growth and change, and to give to the other in return for what one receives."[3] A majority of Americans no longer include being married on their

list of family values, suggesting that marriage has been losing its
legitimacy and social purpose.[4]

The new marriage brings greater freedom and equality, but
greater insecurity and complexity. It reduces the old constraints
but also the old certainty: I am freer to be what I want, but I have
to create my own role; I am freer to leave if I am unhappy, but so is
my spouse. The new freedom, coupled with the fading of traditional
gender expectations, means that spouses now must invent and negotiate career and family roles that were formerly inherited and prescribed. This adds a whole new layer of complexity to marriage and
family life. At the same time, partners come to marriage with higher
expectations than in the past—namely, that it will satisfy emotional
needs for companionship, individual development, and emotional
security, not just for children, a steady sexual relationship, and
maintenance of a home. This makes it easier for them to be disappointed than spouses of previous generations, whose expectations
were lower, with the result that parents now leave marriages at
lower thresholds of unhappiness than in the past.

None of this is to say that marriage used to be easy; it has always
required work. But there is more to work at now and the shifts in
the marital contract do not improve a couple's confidence in permanence or their freedom to be emotionally responsive to their
children. On the contrary, the vulnerability of the marital bond
affects the entire family as it balances its internal and external relations. The ideal of the home as a domestic refuge has been fractured
by everything from our high divorce rate and our workaholism to
our remarkable mobility (we must surely be the most commuting,
relocating nation in the history of the world). The emphasis on
domesticity has been demolished by a new devotion to what Elkind
calls "urbanity." As noted in Chapter Four, Elkind sees the home as
a hub, a junction where busy parents and children see each other
briefly on their way to and from the many events outside the family that engage them. This shift in emphasis reflects a sea change in

the family's basic values. At the heart of the nuclear family was togetherness; for the permeable family it is autonomy. Romantic love, maternal love, and domesticity all required one to place family before self: spouses were to sacrifice for each other and parents for their children's future, and children were to subordinate their own wishes to the family's priorities. Children and adolescents were not highly scheduled into formal activities and routinely spent large amounts of time either at home or nearby in the neighborhood with adults, usually mothers, generally available. The "family first" norm was reflected in the expectation, indeed the necessity, that many adolescents would contribute to the family income.

Today, the focus is much more on the individual's pursuit of personal fulfillment in the world outside the family. One of the features that most distinguishes American families from others around the world is that "the primary loyalty is to self—its values, autonomy, pleasure, virtue, and actualization."[5] These emphases mean that children and adolescents are simultaneously freer, busier, and more alone than in the past: freer in that they have fewer family responsibilities (many teenagers are employed after school but rarely contribute to the family income); busier in that they now participate in so many formal after-school activities (sports, lessons, and the like); and more alone in that they are permitted and forced to spend more unsupervised time on their own. Parents, too, are less bound by family. They feel more entitled to spend money on themselves, even to borrow heavily for material goods, freer to devote themselves to their careers, and freer to leave the family through divorce. In many homes, family meals are a relic of the past. Only 34 percent of Americans say that their whole family eats dinner together regularly.[6]

The Decline of Direct Parenting

The demise of the family dinner graphically illustrates the decline of direct parenting. In the nuclear family the raising of children was understood to be primarily the province of parents, especially of a

warm, nurturing mother. In the 1950s, psychologists were emphasizing the importance of maternal attachment and studying the
effects on children of maternal deprivation. British psychiatrist John
Bowlby, a leading theorist, famously wrote that "leaving any child
under three years of age is a major operation only to be undertaken
for good and sufficient reasons and, when undertaken, to be planned
with great care."[7] It has now become axiomatic that the emphasis
on maternal love as the cornerstone of parental care was exaggerated, even misguided, that it oppressed women, that the Ozzie and
Harriet family celebrated in popular culture really trapped women,
tying them to the home and denying them meaningful lives. This
must surely have been true for some mothers, perhaps for many,
though no one really knows. But there is little proof of rampant
pathology—or even of rampant quiet desperation—among mothers of the 1950s. Nor is there evidence that mothers, or fathers for
that matter, are happier now than they were then. (On the contrary,
as Chapter Eight and Chapter Nine note, there is evidence that
both are less happy, particularly mothers.)

Nonetheless, there has been a definite alteration in the expression of parent-child bonds. The powerful changes brought about by,
among other forces, the women's movement shattered the notion
that homemaker mothers were vital to child development. No one
can now doubt that men can care for children or that women can
have careers and still be good mothers. Childrearing is no longer a
mother's job alone, but a task to be shared by both parents in those
families where fathers participate heavily in the process and also in
those situations where biological parents who don't live together
must arrange visitation and custody. And it is most especially a task
to be shared with nonparental caregivers—and with children themselves. Parents haven't the time.

Whatever else nurture requires, it demands personal time—time
to be with, play with, do for, listen to, and comfort children. There
is no great mystery to parenting, as Cornel West and Sylvia Ann
Hewlitt point out. It is not a mysterious, technical process. It is

something adults have managed on their own for thousands of years. And at its core is "time, huge amounts of it, freely given. Whatever the child-raising technique, a child simply does better with loving, committed, long-term attention from both mom and dad."[8] Time, of course, is precisely what parents who are self- and career-focussed lack. For years, now, social scientists have been reporting declines in the amount of time parents spend with children. The chief reason is the proportion of collective parental time devoted to employment, which has risen steadily. Two factors are operating here. The first is the movement of women into the labor force. As noted, roughly 75 percent of mothers with children under eighteen now work outside the home and those with very young children work every bit as long as other parents. Time has always been a zero-sum game: an addition of time in one place means a subtraction of time somewhere else. When mothers join the workforce, the time they spend in primary child care drops from an average of twelve hours per week to fewer than six.[9]

The second is that almost everyone is working ever-longer hours, fathers and mothers both. Parents' "total contact time" with children, which includes not just playing with or reading to a child but running errands and doing household tasks together, declined massively after 1970. Depending on which study you read, parents spend somewhere between ten and twenty-two fewer hours per week with their children than was common several decades ago.[10] The decline of direct parent availability means that children are now much more likely to be cared for by day-care providers or to be left alone. It also means that the time parents do have with children is more precious and pressured.

Day-Care Dilemmas

Child care itself, once provided primarily by relatives, increasingly occurs at professional centers. Thirty-nine percent of infants and toddlers with employed mothers are in day care at least thirty-five hours per week.[11] The youngest children in day care tend to be there the longest—for example, infants in one study averaged forty-two hours per week in day care.[12] The impact of this third-party child care is one of the most controversial topics in child development. Each year I talk to several thousand educators at their schools and at professional conferences. Most, especially elementary teachers, are deeply dismayed by the numbers of young children who spend long hours in day care. They would agree with Hewlitt that the massive increase in the time adults spend in the workplace (especially when coupled with our high rates of divorce and single parenthood), means, for youth, "little contact with parents and large quantities of time badly spent."[13]

Many studies, of course, have concluded that high-quality day care (provided in an appropriate setting by a trained, consistent staff) does not harm children, either intellectually, socially, or in terms of maternal attachment (some studies have found comparative advantages for children who are in good day-care settings). There is considerable evidence that children who have sensitive, nurturing mothers and competent day-care providers generally turn out to be securely attached to their mothers and cognitively and socially intact.[14]

These assurances are comforting, as far as they go. Unfortunately, they don't go nearly far enough. For one thing, some studies have shown that children who spend lots of time in nonmaternal care have interactions with their mothers that are less positive than those of other children.[15] And careful research has recently confirmed earlier findings that when a mother of a young infant works outside the home, her child is more likely than other children to show lower school readiness by the age of three, especially if the mother works thirty hours or more per week.[16] Other major studies in the United States and Britain have found a correlation between amount of time toddlers spend in child care and the likelihood that they will show greater aggression and disobedience as schoolchildren.[17] But by far the greatest concern is about quality, not quantity. The assurances that day care is safe for children always specify that the day care must be of high quality. And everyone agrees that there is nowhere near enough of this. In fact, there is a broad consensus that much of the nation's out-of-home child care is most definitely not of high quality. Lots of day care is provided in settings that are barely adequate or substandard. Many staff are untrained and poorly paid (they earn, on average, no more than parking lot attendants or dry cleaning staff) and as a result turnover is high. In fact, turnover rates among day-care personnel are among the highest of any occupation, ranging from 25 to 40 percent.[18] The dearth of affordable high-quality child care forcibly shifts what Elkind calls the "need balance" in favor of parents. He points out that when parents have no economic choice but to put the children somewhere, even if they don't have access to good child-care providers and even if they do so with real reluctance, the experience will be hard for them. But in the long run it is likely to be harder for their children.[19]

In addition to the children in day care, a substantial but hard-to-count number of children are, at least for portions of each week, left on their own. The number of these "latchkey children," who return from school to empty homes, began to grow dramatically in the 1970s, rising from 1.6 million to at least 5 and possibly 12 million. Between one-quarter and one-third of twelve-year-olds are regularly left on their own while their parents are at work. Roughly 35 percent of this age group spend at least some time taking care of themselves during the week, and so do 7 percent of six-year-olds.[20]

Some writers argue that the term *latchkey* exaggerates both the apparent neglect by parents and the actual risks that children face when left home alone. They prefer *self-care* as a less judgmental descriptor and this, indeed, is becoming the accepted term used by researchers. But if *latchkey* seems too harsh, *self-care* seems positively Orwellian in its effort to put a neutral face on a negative reality. Whatever we call it, leaving children and young adolescents by themselves *on a consistent basis for significant periods of time* poses an unwise and unhealthy challenge for them, and its impact is unfavorable. An extensive study of five thousand eighth graders found that those who were home alone for at least eleven hours per week—in both upper-class and working-class families—were three times as likely as other children to abuse alcohol, tobacco, or marijuana. A large, comprehensive survey of ninety thousand teenagers showed not only that those who were closely connected to parents were less likely to be suicidal or violent or to use drugs but that the simple presence of a parent in the home after school, at dinner, and in the evening meaningfully reduced the odds of teenagers' engaging in risky behavior. Other research has shown that evening work by parents negatively affects children's emotional and cognitive development.[21]

It's also important to consider the many children who fall into what might be called a *near-latchkey* category. They are what a preschool teacher I know calls "the no-fallback kids": they are dropped off at school extra early and picked up late, and sent to school in spite of illness—all because parents have no child-care coverage. Although their numbers are hard to count, the anecdotal evidence of their presence in schools is abundant. Twenty-five years ago virtually no school in America had an extended day program or day-care arrangement. Both are now common in public and private schools, created in response to parental pressure and requests. Yet nearly every school I visit reports that growing numbers of students are still dropped off before the extended day arrival time in the morning, even when this is quite early, and not picked up at evening closing time, even when this is quite late. And each year I visit several dozen schools, private as well as public, that must write letters to parents reminding them—sometimes begging them—not to send children to school who have a fever or are vomiting.

Twin Myths: Quality Time and Family Efficiency

The reduced quantity of time that parents spend with their children is one thing, reduced quality is another. It's not just that parents are with their children less, it's that when they are together, the pressure is often high and the energy often low. For some years there was, unbelievably, an actual debate about the concept of "quality time," with some writers proposing that positive intensity can make up for lengthy absence, that brief, ordinary moments can be made especially influential and meaningful to children. There were even whole books promoting this myth. The debate is over: trying to rely on quality time as an approach to raising children is hopelessly self-defeating.

The immediate issue is that being forced to have high-quality interaction is an impossible burden for both parent and child. Imagine that you were instructed to put this book down and engage for ten minutes in a high-quality conversation with a companion. You could discuss anything you wanted, but the discussion had to be of high quality. The command is paradoxical and disabling. You might well have a high-quality conversation with any number of people on any number of subjects, but not if you are required to do so. This can only lead to forced and artificial interaction, not to genuine high-quality communication.

A much larger reason that parents can't make do with small bits of high-quality time is that children need and provoke huge quantities of *low*-quality interaction. Of course they have wonderful moments where they say adorable or funny or surprisingly thoughtful things, and every parent has many moments to cherish, but these occur at widely spaced intervals and we pay for each of these gems long before and long after they appear. I am living proof.

In 1982, back when the Boston Celtics were perennial powers in professional basketball, I endured a solid winter of complaint from my sons: I was, they were sure, the only father in the entire greater Boston area who never took his children to a Celtics game. Then on a Wednesday two friends each offered me a pair of tickets. I bought both so that our whole family could attend. It turned out that the opponents were terrible—that's why the tickets were available—and the Celtics won by 30 points. Near the end of this rout my wife and I got ready to leave. My younger son, then eight, wanted to stay to the end; he always wanted to stay to the end. We ended up with him clinging to the railing in front of his seat while I tried to extricate him from the stadium in full view of the few remaining fans who had stayed, a brief but intense spectacle more dramatic than the game itself.

When we got home I said, "OK, time for bed."

My son said, "I'm hungry."

I said, "It's ten o'clock, it's a school night, you're in third grade, we ate before we left, you had two hotdogs and a big pretzel. Upstairs."

He looked at me and said—I've never let him forget this—"You never do what I want."

Here I was, out more than $175—in 1982 dollars—for a boring one-sided game on a school night and I never do what he wants. There may be many things you can do with a child in such a moment, but having a high-quality interaction is not among them.

And that's just the point. It's not just that children *will* provoke such low-quality moments but that they *need* to. These are often crucial learning opportunities. If they never behaved this way, how would they know what to do when they become parents and their children do this to them? When your children have finally gone too far and you have to settle their hash, you always speak to them in someone else's tone of voice. It's either your mother's or your father's—even if, like me, you swore you'd never do that. My father specialized in the rhetorical question: "Do you think that's a nice way to treat your sister and brother?" I sometimes wanted to shout, "Yes, they deserved it!" But I had to say, "No, that's not a nice way to treat them." I remember standing in the kitchen at twelve years old during one of these episodes, promising myself that I'd never inflict this on a child of mine. But I later heard myself say—many times—in my father's very tone, "Do you think that's a nice way to treat your brother?" This is how we pass culture on. This is how children learn to be parents. And to do so they need all kinds of time—a sufficient quantity so that it can include both high-quality and low-quality, not just the high pressure of forced high quality.

How much is enough? T. Berry Brazelton, America's best known pediatrician, says that for parents raising young children a combined total of three hours per day is the minimum. He means three hours between both parents, not three hours each, and he includes getting dressed in the morning, eating dinner, getting ready for bed, and so on.[22] If we were to enforce such a dictate, this nation's entire economy might fall into depression. After all, the typical working parent spends, by some estimates, barely half an hour per day in interactions with the kids—about half as much time as in commuting.[23] By the time children reach adolescence, this meager amount dwindles further; the typical father and teenager may spend no more than three minutes per day alone together.[24]

Trying to find sufficient time, many working parents pursue a solution—greater efficiency, better time management—that ends up, paradoxically, adding to their problems. They hurry up so they can slow down, says Arlie Russell Hochschild. They multitask, doing several things at once. They organize, plan, and outsource some functions. Family life becomes more a matter of scheduling people and coordinating activities. Efficiency thus becomes both a means to an end—more home time—and an end in itself. Unfortunately, it is a bad fit for children. It disregards powerful, emotionally meaningful symbols that children (especially young children, who love rituals and repetition) associate with particular times. When parents schedule activities closer together so as to fit everything in, they cramp or skip the "framing" around each one, "those moments of looking forward to or looking back on an experience, which heighten its emotional impact." In so doing, "they ignore the contribution that a leisurely pace can make to fulfillment, so that a rapid dinner, followed by a speedy bath and bedtime story for a child—if part of 'quality time'—is counted as 'worth the same' as a slower version of the same events."[25]

But children, as virtually every parent discovers, resist tight schedules and planned sequences. The rhythms and rituals of daily life have a special importance in a family, particularly for small children. Children's needs are often simple, mundane, repetitive, but they are essential. When parents can't or don't make time for them, many children, especially young ones, object, sometimes strenuously. Their resistance complicates parents' lives further. They must endure their children's protests, resistance, and grudging acquiescence. They must respond to their children's stubborn demands, whining requests, and resistance to organizing the home more and more like the workplace.[26] When parents' busy-ness interferes *consistently* with the rhythms and rituals that make family life meaningful, it deprives children of the essential core of childrearing, the nurturing that makes family, family. Apart from the immediate stress this tendency causes, it brings with it a larger loss: it erodes what the late Harold Howe II, a former U.S. Commissioner of Education, called "the intergenerational exchanges on which maturity is successfully built."[27]

The dinner table has always been a key site for these intergenerational exchanges. For me, nothing captures their erosion more vividly than the vanishing family dinner. "A household where the members do not sit down at dinner together nearly every night is a convenience store, not a home," says Miss Manners.[28] The transformation of homes into convenience stores—the weakening of family ties, the decline of direct parenting, and the myths of quality time and family efficiency—all can be seen in the epidemic spread of the late, hurried, partially attended dinner. The loss here, as the journalist Francine du Plessix Gray argues, is not just symbolic:

> We may be witnessing the first generation in history that has not been required to participate in that primal rite of socialization, the family meal. The family is not only the core curriculum in the school of civilized discourse;

> it is also a set of protocols that curb our natural savagery
> and our animal greed, and cultivate a capacity for shar-
> ing and thoughtfulness. . . . [Children] are deprived of
> the main course of civilized life—the practice of sitting
> down at the dinner table and observing the attendant
> conventions. Like the Passover Seder or the Commu-
> nion bread, the ritual of nutrition helps to imbue fami-
> lies, and societies at large, with greater empathy and
> fellowship.[29]

Like all rituals, the home meal requires a sacrifice; it demands large amounts of patience, compassion, and self-discipline—traits which, in return, it nurtures. Their disappearance risks a cumulative impact that cannot be good for our children or our nation's future.

6

· ·

Abandoning Authority

Structure, like nurture, suffers badly in the fragile family. Embedded in the shifts in family feelings and values is a radically diminished role for parents as prescribers and shapers of children's behavior and priorities, both within and beyond the home. The nuclear family (like all its predecessors) was unmistakably hierarchical in its basic assumptions and functioning. Romantic love tended to see women as dependent on men, maternal love saw children as dependent on mothers, and domesticity required the personal wishes of all to yield to the greater good of the family.[1] In such a framework parental authority, though not always absolute, was often nonnegotiable. No longer. To many teachers, this is the most dramatically visible of the changes in the American family: parental retreat from structure, or in Elkind's terms, the replacement of unilateral authority by mutual authority.

"Because Your Goddam Father Says So"

Unilateral authority is most easily captured in anecdote. I encountered a particularly vivid example when, as a doctoral student in psychology, I attended a seminar that met evenings at the home of an eminent Boston psychologist. Arriving early one night in June, I entered to hear the sound of children shouting distantly above me, perhaps up in the third floor. Then suddenly I heard the eminent psychologist's voice, right at the top of the stairs, boom out, "Because your goddam father says so, that's why!" I was stunned. I didn't have children yet, but I imagined that if you were trained as a psychologist you would never have to speak to your offspring this way because you would always know how to get them to comply. And I was certain that the eminent psychologist would be embarrassed that a rookie had overheard him in a most unpsychological moment. As I was debating what to do, he came down the stairs and, with his customary cheer and no trace of embarrassment, said, "Hi. How are you?"

It had been a hot day. His sons, aged ten and twelve, were sweaty and dirty, and he wanted them to take baths before his seminar started so that they would be ready for bed when it was over. He called up to get their attention—once, twice, three times. No answer. The fourth time they yelled back, "What?"

"Come down here," he told them.

"Why?" they yelled back.

So he told them why. Often, this is the only answer a parent can give: "Because I say so." When you have explained to children three times why they must do something they don't want to do, or can't do something they do want to do, what else can you offer? Repeating yourself a fourth or a fifth time is unlikely to cause them to say, "Ohhh, now I get it. Thank you for persevering. I see that you were right and I was wrong. I withdraw my objection."

In the light of today's cultural norms and mores, unilateral authority can seem more than old-fashioned. After all, stories about stern parents who commanded respect and brooked no insolence were already old hat decades ago. But though it is easy to ridicule, unilateral authority had at least four important qualities. First, it provided a vital clarity for children. It helped them know where they stood and how far they could push. It confirmed that their parents, and, by extension, all adults (teachers, for example) were to be respected. Preaching respect, by itself, never produces respect. Respect needs to be demanded and modeled as well as professed.

Second, it was by no means always punitive. It was firm but not hostile. My professor's explanation to his sons was forceful but his tone was matter-of-fact; there was almost a lightness about it, even though his sons could not doubt that he meant business. Third, unilateral authority was often applied indirectly. When my mother didn't want my sister and brother and me to play certain games or use certain toys, she didn't just prohibit them and leave it at that. Although she was very clear about declaring something off limits, she frequently offered us a range of other options. Authoritative parents learned to "childproof" parts of the house or distribute certain play materials so that toddlers would not cause trouble or endanger themselves—and so that adults wouldn't have to constantly reprimand and remove the children. Fourth, unilateral authority gave parents room to maneuver. As their children grew, parents could adopt a more mutual, negotiated stance without losing their overall influence and credibility. This is what much of the friction of adolescence was about: teens, insistent and assertive, pressing for freedom from constraint; parents, reluctant but hopeful, looking for proof of judgment and conscience. The transition from unilateral to mutual could often be difficult, but it produced valuable learning, and it helped adolescents reach adulthood on a sound footing.

Families today operate much more on a basis of mutual authority from early on. Consensual love and shared parenting both assume a reciprocal, negotiated balance of power between husband and wife, and urbanity does the same for the family as a whole, reducing the priority on the unit and enlarging the opportunities for all individuals to be out in the world pursuing their own activities and interests. Negotiated authority may be a good fit with the trends in public, political, and economic life in contemporary America, which seem to be fostering ever more vigorous pursuit of individual fulfillment, but its spread has left large numbers of parents too lenient and unassertive in their monitoring and discipline of children.

What has vanished from many homes is not simply old-fashioned unilateral authority but also milder forms of limits and expectations, even about the most basic aspects of life, from manners to bedtime. To the continual amazement of educators everywhere, parents fail to establish guidelines for conduct and consequences for misconduct, to insist on expectations and responsibilities, even about the most routine of family chores. They are far more likely to negotiate with children about all sorts of decisions, from the smallest to the largest.

At school, teachers must spend more and more time teaching students the basics of social comportment and consideration for others, beginning, as a principal told me, "with 'please' and 'thank you,' with taking off your hat when you're inside, with looking at someone when you speak to them." A first-grade teacher adds, "We're continually surprised by all this, despite how much of it we now see. We still can't get over the way the kids speak to each other, and to us—and then we hear how they bawl out their parents. Right in public, they disagree and complain and order their parents around." In poor urban schools and wealthy suburban schools alike, educators report that more and more students now see the word *No* as the start of a negotiation. Pediatricians and psychologists notice similar changes; they regularly field questions of a kind that parents almost never used to ask, such as, "Can I tell my five-year-old what clothes to wear if it takes him too long to make up his own mind?"

Friction Deprivation

As children become preadolescent and then full-fledged teenagers, the consequences of parents' retreat from structure grow more evident and ominous. Adolescence used to be understood as a period of preparation for coping with the demands and dangers of the larger world, a time when immature, bewildered, temperamental youth needed adult guidance as they grappled with the tensions between growing freedom and growing responsibility. Because of the definite distinctions between the perquisites and requirements of youth and those of adulthood—about such things as sex, for example—adolescents were caught in the middle, a position that led to inevitable friction with adults. This was understood as a normal part of the adolescent transition.

The ideal outcome of this normal tension is that a teenager gradually develops a firm, positive sense of identity, one based on both differentiation and integration. *Differentiation* means learning to distinguish ideas, emotions, and roles (how am I different from, and similar to, my father, for example). *Integration* means assembling these various perceptions and experiences into a concrete whole (what defines me as my own person). Both proceed best when child-rearing has included strong doses of nurture, structure, and latitude. Friction is common as teenagers try to establish themselves as individuals, but even as adolescents turn away from parents, they also draw heavily on them. If, through structure, parents have offered an example of strong identity—consistently supporting, modeling, and enforcing certain standards of conduct—teens have an easier time developing their own identity, even if it differs from their parents'. Such adolescents tend to be self-directed and able to delay immediate gratification and pursue longer-term goals. By contrast, those who grow up without sufficient structure, without a model of consistency to imitate and oppose, are often left to construct an identity by substitution—not a full, coherent inner sense of self, but a loose compilation of attitudes, concepts, and feelings, a kind of "patchwork self."[2] They tend to be much more other-directed, present-oriented, to have difficulty delaying gratification, and to be more vulnerable to peer influence. The permeable family inclines kids toward the latter.

In contemporary America much of the growth-promoting normal tension of adolescence has vanished because the distinction between being adolescent and being adult has faded, taking with it much of the modeling and constructive friction that structure provides. Adults have come to accept adolescence almost as "a different

form of adult life" with a sophistication all its own. Teens are allowed (indeed, expected) to be "worldly-wise in matters of sex,
drugs, music, computers, and consumerism."[3] Most parents do not
know as much about computers as their children, for example. And
most take very little action to resist the negative influences of music,
films, TV shows, video games, and the Internet. At the same time,
the distinctions between childhood and adulthood have been dis-
appearing.

Life has always been a process of moving through different stages
(preschooler, college student, grandparent, and so on), each indicated by markers—external signs of progress to a new status. In
addition to ceremonies (first communions, bar mitzvahs, and the
like) there were other markers—notably dress—that separated
childhood from adolescence and adolescence from adulthood. Different modes of dress for teens and adults signified an expectation
of different modes of behavior; growing up meant leaving the one
and adopting the other. But since at least the late 1980s the dress—
and behavior, language, and attitudes—of adults and children have
been growing more and more similar.[4] Now firmly established, this
trend has a name among marketing researchers: "generational blur."
It consists of adults' dressing children in grown-up ways, rather than
in separate children's clothes, while at the same time trying to
"young themselves down." We should thus not be surprised when
parents fail to support schools' proposals for even minimal standards
of dress.

The larger evidence of the decline in authoritative parenting is
all too common. What appear to be substantial numbers of pre-
adolescents and adolescents are largely left to run their own lives.
For example, they are given, as a group, unprecedented amounts of
both spending money and unsupervised time. Many hold part-time
jobs, but their earnings are typically for their own use, not for sup-
plementing the family income.[5] And many who are not employed
have enough money from their parents that they have become an
enormous marketing bonanza. Teenagers' unprecedented personal

spending power has made them prime targets for luxury clothing designers who used to concentrate on adults. This financial freedom begins early. The purchasing power of preteens and very young adolescents is so great that they have acquired a label of their own: "Tweens." Malls are full of these young consumers, even on school nights—collectively, youth aged twelve to nineteen spend over $50 billion per year on clothing.[6]

As with money, so with supervision. It is hard to know whether parents are more indulgent or just more disengaged. What is clear is that in communities across the country many parents regularly let their teenagers go out without monitoring where they'll be going and what they'll be doing, and also leave them home alone on weekends. Less supervision means more substance abuse and more sex. For decades now evidence has indicated that teen drug and alcohol use is, on average, high. The drug of choice changes, but the problem remains. In recent years, many communities have been concerned about alcohol, specifically about binge drinking, and about the onset of this behavior among middle school students. It would surely be a rare weekend in most suburbs without at least one party at a home where parents are away—or another at which parents are present and permit alcohol to be served. I regularly ask about this in schools I visit and someone—a teacher, a counselor, a principal—can always cite a recent example.

R-Rated, Pre-Jaded

Adolescents who are undersupervised are likely to engage in more and earlier sexual experimentation. The hormonal pull is powerful, old taboos are growing weak, and advertising is sex-obsessed, as is much of our public life. These external influences are strong, but as a high school nurse once told me, "whenever one of our kids gets into a lot of premature or unwise sex, we almost always find under-involved parents." Although concerns about teens' sexual behavior are hardly new, there is worrisome evidence of an earlier and more extensive onset than ever before. A 1997 study found that 17 percent of seventh and eighth graders reported having had intercourse. Other studies have shown a sustained trend toward precocious sexual activity. In the early 1970s, for example, fewer than 5 percent of fifteen-year-old girls and fewer than 20 percent of fifteen-year-old boys said they had had sex. Thirty years later, the respective figures were 38 percent for girls and 45 percent for boys. Newspapers in major cities have been describing an increase in sex—and most recently, oral sex—among young teens and pre-teens. In the wealthier precincts of New York City and its suburbs, "groups of seventh and eighth graders rent limousines to take them to clubs . . . where they get drunk, grind [freak dance] on the dance floor and have oral sex in dim corners." A movie producer, responding to one of Congress's periodic (and brief) bursts of outrage over the sex and violence in films targeted at youth, dismissed the criticism by saying, "Who's kidding who? The reality of teenage life is R-rated." Or worse. A writer at a magazine that covers the pornographic film industry told the *New York Times* that today's teenagers, having grown up with cable and VCR, "come to the table already saturated with sex. . . . They've never known a time without Calvin Klein ads and MTV. By the time they see porn, they've already seen so many naked people they're pre-jaded."[7]

Pre-jaded indeed. The Public Broadcasting System's *Frontline* offered a particularly graphic example in its portrait of *The Lost Children of Rockdale County*. In 1996, in Conyers, Georgia, a comfortable, largely white suburb of Atlanta, a community "steeped in Christianity," its streets virtually empty on Sundays because its more than a hundred churches are so full, there was an astonishing outbreak of syphilis among teenagers. Seventeen young people contracted the disease; another two hundred students were exposed and treated. As public health officials investigated, they began to discover an epidemic of sex, including a stunning amount of extreme sexual behavior among students as young as fourteen.[8]

This case is not typical, but it is not just a fluke, either. When I mentioned the *Frontline* program at a conference of middle school principals from suburban schools, 20 percent reported recent episodes of girls performing oral sex for a series of boys, sometimes in school. What Conyers illustrates is that even in middle-class, white, churchgoing communities, being a typical, everyday teenager can mean being a significantly understructured teenager. In fact, the evidence of this is overwhelming in other domains, notably children's access to electronic media. Perhaps nowhere else is parents' abandonment of authority more visible than in the unsupervised access they grant their children to media and technology, from television and movies to video games and computers.

In very large numbers, parents oppose the influence of the media on their children, and in almost equally large numbers do little about their concerns. The Kaiser Family Foundation reports that the typical American child devotes an average of more than thirty-eight hours per week—almost five and a half hours per day—to "consuming media" outside of school. For children eight and older, the average is nearly seven hours per day. The medium they are consuming is overwhelmingly television. American youth average more than fifteen hundred hours per year watching TV (versus less than nine hundred in class at school, and less than a hundred in one-on-one activity with a parent). They see twenty thousand commercials per year.[9]

What they are watching, of course, is without question not good for them—or for us as a nation. Television negatively affects children's academic and social development, their attitudes and behavior, and their knowledge of the world they live in. As far back as the 1970s researchers were reporting that watching TV more than ten hours per week diminished children's academic performance.[10] Recent studies have shown a strong negative correlation between TV watching and reading skills.[11] In addition to these consequences, the negative impact of television on children's attitudes and behavior with regard to violence and sex has been confirmed in numerous studies. Most of us have heard the statistics: violence on TV occurs at eight times its actual rate in American life; by the age of eighteen, the average child has seen sixteen thousand murders and two hundred thousand violent acts, and so on.[12] The film industry, of course, has long perpetrated its own glut of gore. As for sex, beginning with the deregulation of TV standards in the Reagan era and accelerated by the public excesses of the Clinton era, the commercialization of sex and its movement into the daily orbit of the media and thus of children has been phenomenal. During the 1999–2000 television season, for example, 68 percent of all programs and 75 percent of those shown in prime time contained sexual content.[13] Even a casual viewer would have to conclude that the percentages have continued to rise since then.

The broad case against the media is so clear and compelling and widely acknowledged that I will not belabor it. What is important here is how little effort parents make to counter the impact or control children's access to the media. The saddest of all facts about television is that parents overwhelmingly want to limit what their children watch, but do not. When asked, nearly three-quarters say that they would like to reduce their children's television consumption, but few do so. More than a third of parents of young children say the TV is on in their homes most of the time. Over 60 percent of children surveyed report that their parents have no rules about TV watching. Those parents who do set rules do not seem to be particularly firm: fewer than 10 percent require children to do their homework before turning on the tube. Parents report that they watch TV together with their children a bare 5 percent of the time. Worse, most buy their children televisions. *More than half of children over the age of five now have a TV in their bedroom; by sixth grade, more than three-quarters do.* Large proportions of young people are essentially free to tune in to whatever they want whenever they want— and by themselves. One study found that fully one-third of school-age children were watching TV at eleven P.M.[14]

It is hard to know whether this parental passivity, this refusal to structure children's viewing, reflects helplessness, denial, or—more worrisome—a value shift. TV is often a substitute baby-sitter or companion, freeing harried, overworked parents for some time to themselves or for household tasks. But why put a television in a child's room? Chiefly, it would seem, so that the family doesn't have to watch together and thus fight over which programs to see. Of course, there is always the possibility that parents' apparent disapproval of the media is just lip service—saying what sounds right when the pollsters call—that many don't find the blizzard of sex and violence unacceptable. This would be truly worrisome.

Technology versus Childhood

Television and movies are obvious villains. Less clear-cut but potentially just as damaging are technology and the Internet. Today's school-age children are the first in all of human history with access to large amounts of information and other material not filtered by their caretaking adults—parents and teachers. This has never happened before in any society. Although technology opens some wonderful doors, it also opens some very dangerous ones, and in so doing it undermines the roles of parents and teachers. And just as they do with TV and movies, most parents adopt a permissive stance about their children's access to their PCs.

Computers and the Internet are classic examples of "disruptive technology"—developments so radical in their impact that they upset and destroy a whole way of working, living, thinking, and relating. Disruption, of course, is integral to progress. The steam engine was a disruptive technology, as were the telegraph, the telephone, and the automobile. Each undermined and ultimately transformed the very patterns of daily existence. The wonders of the electronic age continue to be widely celebrated and seen as the core of America's—indeed the world's—economic growth in the twenty-first century. But for all the power and potential technology promises, all the fun and fascination it provides, it is proving to be profoundly subversive of childhood, education, and civility because it undermines authority, reflection, and relationship.

Childhood and society both have always depended, as the late Neil Postman observed, on "managed information and sequential learning." Postman, professor of media ecology at New York University and a widely read cultural critic, pointed out that adults know and children don't. To become a grown-up, to gain the privileges and perks of adulthood, has always required a lengthy process of learning and initiation. Civilization rests on the acquisition of skills such as literacy, and, most crucially, on the control of impulses, particularly those toward aggression and immediate gratification (society literally cannot exist unless these are contained). Hence the importance of manners, among other things—and of shame. From the child's point of view, "shame gives power and authority to adulthood." Adults, for example, know which words and subjects are shameful, which acts are to be kept private. Children need help to learn the control civilization requires and, as they struggle to do so, to figure out what it means to become adult, they confront "a world of secrets, surrounded by mystery and awe; a world that will be made intelligible to them by adults who will teach them, in stages" the standards of conduct and behavior, including the distinction between what is public and what must be kept private. As adults gradually reveal to young people the secrets of the adult world and initiate them into the rules of social behavior, they are, in part, turning shame into a code of conduct.[15]

This staging has always been the province of parents and teachers. But communications technology has intervened pervasively, usurping their control over the dissemination of information. This transformation actually began with the invention of the printing press in the fifteenth century, but its direct modern roots can be traced to the advent of the telegraph in the mid-nineteenth century. It has accelerated steadily since then, especially since the birth of computers and the Internet. A hallmark of both is their ability to undercut and circumvent established authority, to empower individuals by distributing information widely and quickly. They flatten out organizational hierarchy by disempowering (and often by replacing) those whose status depends on transferring information—corporate middle managers, for example. Within the family and the school, the new technology operates similarly, but it is parents and teachers who end up disempowered. As "the electric media's rapid and egalitarian disclosure of the total content of the adult world" invalidates distinctions among age groups and thus subverts the very idea of a hierarchical social order, we are relinquishing traditional adult authority over children. A boundaryless information environment that keeps no secrets from the young disempowers shame (not to mention manners). But if we simply "turn over to children a vast store of powerful adult material," Postman pointed out, "childhood cannot survive."[16]

This risk plays out in many ways. The most obvious is that children and teenagers can gain access to all sorts of information and communication that have traditionally been reserved for adults and for the private (as opposed to the public) realm, and thus erode adult authority and social conventions. Even if children don't seek out such material, they are likely to encounter it. One study found that 19 percent of youth who used the Internet regularly were the targets of unwanted sexual solicitation.[17] It is not only sexually oriented material that is at issue here, though that is a prime concern of many parents, but all sorts of influences and viewpoints, including those that are diametrically opposed to parents' own. And much of what children encounter over the Internet is provided by people whose interests are strictly commercial, not educational, who simply want to create demand for their products by reaching youth directly rather than through their caretakers.

For their part, educators worry about, among other things, the growth of antisocial Web sites and electronic bulletin boards devoted essentially to character assassination and personal harassment. These include sites created for students to post attacks on other students and on teachers, attacks that are often more than scurrilous and include sexual innuendo, threats of bodily harm, and so on. In one case, an eighth grader created a site called "Teacher Sux" about a particular teacher; it contained, among other things, a list of reasons why he should be fired and should die, and a section soliciting funds to "help pay for the hit man."[18] Educators feel virtually helpless in the face of this kind of use of technology. "We can't control it," says an assistant principal. "It can spread like a virus."

A less discussed but equally grave danger of technology is its emphasis on speed and data. Computers are addictive in their power to crunch ever larger volumes of information ever faster. Speed and data are important to all sorts of commercial and research activities, but they rarely promote contemplation or creativity. Web sites provide an abundant but superficial collection of facts, and can easily give students the illusion that they understand a topic even when this isn't true. Worse, much of the Internet's appeal is overtly anti-intellectual. Many popular sites make fun of learning, studying, tradition, and authority. Others facilitate cheating and plagiarism by offering thousands of term papers for students to download and hand in as their own work. But the larger problem is the medium itself: "Its methods, pace, and style constantly denigrate the values essential in schooling: concentration, disciplined analysis, wrestling with complexity, and pursuit of understanding."[19] Technology's emphasis on speed and data risks creating a national attention deficit epidemic, a loss of concentration and patience in children that is antithetical to many of the virtues of family life, schooling, and ethical behavior. On-line companies like Mattel, Disney, and others who market to children design their Web sites to capture attention within eight seconds—anything else is too long. No wonder teachers at all levels report that more and more students equate education with entertainment and seem to lack the motivation to tackle and persevere at demanding tasks.[20]

Disengaged

If our electronic access links us to a much wider world of contacts, it does so mostly in shallow, superficial ways. Virtual connection is, in most cases, a poor substitute for its face-to-face counterpart. It is, however, the appropriate mode for the fragile family. Too few parents invest themselves in their children directly and personally enough to establish the limits and expectations that healthy growth requires. Like nurture, structure demands active, sustained engagement with a child. Recall that the combination of high nurture and high structure can be especially powerful because well-nurtured children are more reluctant than others to lose their parents' esteem and yet at the same time better able to tolerate parental correction because of their confidence in the overall relationship. It is unfortunate, therefore, to find both nurture and structure in such decline.

To many educators, parents' pronounced reluctance to set limits and maintain expectations reflects a combination of self-centeredness and blindness. As one principal says, "Sometimes I think the parents just don't care enough; other times I think they're just lost." Some surveys have shown that more and more parents report feeling helpless, incapable of influencing their children's choices about such things as sex and drug and alcohol use. But even if we see parents as selfish or permissive or powerless, we must also see them as driven by guilt.

Being away from their children so much makes many parents feel they are letting the kids down. If they have relatively little time to spend together, they don't want it consumed by negative interaction (hence the appeal of the "quality time" myth). This makes them less willing to put their children (and themselves) through the discomforts of creating structure. Setting expectations and limits, drawing guidelines, and enduring the displeasure they can cause takes time and trouble. When parents feel guilty about not being available enough, they are also less likely to hold the line or insist.

And this reluctance will be intensified if they have read enough books that caution them against disciplining children.

As I talk with teachers, physicians, and fellow psychologists about the decline of parental authority, I hear over and over two observations: parents spend too little time with their children and they seem to want to be their children's friends. They aren't present enough to know their children as well as they should, but when they are with them they go out of their way to avoid the young people's displeasure. The postmodern emphasis on personal fulfillment may have given parents the upper hand in that it freed them to pursue their own careers and required children to adapt to these work-driven schedules, but when they are with their children, many parents seem overanxious not to displease them, let alone to set limits and tolerate the friction that structure demands. This may be especially true of high-achieving parents who work long hours and have lots of disposable income; they can be particularly prone to avoiding the challenges of structure and to appeasing their children. In so doing, they create the worst of two worlds: fragile families become child-dominated without being child-centered.

Building Résumés

Latitude lives a difficult life in the permeable family. Superficially, children and teenagers seem to have lots of it. Many of them are indeed allowed great freedom to express themselves and to do much as they please. But latitude doesn't mean license; it means support for autonomy, support that includes not only the chance to voice one's views and try one's hand but to learn from the consequences of doing so—and in many families this freedom has declined sharply. Many parents try so hard to fast-track their children and to smooth their path, or simply to keep them from suffering unwelcome consequences of any kind, that they allow them little scope to solve problems and less to learn life lessons from their choices and conduct. There is a great irony in this duality: it is rooted in a view of childhood that emphasizes its competence rather than, as used to be the case, its innocence, and yet it leads to a kind of childrearing that in key ways stunts competence. It makes childhood less childlike and damages the very things it means to encourage: performance and self-esteem.

Not So Fast: Precocious Competence

In the 1950s and '60s, it was assumed that children were not only vulnerable and in need of adult nurturance and protection but innocent explorers who required time and space to discover the world on their own. Back then most parents—and most pediatricians, psychologists, and educators—saw childhood as a time of innocence and adolescence as a time of immaturity and both as periods of exploration during which young people could learn from the consequences of their exploring. There was broad agreement that children developed at different paces. No doubt, mothers and fathers were proud to have precocious performers who acquired skills early. But differences in maturation and skill were acceptable. It was permissible, for example, to have a child who might be a late bloomer. There was even a popular children's book called *Leo the Late Bloomer*.[1] The book is still in preschool and elementary school libraries, but the concept has withered. Where once we emphasized childhood innocence, now we stress its competence. We look for early evidence of aptitude and skill in a wide variety of academic and nonacademic domains, from reading, math, and keyboarding to higher-order thinking, and from athletic prowess to tolerating frequent turnover of day-care staff. And where once it was accepted that learning from experience meant coping with the consequences of mistakes, now many parents feel it vital to protect their children from any errors or negative outcomes.

Although the emphasis on childhood competence is more than twenty years old, it spread rapidly during the 1990s, sparked by a burst of interest in the first three years of life as a crucial, make-or-break interval that dictates future cognitive and psychological development. Articles in major magazines and newspapers and books on childrearing misunderstood and misapplied a range of research, including studies showing that human brains undergo explosive growth of synapses (connections between cells) during the first three years of life, followed by a sharp reduction. This misguided publicity fostered the impression that it was not only possible but vital to avoid the die-off of brain synapses and to stimulate the brain to even greater synaptic density, which, advocates claimed, would enhance children's cognitive and personal development. Infants and toddlers required enriched, stimulating environments. By 1998, twenty-five states were citing research into early brain development as the rationale for various child development programs. The then-Governor of Georgia, Zell Miller, sought state funding for classical music CDs and tape recordings for all infants.[2]

The early years of life are surely important, but the case for forcing development is weak. The synaptic density of the brain does, in fact, rise rapidly in the first three years and then decline back toward its level at birth. This, it turns out, is not only normal, it is necessary: too many connections between the cells of the brain compromise its functioning. Indeed, it is only after the pruning of cells that much of the sustained rapid intellectual growth of childhood and adolescence occurs. As for the impact of music—the "Mozart effect," as it has come to be called—it hasn't actually been shown to exist. This hasn't stopped eager entrepreneurs, including one who has sold several hundred thousand books and tapes to help parents produce the mythical effect at home.[3]

For a variety of reasons not primarily related to zero-to-three hysteria, educational policymakers have shifted their emphasis on schooling from one that was primarily child-centered to one that is strongly curriculum-centered and that gets much more serious much, much earlier. The explosion of information and of new knowledge, particularly in the sciences, coupled with widespread anxiety about America's competitive strength during the 1980s, helped spawn an epidemic of worry about the state of our schools and the preparedness of our students. This led in many directions. Most promising were those that sought to help students master essential thinking skills and habits of mind that would make them effective lifelong learners and that advanced our knowledge about students' different learning styles.[4] Approaches like these aim at helping schools concentrate on depth in student learning.

Much less promising, but currently ascendant, has been an effort to promote across-the-board proficiency, starting in elementary school, in state-mandated curriculum frameworks—mastery measured by "high-stakes" tests that students must pass in order to be promoted or graduate. In good part, this movement has been advanced by political conservatives who have exaggerated the shortcomings of students' performance and have attributed these almost entirely to the schools themselves. Their attacks have led to remarkably shortsighted and child-unfriendly measures. Many school districts, under pressure by state officials to improve test scores and by parents to provide early brain enrichment, have been making their kindergartens more academically rigorous. Others have moved to abolish recess. These latter districts have decided, incredibly, that to maximize instruction and improve scores, children should stay at their desks straight through the day except for lunch. (Even ignoring the loss of social learning that recess permits, one is hard-pressed to imagine recess-deprived seven-year-olds attending eagerly to academics—or the heroics required of teachers to keep them focussed.)

The Rising Tide of Anxiety

All this new pressure on schools and children has yet to improve students' learning, but it has helped increase parents' anxiety. Consistently, in nearly every school I visit, educators report that parental worry about student performance is on the rise. This is particularly true, ironically, among better-off, better-educated parents whose students go to better schools. It is less common in urban areas; educators there do not report such a feverish intensity, though they, too, have seen an increase. Of course, parents' anxiety didn't need a boost; it has been elevated by other factors, notably a growing uncertainty about the shape of the future and what it will take to be successful in the coming decades. With so much changing so rapidly in the way we live and work, with the increasing transience and fungibility of workers and companies, most parents are less confident than they would wish to be about their children's future and eager to do anything to assure their well-being. Too often, the result is what a Texas principal calls "heavy-duty grade grubbing and résumé padding."

Grade grubbing and résumé padding may not always be heavy-duty, but they are abundant. As I noted at the outset, elementary teachers in a premier suburban school district recently told me they wished they could stop giving report card marks because they now get so many calls from parents. What trouble them most are not the complaints from parents whose children who receive a C but from those whose children receive an A-minus. It would be one thing if this anxiety were about helping students develop habits of excellence (reflection, love of learning, and so on), but it is much more about getting a leg up on the competition. Teachers everywhere say that parents now concentrate more on students' relative standing than on their actual mastery. Of course, all parents want their children to be well educated and knowledgeable, and grades are the primary and official indicator for learning and performance; parents have always paid attention to them. What schools see now, however, is a shift in emphasis, with parents' zeroing in almost exclusively on the grade itself rather than on the effort and result it should betoken.

By high school, of course, with college looming, transcripts are serious business. Growing numbers of parents want their sons and daughters to take honors-level and advanced placement courses because these present a stronger admissions profile. Parents pressure their teenagers to sign up for such courses and lobby the school to allow them to enroll in these classes, even when the record suggests they are unlikely to do well. Then, when the students do find the going tough, parents ask for exceptions. A biology teacher at a New England boarding school describes the pattern this way: "Parents want the grade, but not if it comes at a high price in terms of hard work or slow improvement. What lots of them really want is what I call 'achievement lite'—the trappings, not the substance of high performance." A guidance counselor at an elite Catholic school shrugs her shoulders. "Parents want the college admission and they read that Harvard rejects more than two thousand valedictorians a year, that Princeton has to turn down an entire second class that's the equal of the one it admits, and so forth. No wonder they pressure their kids and look for every edge they can find."

Competitive schools, of course, are not just passive observers of drivenness and anxiety among students and parents; they help foster it. Although teachers in America's better schools complain about the expectation that they will cover ever more material at an ever higher level, they themselves help generate the very stress they decry. Talented teachers keep pushing the envelope, looking for ways to increase the quantity and quality of students' achievement. The head of one of the nation's leading independent secondary schools calculated that a student who practiced for a sports team, a play, or a music performance while also doing the required homework for a full five-course academic schedule could never get to bed before one A.M. Presented with this finding, the faculty readily agreed that students had too much to do and were at risk of becoming "a mile wide and an inch deep." Discussions about how to reduce and concentrate the student workload quickly collapsed. Every department felt that some other department should scale back its requirements, but none would compromise its own expectations.

Anticipating the later challenges, more and more parents of young children exhibit a preparatory, future-focussed anxiety. This is evident, for example, among the mothers who concentrate obsessively on getting their elementary children placed in the classroom of the absolute best teacher, even to the point of asking young female teachers whether they plan to get pregnant during the coming year. Spring is now a tension-filled, anxiety-laden interval for principals and teachers in America's middle- and upper-class communities as they deal with the intense, anxious shopping and lobbying for classroom placements. Most schools do not permit parents to request a specific teacher, but many let them write a description of the kind of class placement they feel their child requires, which,

of course, turns into a thinly veiled request for a specific teacher—
and, often, for specific classmates. Says an elementary principal: "I
literally get letters every year saying 'My son would do best with a
tall, blonde teacher,' and 'Here is a list of the ten students my
daughter should be with to preserve her self-esteem.'"

New Bull Markets

Anxiety like this, once spawned, is infectious, and has been sweep-
ing through many of the nation's schools like an epidemic. It has
created two bull markets. One is in treatment for apparent learning
disabilities, including most notoriously attention deficit disorder
(ADD). Those who specialize in the problem disagree about
whether ADD is actually more prevalent now or just more frequently
diagnosed, but educators everywhere know that growing numbers of
parents disappointed by their children's grades or behavior are convinced their children must have the condition. They are now used
to parents' searching until they find a psychologist or psychiatrist
who will provide such a diagnosis and recommend both medication
and special accommodations at school, such as untimed tests.[5]

The second bull market is for after-school tutoring and for
summer camps devoted to college prep courses, to math, science,
and computing, and to such skills as test taking. To improve their
children's prospects parents have become eager purchasers of these
services, which add to the already overloaded schedules of many
students. The *New York Times* reported a classic case of a suburban mother taking her fourteen-year-old son, "still sweaty from
soccer practice and headed for a classical guitar lesson," to a tutoring center to improve his test-taking skills to that he can be admitted to a private high school. "I should just ignore what
everybody else is doing," she told the *Times*, "but we are competitive, overachieving parents. I look to the left and I look to the
right and I panic."[6]

As this example illustrates, concern about building a competitive résumé and getting a leg up on the competition not only begins early, it extends well beyond the classroom. It is a key contributor to the overscheduling of children outside school. What was once characteristic only of "pushy" parents is now ubiquitous, and what used to be children's play time is now dominated by formal adult-supervised activities, sports, and educational enrichment. Suburban children routinely participate in three or four weekly activities outside school. These begin with sports of all kinds and include music and dance lessons, as well as tutoring and religious instruction. In many communities it is not uncommon for children as young as ten to be playing two sports in a single season (both baseball and soccer in the spring, for example) as well as taking a music lesson and a religious education class, and spending some time in day care or with a baby-sitter. Nor is there any letup in the summer, when specialty camps of all kinds encourage children to pursue all these activities more intensively.

Few of the activities that clog children's calendars are truly recreational. Most of the athletics and lessons are performance-focussed, or, more accurately, victory-focussed, and, increasingly, pursued in serious, sustained ways. Elaborating on the blurring of lines between childhood and adulthood that I discussed earlier, Neil Postman argued twenty years ago that its most obvious symptom was the disappearance of children's games. A children's game didn't involve instructors, umpires, spectators, or special equipment, and it was chiefly played for pleasure. By contrast, organized youth sports are not only adult-led but modeled closely on big league sports, complete with referees, expensive equipment, and raucous spectators. In such a context, "it is not pleasure the players are seeking but reputation." Instead of being self-initiated and played for pleasure, the games children now play have become "increasingly official, mock-professional, and extremely serious."[7]

Communities across the nation have not only heavily populated general soccer leagues open to all boys and girls but a growing number of selective "travel teams" with their own practices, games, tournaments—and fierce fans. More and more, it seems, adults want their children's teams to be fast-tracked early and win at all costs. As I began this chapter a youth baseball coach in Florida broke an umpire's jaw and a father in Massachusetts killed another in a fight at a boys' ice hockey game. Hardly a month goes by without such events being reported. The assaulting of referees and coaches in youth sports has become a chronic dysfunction instead of an occasional aberration. The National Alliance for Youth Sports maintains at its Florida headquarters a "Wall of Shame" filled with newspaper clippings about misconduct at games: a coach of six-year-old baseball players choking an umpire; a man paying a Little League pitcher to throw at an opposing batter; more than a hundred adults in a wild melee at a Pop Warner football game, and so on. The Alliance reports that 15 percent of games involve verbal abuse of some sort by parents or coaches (triple the rate of the mid-1990s). No wonder 20 percent of high school coaches quit every year.[8] To restore sanity and balance, the Northern Ohio Girls Soccer League resorted to a "Silent Sunday," during which players could encourage each other, but parents and coaches had to be quiet. "The kids," a League official said, "had a ball [and could] make decisions on their own without being questioned or yelled at." For at least one day, the girls got some latitude back.[9]

All of this pushing of students to compete and excel both in and out of the classroom is easy to satirize and dismiss, but as it spreads and intensifies it brings with it some serious risks. For some time now research has suggested that much drug and alcohol use among teenagers involves an element of self-medication, that adolescents who are stressed are more likely to misuse substances. Several recent studies have not only confirmed these findings, they have also reported drug use to be higher among upper-income suburban youth than among their low-income urban peers—and to be most likely among youth who felt strong pressure to achieve academically and in extracurricular activities and also felt isolated from their parents.[10]

No Consequences

The focus on résumé- and reputation-building is related to a parallel unwillingness to let children encounter reverses and learn from experience in the realm of social and personal responsibility. Even as they provide less structure and exert less control over their children, parents go to greater lengths to insulate them from the consequences of errors and misconduct, even the most minor. The dean of students at a boarding school recently told me that no matter what a student's offense, including the most serious, "Parents invariably go from, 'Having this on his record could affect his college chances' to, 'What he did really wasn't that bad.' They almost never see that holding the line and having a consequence is not just vital to the school as an institution but an important life lesson for the student." More and more middle school and high school principals I meet have grown used to a prevalent form of unethical parental behavior that one calls, "covering for cutters." Students who cut class or skip school are typically subject to detention and eventually to losing credit for courses if they accumulate too many unexcused absences. More and more parents now write notes to excuse their children's absences. "It's not that they want their kids to skip," says an assistant principal, "they just don't want them to suffer any negative consequences for skipping. These days, protecting kids from consequences knows no limits."

He means *no* limits. In fact, it sometimes seems that the greater the student's behavioral lapse, the more likely parents are to seek to avoid consequences. Not long ago I visited four high schools, public and private, where shortly before graduation seniors committed expellable offenses (smoking marijuana on campus, vandalizing thousands of dollars' worth of computers, and so on). Each school's policy, printed in its official handbook, permitted such a student to graduate but not to participate in the actual ceremony. As they considered their response, each of the four principals predicted what would happen when the policy was invoked: the students' parents would not fall on their swords in shame or even apologize, and they certainly would not accept the school's decision. They would hire lawyers to try to convince the school to relent and threaten court action if this didn't work. Throughout, they would attack the school's procedures rather than address the students' behavior. None of the parents surprised the school by acquiescing. None of the administrators backed down, but each paid a heavy price in time and aggravation.

It would be an error to imagine that all this protection from consequences is solely a matter of résumé- and reputation-building. It reflects an anxious perfectionism among parents who want nothing but the best for their children, and who are determined that nothing should go wrong. This is why they place sound monitors in their infants' rooms twenty-four hours a day, so they can hear every rustle. This is why they pressure schools to forbid dodgeball as too dangerous. What this effort to micromanage childhood fails to consider is the risk to children of avoiding all risks.[11]

Limiting Learning

Many parents are aware on some level that what they're doing isn't healthy, that overscheduling and an early, intense focus on competitive success can be harmful, but, as a *Newsweek* story suggested, "they aren't sure how to cut back without depriving their kids."[12] And they aren't sure how to let children learn from their own mistakes or solve their own problems without harming their résumés. The irony, of course, is that *not* cutting back and letting go is what is truly depriving and harmful to children. Childhood is losing its unfettered informality—and all the vital social and personal learning this permits—and becoming a kind of apprentice adulthood.[13] Even as children are involved in more activities, even as their parents press them toward greater, broader, earlier achievement, their latitude shrinks in ways that are disadvantageous, even dangerous. Among the casualties are self-regulation and social skills, a tolerance for losing, a sense of fair play, a work ethic, and ultimately their self-esteem.

Overscheduling and the replacement of children's games by adult-led sports and activities not only take much of the fun out of childhood, they complicate the development of the ability to manage oneself and one's time and the development of social skills. Time is no longer something children pass, it is something they spend as they hurry between school, practices, games, and lessons, pursuing skills and reputation more than pleasure, having less and less leisure. This, of course, might seem ideal preparation for later life, given the speed, frazzle, and fragmentation that now mark so much of adult existence. But we are at risk of creating an entire generation of individuals who lack the capacity to be alone and who are even less self-sufficient and more other-directed than their predecessors. Growing up overscheduled makes it hard for children to learn how to amuse themselves, how to fill time that isn't externally organized. Each year, in talks to PTAs and other groups, I hear from hundreds of parents that their children are bored and adrift without the TV or a computer, that they don't know what to do with "down time," that they can't engage themselves on their own without sources of stimulation. A youth minister at a local church complained to me about parents who complain to him that their children "can't amuse themselves, that when they go on vacation a rainy day is a disaster. I want to ask them what on earth they expect," he said. "Their children have never *had* any time to themselves. How could they know what to do on their own?"

More important, the growth of intense, professionalized sports and lessons damages children's ability to organize their own play— a key vehicle for social learning. Having to create and manage their own games provided children a wonderful natural laboratory for socialization. Playing together and inventing guidelines, rules, and scoring systems helped them develop valuable life skills: they learned about competition and cooperation, about making regulations and making exceptions, about how to come out on top and how to soothe hurt feelings. The withering of opportunities for this natural learning has brought consequences that are visible in the daily behavior of schoolchildren. I still remember my surprise when, in 1993, an elementary principal told me that groups of boys had begun asking him to set up games for them on the playground at recess because they couldn't do it themselves. He, too, had been taken aback at first, he said, until he realized that "they have no experience simply starting a pickup game together; they actually don't do it anymore and really don't know how." In the years since then I have met scores of principals and teachers who field such requests and who see the same inability in students. Most are convinced that the decline of children's games contributes to other trends among students, including a decline in politeness, cooperativeness, and empathy, among other symptoms of growing social weakness.

It is not just the sheer extent of formal, adult-led activity that is problematic, but its intensity—specifically, the insistence of parents that children succeed and their reluctance (often, their refusal) to let them encounter negative consequences or feedback, even in small ways. This inhibits the development of self-restraint and of a respect for rules and fair play. Today's young athletes betray a growing competitive ferocity that doesn't just break the boundaries of sportsmanship, it often obliterates them. The National Alliance for Youth Sports Wall of Shame doesn't stop with stories about adult excesses, it includes stories about players' own, like the high school wrestler who head-butted a referee, knocking him unconscious, and the high school basketball player who earned a prison sentence for deliberately elbowing an opponent in the face, breaking his nose and giving him a concussion.[14]

Growing up in a high-stakes, winner-take-all world that concentrates intensely on competitive standing, even to the point of "achievement lite," also risks damaging children's perseverance and self-esteem. Recall that latitude is not only about resigning oneself; it stimulates effort, as well. Falling short and failing at tasks are irreplaceable learning opportunities. Properly handled, they can foster persistence. But not when adults place an undue emphasis on winning rather than on trying one's best. As some writers have been pointing out for years, students who are strongly encouraged to value grades and competition, extrinsic rewards, and winning are prone to a significant vulnerability in this regard. For example, researchers studied hundreds of fifth graders, looking at occasions when they succeeded and failed in school. They compared the goals and behavior of those who were praised for intelligence and those who were praised for effort and hard work. The former came to value performance, and, when they performed poorly, tended to blame their own lack of intelligence. The latter came to value opportunities to learn and, when they did poorly, tended to criticize their effort as insufficient and to show a determination to work harder and improve.[15]

The point in all this is not that we shouldn't want children to do well or let them participate in organized activities and sports. Large numbers of children have great fun playing in sports leagues, as mine did, or studying a musical instrument or pursuing other courses and interests. Many parents, including those who very much want their children to win and who sometimes criticize the umpire too much (I was one), still manage to keep their aspirations in perspective. Unfortunately, their numbers seem to be dwindling.

In too many cases, parents who devote relatively little time to their children are spending much of the time they do have on the sidelines or in the audience. There can be real harm in *concentrating* much of one's contact with a child on competitive performance. It can skew the relationship away from a balanced combination of nurture, structure, and latitude toward what I think of as "Vince Lombardi parenting." Lombardi, the legendary coach and icon in the National Football League, famously said, "Winning isn't everything, it's the only thing." Parents for whom an A-minus is insufficient, parents who focus primarily on whether their young athlete or violinist beats others, teach children that they are worth only what they achieve, and that no matter how successful they may be, they are only as good as their last victory. This, of course, is injurious to their confidence and competence, which is precisely the opposite of what parents intend. As noted earlier, when concern to boost a child's self-esteem causes parents to overprotect the child from appropriate disappointment and from any negative consequences, it can become counterproductive in this way. Losing is inevitable. To make it intolerable puts children in a terrible bind; it turns the unavoidable into something shameful. And it sells them short. They have much to learn from their failures, not just their successes. Within broad limits of safety, they need latitude for all their efforts to negotiate the realities of the world.

The New Insecurity

Many educators have found it helpful to understand the increasing challenges presented by students and parents in terms of the deficits in nurture, structure, and latitude, but this still leaves them wondering about the origin of the deficits, especially on the part of parents. As a kindergarten teacher told me, "Now I have a framework for *what's* gone wrong, but I still don't know *why* they would do this to their kids." The question is important: as I have noted, it's natural to react differently to someone's problem behavior depending on whether it comes across as *won't* or *can't*, as a deliberate refusal, say, to respect the requirements and boundaries of social comportment and school life or as an inability to do so. Though I meet many teachers who are uncertain, I also meet many who have a diagnosis: they trace the problems back a generation to the Baby Boom parents, those who came of age during the social upheavals of the 1960s and '70s. "The parents of today's parents were into freedom, not responsibility," goes this view. "They didn't raise their children well, and now that those children are parents they in turn don't know how to be responsible parents."

There is clearly something to this charge. The boomers were raised amid historic affluence and indulgence. Compared to their predecessors, they have been, among other things, much more likely to divorce, much more cynical in their attitudes, and much less trusting and respectful of institutions.[1] Nonetheless, the developmental decline of the family cannot be blamed on them alone, as though it were something they created or planned. It surely reflects choices by parents about where to invest their time and energy, choices whose effect—not intent—is to undermine their provision of nurture, structure, and latitude to children. But these choices are an outgrowth of shifts in the ways we live and work and in our national fixation with personal freedom. They are an acceleration of a long-term trend driven by changes in technology and also in systems of philosophical and political thought, which, together, have repeatedly upset social norms and customs, forcing society to revise its guidelines and expectations.[2]

In less than fifty years, much of the predictability of life has been swept away. America and, increasingly, other Western nations have moved from a fairly stable, standardized life cycle based on long-term employment and long-term marriage to a destabilized, destandardized life cycle based on much less permanent employment and marriage. Throughout the twentieth century, declining child mortality and rising longevity made people's lives more predictable; rising economic strength and steady work made their careers more predictable.[3] To mid-century and beyond, all this was accompanied by much lower levels of individual autonomy than we now take for granted, and by a much stronger consensus about many basic values. Today, as Arlie Russell Hochschild says, "fault-line shifts in family and work life" have created a climate of "advanced insecurity." Our old society based on stable marriage and employment has yielded to a new one based on "marriageability and employability. . . . You can marry, but will you stay married? You can work at a job, but will you be able to stay in that job?"[4]

Economists, psychologists, sociologists, and political scientists have all weighed in on the changes that have transformed public and family life.[5] They agree that the causes are multiple, though not about which ones are primary. From my perspective the central factors are economic and cultural: changes in the way we work and in the value we place on individual fulfillment. These have the greatest implications for schools because they lie, I believe, at the core of the family's developmental decline, affecting most directly the actual behavior of parents as they raise children and hence the actual behavior of children and parents at school. These are enormous topics in their own right and I cannot begin to present them here in their full complexity. But I do want to outline some of their key aspects, because they are vital to the important question of what society should expect of educators (and what they should expect of themselves) and to the practical question of how schools can cope with the changes in students and parents. This chapter explores some of the key economic causes. The next will take up individualism.

Hard at Work

Reversing a century-old trend, America has made a massive national shift of time and energy toward the workplace, one that has brought with it a great paradox: we are earning more and living better materially but working longer and more frenetically, and we have less and less time and energy for our personal and family lives. The decline in direct parenting reflects a huge transfer of adult resources out of childrearing and into the workplace. Most Americans do still work fewer hours and have more leisure time than almost all but our immediate forebears. But the last thirty years have seen a sharp increase in the amount of time people spend on the job, a remarkable shift in the balance of life that has had enormous implications for families and children. For fully a century, workers at all levels had been working shorter days and weeks and years. But in the 1960s this trend began to reverse with a vengeance. By some estimates, the typical American is now working roughly four hundred more hours per year than was common then. Overwork is now ubiquitous. The proportion of people working fifty hours per week or more has risen by nearly 35 percent since 1985. We even outwork the notoriously industrious Japanese.[6] We are the world champions of workaholism.

Not surprisingly, then, agreement with the statement "I always feel rushed" has jumped by more than 50 percent since the 1960s. Some pollsters report that over the past twenty-five years, free time has declined a stunning 40 percent—from a median of twenty-six hours a week to fewer than seventeen. Fully half the participants in one survey acknowledged guilt about not spending enough time with their children; three-quarters find balancing the demands of work and family a major source of pressure. How are such parents to spend enough time with the kids to avoid the "quality time" dilemma, to set the limits on the big issues, and to create the latitude that leads to constructive problem-solving? Clearly, it is growing more difficult to make both a living and a life.[7]

At least three key factors have helped to upset parents' abilities to be parents: a remorseless new economy in which the very forces that improve people's lives as consumers complicate their lives as workers, a relentless work-and-spend mentality that keeps them wanting more no matter how much they have, and the lure of work itself—Americans are not just prisoners of a time bind created by the demands of their jobs, they are architects of it, often preferring the burdens—and attractions—of work to those of raising children.

Buyers and Sellers

The opportunities and necessities of the new economy are rapidly invalidating those of the old and of the way of life that accompanied it. As a practical matter, they dictate that people pay more attention to work and less to their personal lives. Looking back on mid-twentieth-century America, it's clear that employment had come to be governed by four principles: steady work, mutual loyalty, predictably rising pay, and limited effort. Despite occasional recessions, America was in a period of remarkable long-term growth, with real per-capita incomes rising at an average annual rate of 3 percent during the 1950s and '60s. At all levels of the workplace there was an assumption of mutual loyalty and an expectation that employee and employer shared similar goals. Compensation was based on seniority more than effort or actual contribution to profitability. People could thus expect their salaries to rise over time. America's companies could be such comparatively stable, rewarding employers and could organize work according to these four principles because of their own strong, stable positions and the sustained expansion of the marketplace. This was the heyday of the old industrial economy.[8]

What happened next is now a well-known story. The new, technology-driven information economy began to destroy and restructure, with astonishing rapidity, the entire edifice of American work life. Electronic communication, deregulation, and globalization upset the longstanding security of corporate oligopolies. A dynamic renewal of American entrepreneurship transformed America's companies from fat and happy to lean and mean. It generated unprecedented growth in innovation, but it also caused enormous economic and social dislocation. America, as Robert Reich says, has entered "the age of the terrific deal." Life has improved hugely for most of us when we are buyers, but has declined sharply for most of us when we are sellers.

Our new economy is offering unprecedented opportunities, a remarkable and constantly expanding array of products, services, and investments. It grows ever easier to find ever better deals from a wider range of sources, both virtual and actual. The proliferation of the Internet and communications technology has greatly intensified competition among sellers of products, shortening the shelf life of innovations, which in turn begets even more innovation and productivity because to survive, organizations must keep cutting their costs, adding value to their existing products and services, and creating new ones.

This brave new world has brought the material standard of living of the professional class to impressive levels, but its impact on the parts of people's lives that depend on relationships, continuity, and stability—marriage, family, childrearing—has been malignant. "The easier it becomes for us as *buyers* to switch to something better, the harder we as *sellers* have to scramble in order to keep every customer," notes Reich. And "the faster the economy *changes*—with new innovations and opportunities engendering faster switches by customers and investors in response—the harder it is for people to be confident of *what any of us will earn* next year or even next month, what they will be doing, where they will be doing it."[9]

The old stability and the assumptions in which it was rooted are gone. Work is no longer steady and pay doesn't rise predictably. It is now more difficult for companies to count on their own income, and they increasingly hire workers by the hour or by the project, without benefits, and emphasize pay-for-performance. Effort must now be continuous, even for veterans. Loyalty is turning into an unaffordable luxury: as it diminishes between customers and companies, it is vanishing between companies and employees. Everyone is now free to seek better deals, even in medicine and law, once bastions of stability. The new economy has also vaporized factory jobs and crushed the incomes of those who perform routine work, widening the income gap between the skilled and the unskilled.[10]

The extent of this destabilization is hard to exaggerate. In this new age of uncertainty all sorts of workers must now concentrate not just on their employment but on their employ*ability*.[11] Warren Bennis of the University of Southern California, one of America's leading management experts, says, "No job is safe. Never will be. The half-life of any particular skill set is, at most, five years."[12] Just as companies can no longer predict the future and make long-term plans, so workers from top to bottom cannot forecast a career path. They have to be ready to jump, either because they find a better deal or because their company or the company's customers have done so. This means they have to focus more on themselves and the immediate future,[13] thus contributing to a rise in individualism, a preoccupation with self, and a decline in trust of others that has worrisome implications for family life.

Prisoners: Work-and-Spend

If rising uncertainty about future income and job security is one clear source of greater work involvement, there is a second: rising materialism. American engagement in work was accelerating well before the competitive pressures described here began to intensify. And though it may be easy to see why people who have lost ground would feel less confident about their jobs and futures and hence devote more time and effort to making money, it is the greatest beneficiaries of the new economy, the highest-level professionals and managers in the best-paid jobs, who are logging the longest hours.[14] Many economists explain this behavior by saying that we are rational agents who get what we want; if we are working more it is because we choose to. In fact, notes social economist Juliet Schor, the reverse is more true: we come to want what we get. America is locked in a cycle of consumerism—"work-and-spend," she calls it—that now dominates our economic and social life. And, she points out, overwork is also common among the poorly paid who, unable to make ends meet on one job, take a second.[15] We have turned more and more to consumption for satisfaction and meaning in our lives, translating progress into possessions instead of time at home.[16]

This would not have surprised Alexis de Tocqueville, who—two centuries ago—saw the roots of work-and-spend as embedded in American democracy itself, a natural outgrowth of the commitment to freedom and equality (each person believes that it ought to be possible to achieve as much wealth and status as anyone else, rather than having to accept a fixed station in life).[17] It certainly wouldn't have surprised Thorstein Veblen, who, a hundred years later, coined the phrase "conspicuous consumption" to describe the extravagant materialism of tycoons and robber barons, noting that possessions are a way of seeking status. The rich spend to prove to others that they can.[18]

Of course, the impulse to seek status is universal. Materialism is not unique to the wealthy; they are simply in a better position to gratify their desires than the poor, doing what the poor would do if they could. In fact, statistically, whether a family has a large-screen television is likely to depend less on its income or the television's cost than on how many neighbors have one. We devote much more time to shopping than any other nation. We own twice as many cars per person and dine out more than twice as often as in 1957. Most homes are full of appliances that would have been unimaginable then. The homes themselves are ever more spacious and costly; the average individual now enjoys as much living space as a family of four had in 1950. We spend nearly $40 billion per year on lawn care alone. The latest round of conspicuous consumption (boom markets for second homes, expensive cars, yachts, deluxe watches, and cosmetic surgery, and so on) has been summed up as "luxury fever"—and it does often resemble a disease more than a source of contentment.[19]

Work-and-spend could be said to represent the ultimate success of our market system, which is why a president of General Motors, Charles Kettering, famously defined the mission of business as "the organized creation of dissatisfaction." Consumerism is insatiable: a new luxury quickly becomes a taken-for-granted necessity. We rapidly become habituated to each new level of affluence, power, and status, and measure our success not by some absolute standard but in comparison to those who have the most—or at least more than we do.[20] Possessions turn out to be like health; not having them makes you unhappy, but having them doesn't automatically make you happy—at least not for long. In polls, Americans report themselves no happier today than in 1940, when most homes contained more people than rooms, and no happier than in 1957, when per capita income was less than half its current level. And during these decades we have seen the divorce rate double, teen suicide triple, violent crime quadruple, and depression, especially among adolescents and young adults, skyrocket.[21] Meanwhile, in one area—family time—we have grown steadily poorer.

Architects: The Lure of Work

From one perspective, work-and-spend is a cycle we keep perpetuating, choosing it without even consciously doing so. But working parents are not simply prisoners of the new economy or of marketers' manipulations. On the contrary, many are also creators of the time bind that causes them so much stress. Although they tell pollsters they want to spend more time at home with children and feel guilty about not doing so, the full truth is much less clear-cut. When asked about their work preferences, only 10 percent of employees say they want to work fewer hours; the rest want to keep their current schedules or work even more. When their companies adopt family-friendly policies, the programs parents prefer generally are the ones that make it easier for them to be on the job, such as creating a day-care center at the workplace (even when parents have to pay tuition), rather than the ones like flextime that improve their ability to be at home with their children. Something other than economic uncertainty and work-and-spend must be involved here.[22]

That something else is a widespread increase in the lure of work, a draw that stimulates people to choose to invest more of themselves in their jobs.[23] The lure has three major magnets. One is that the new economy has opened tremendous professional possibilities and rewards to those with the right skills. In the high-tech, telecommunications, and biotechnology fields, for example, people have had unprecedented opportunities to tackle exciting, intellectually challenging, cutting-edge projects. As options for creativity have expanded and the successes of entrepreneurs and innovators have been celebrated, more professionals have come to treat their employment as a special commitment, a form of self-expression, a source of personal growth that invites a full personal investment. Even when the work itself lacks innate appeal, when its interest, challenge, and pay are low, it can nonetheless be more attractive than childrearing, which is often hard, unglamorous, unsettling labor. Work is generally easier to deal with than home life; at any rate, some studies have suggested that crises at work tend to cause lower and briefer levels of stress than those of managing children and family.[24]

A second magnet is that, despite all the political rhetoric about "family values," Americans esteem work more highly than childrearing. Most of the professional people I know complain about how much they work, yet are proud of being so busy and important. They acknowledge that they feel like workaholics and should cut back, but they quickly move to talking with interest and energy about the projects they're involved in. They are in demand, they count.

Feminism has made a key contribution here. It is overwhelmingly about liberating women from domesticity, about professional freedom (equal access to interesting, well-paid jobs and career advancement), and personal freedom (birth control, abortion, no-fault divorce). Men, as we know, have always concentrated on work more than parenting. Women, as they have made headway in formerly male domains, have, understandably, become more like men, increasing their concentration on work. This has helped to devalue *parental* childrearing. Many feminists have actively sought the expansion of affordable, high-quality *paid* child care, but this, in itself, confirms that both parents have more important things to do. Necessity has helped to make a virtue of this view. As the economy has become more competitive, as intact families have needed two incomes to get by, and as legions of single mothers have had to support their children, the logic of women in the workforce has grown more compelling.

A third magnet is a major role reversal between the workplace and the home. As Hochschild points out, work has made itself more attractive by assimilating the best qualities we associate with family life, while home has taken on what used to be seen as the worst features of work. As we become more engaged in our employment, our lives are increasingly shaped by its deadlines, cycles, pauses, interruptions—and its overtime. Even when we are at home, work comes with us via cell phones, pagers, laptop computers, and e-mail backlogs that inevitably encroach on family time. As activities once performed at home (music lessons, tutoring, after-school play, birthday parties, and so on) are outsourced to paid providers, family life must be tightly scheduled, acquiring a kind of cult of efficiency. Meanwhile, work, its hours ever longer, grows more "hospitable to sociability—periods of talking with friends on e-mail, patching up quarrels, gossiping." In her research, Hochschild met many men who were better fathers to their staff than to their children, and many women who voiced strong support for family-friendly policies but concentrated their lives on their jobs, bringing a maternal presence to the office and an administrative presence to the home.[25]

Masculinizing and Minimizing

The work-home role reversal has led to what I think of as the hypermasculinization of the parenting pair. There is a sharp difference between the outlooks, attitudes, and traits that breed success in the workplace and those vital to successful childrearing. The world of work is much more instrumental—factual, rational, technical, product-oriented, and the like; it calls upon characteristics that, to oversimplify, are more typically male. The world of childrearing is much more affiliative—empathic, emotional, interpersonal, spontaneous, and so on; it calls upon characteristics that are more typically female. Parenting is surely work, but it doesn't call for the virtues of the workplace. In fact, attitudes and habits that lead to professional success often run counter to those required by good nurturing. Table 8.1 offers a schematic summary of the key differences.

Table 8.1. Parent Qualities and Career Qualities

Parent Success Qualities	Career Success Qualities
Loyal Agent	Free Agent
Altruism	Self-Concern
Stability	Mobility
Tolerance for Disorder	Efficiency
Spontaneity	Planfulness
Present Focus	Future Focus
Acceptance	Drive
Relationship Orientation	Task and Product Orientation

Source: Adapted from Hewlitt and from Brooks.[26]

The more one cultivates the career qualities on the right, the harder it tends to be to shift modes at the end of the day or on the weekend, to express in a natural way the parent qualities on the left.

Though these differences have always obtained, they used to be better balanced in a family *as a whole*. Fathers and mothers used to divide the two roles. When it was overwhelmingly the father who assumed the marketplace role, and who had the skills and attitudes to match, his instrumental focus was balanced by the homemaking mother, who was both available and inclined to master parenting skills. For another, back then the key career qualities were less extreme than they have become, due to the rules of employment in a stable workplace. As "workaholism *à deux*" has become common, especially in professional circles, the perspectives and attitudes of the business world have increasingly overshadowed their parental counterparts.[27] As more and more families have had to rely on two incomes, as we have increasingly valued career over homemaking and childrearing, as loyalty and job security have diminished, as competition has gone global, as we have come to worship entrepreneurship, and as all sorts of jobs require more market-driven, product-oriented, technical competence, the career qualities in the right column of Table 8.1 have moved further right. And this is now true not just for men but for many women in the workforce. To preserve their employability, they need to develop their career strengths. "Instead of humanizing men," says Hochschild, "we are capitalizing women."[28]

The end result is that parents' priorities have shifted in ways that make them less ready—less inclined, less practiced, less available—to provide nurture, structure, and latitude. Thus the essential components of good childrearing, the nonmarket values and skills, have been marginalized in American life.[29] For many, this has enhanced the potential for guilt. When I ask parent audiences to compare their performance at work and at home, the embarrassment and dismay on their faces is often striking. I remember vividly one mother who blurted out, "I can't even do this. I know I should just be giving more of myself to my kids." And it is a tiny, quick step from feeling guilty to rationalizing. The same mother raised her hand a few minutes later to add, in a defensive tone, "I know I should be with them more, but I also think my kids need to learn to fend for themselves." Heads around her nodded. She smiled, visibly relieved.

She does, in fact, have lots of company. Minimizing children's need for parental contact and care is one way busy mothers and fathers comfort themselves. They "define down" children's needs for security and contact. I have met lots of parents, especially those who spend very little time with their children, who mention the importance of independence training for children. Rushed and harried, they need their youngsters to hurry their development, to curtail dependence and forgo nurturance. A father whose three-month-old son was spending nine hours in day care every day told Hochschild, "I want him to be independent"; another explained, "We don't really need a hot meal at night because we eat well at lunch."[30] Guilt and anxiety also minimize parents' willingness to set limits on children's behavior and let them learn from experience. Guilt turns them into buyers; anxiety, into sellers. The pressures reviewed here make it understandable that so many parents abandon authority, downplay the need for holding the line, and appease their children, buying them gifts for good behavior, say, instead of expecting (and insisting on) it. And they make it understandable that adults who can't be confident about their own future, let alone their children's, would want their sons and daughters to demonstrate precocious competence, avoid missteps, have flawless résumés, and get a leg up on the competition. They will be sellers soon enough. Why not start early?

9

The New Individualism

As powerful and far-reaching as they are, economic forces are not the strongest influences on the way we live. All human behavior, including economic behavior, reflects not just the conditions of the marketplace and our choices as buyers and sellers but the cultural norms and beliefs that shape our understanding of those conditions and choices. Many Europeans, for example, facing the same global competitive pressures Americans do, have chosen a different trade-off between making a living and making a life: they work less and shop less. Of the cultural factors relevant to the developmental decline of the family, one stands out in bold relief: rampant individualism.

America has always been a most individualistic nation. Personal freedom is proclaimed in our Declaration of Independence and detailed in our Bill of Rights; Americans have prized it since our birth as a country. But to survive, let alone to thrive, every society depends on a core of shared norms and values. Without them, collective action of all kinds—political, economic, social—is severely compromised and so, therefore, are family and community life—and schooling. When broadly shared, values such as reciprocity help organize social behavior at all levels, from the classroom to the marketplace to the town hall to the boardroom. Indeed, a key reason we refer to a society's shared values as "social capital" is that just like financial capital (material resources) and human capital (skills and knowledge), these values help individuals cooperate to generate wealth.[1]

America has a long history, dating back to the Founding Fathers, of concern about excessive individualism and its close cousin, materialism. Much of this worry has concentrated on the risks to democratic governance. What matters here is related but different: the rise of an exaggerated emphasis on self-fulfillment and personal freedom that has inspired adults to pursue their own interests ahead of those of family and community (or at least to weight their priorities more heavily toward themselves) and so undermine child development and schooling. This trend has been a perfect complement to the self-centeredness bred by the changing dynamics of the workplace.

Freedom and Fragmentation

I have already noted that American families differ from those of other cultures in their emphasis on the individual as the basic unit rather than the family itself. Historically, in almost all cultures around the world, things have been quite different and still are today. Individual fate has been largely outside personal control. A man could not decide on his own where he would live, what he would do for a living, whom he would marry, or how many children he would have, and could do little to affect how healthy and long-lived they would be. A woman typically enjoyed even less choice and control about these things. In most societies the trajectory of life has depended heavily on the strength, skills, and status of the kinship group. Naturally, these societies have emphasized in their social relations and their childrearing practices the importance of cooperation and harmony rather than individual initiative. For much of the world, interdependence is a stronger norm than independence.[2]

Although we have always prized independence and self-determination, until the mid-twentieth century American individualism could fairly be called communitarian. It embraced a belief not just in personal choice but in the importance of social units—family, neighborhood, school, church, town. We have, for example, traditionally been a nation of joiners. From Rotary and bridge clubs through PTAs and political parties, American participation in groups of all kinds has always been higher than other nations'. This "art of association," as Tocqueville called it, has included a prominent emphasis on values such as honesty, duty, service, and reciprocity that emerge from the Puritan, Protestant tradition of our nation's founders and helped to bind the nation together.[3]

Today, this traditional individualism has lost out to a radical, expressive version focussed mostly on self-interest, even self-aggrandizement.[4] Over the past thirty years, growing numbers of Americans have come to see self-fulfillment as their primary goal, to the virtual exclusion of self-sacrifice, service to others, or institutional obligation. Indeed, never before have so many people been able to live essentially the life they prefer, free of material or cultural constraints. Large numbers of us can pick the kind of career we want and the location where we want to pursue it. We can choose a lifestyle and an identity. We can select a mate virtually without religious, ethnic, racial, class, or even gender barriers; we can decide whether and when to have children, and whether to raise them inside or outside a traditional marriage. If we marry but later regret doing so, we can seek a no-fault divorce. We take for granted a freedom of choice that would have been unimaginable throughout human history and remains so in most of the world.[5] And we appear to be pushing the outer limits of how much freedom we can stand.

Embedded in America's rising individualism is a growing distrust of other people and institutions and a consequent fragmentation of our society and a disabling of communal institutions—including our schools. The relationship between individualism and trust is reciprocal: a glorification of personal freedom both reflects and promotes a breakdown in personal relationships and a diminishing sense of mutual responsibility; a widespread distrust of others and of institutions inclines people to look out for themselves. Throughout America, the "radius of trust," in Francis Fukuyama's phrase, is shrinking.[6] A scholar of public policy at George Mason University, Fukuyama has traced the decline of trust in detail, but anyone can confirm it in the course of an ordinary day. You can't read a newspaper, watch television, see a doctor, go to the bank, sit in a traffic jam, dine in a restaurant, or board an airplane without encountering evidence that we are more uncivil to one another, impose on one another more, ignore one another more, doubt one another more, threaten one another more, sue one another more—and spend more time preparing ourselves for and protecting ourselves against the incivility, imposition, ignoring, doubt, threats, and lawsuits of others.

During the late 1950s a majority of Americans voiced confidence in both their fellow citizens and their government; by the early 1990s only a small minority did.[7] The collective effect is to erode the authority—indeed the legitimacy—of virtually every kind of institution. Government, religion, the professions—none are immune, and certainly not marriage and the family and certainly not schools. It is one thing to live in the land of the free—something most of us cherish—but something else again to live in a land of free agents.

Free agentry has gotten an enormous boost from technology. Of course, technology has been helping to destabilize social order since at least the 1700s. The upheavals in American life and work brought about by computing technology and electronic media are the latest chapter in a story that dates back to the Industrial Revolution. The creation of steam power and factory mechanization spawned whole new industries such as railroads and textiles, which in turn transformed the face of life and the nature of work. In little more than a century rural agricultural communities became predominantly urban industrial societies, and the ancient rituals, values, and customs of village life and rural society began to be replaced by new norms of the factory and the city. A world with minimal individual freedom in which relationships were dictated by status (lord, peasant) that carried permanent moral obligations yielded to a world with growing autonomy and relationships based on negotiable contracts. From an economic perspective, this is an example of "creative destruction"—disruptive change sparked by technological innovation that leads to material progress.[8] From a social perspective, a parallel destruction was caused in the world of community and family relationships, though how purely "creative" this was is open to question. The benefits of modern civilization are hardly without cost—compared to primitive hunter-gatherers, for example, we receive much better medical care, are less likely to be murdered, and live much longer, but we lack the high levels of social support provided by extended families, kinship groups, and village life, and we work longer and harder.[9]

The disruption that occurred in the late twentieth century constitutes a similar but even more rapid and dramatic instance of creation and destruction. Although our fast-changing information economy has brought many advantages, it has also brought enormous social and moral challenges. The ability of communications technologies to diffuse data rapidly, bypassing and disabling older, hierarchical systems of information, enhances their power to innovate and to undermine. In this they dramatically further the spread of individualism, which inspires change and growth in the marketplace but which, says Fukuyama, has "corroded virtually all forms of authority and weakened the bonds holding families, neighborhoods, and nations together."[10] A work world that always asks, "What have you done for me lately?"—a work world in which people are forced to concentrate on their employability, to stay flexible, and to keep themselves ready to relocate, to change roles, employers, even careers—does not foster the putting down of roots, the deepening of relationships, the sustaining of communities, or the stability of families. And it certainly does not support the efforts of the schools to function as constructive communities.

Paradoxes of Liberation

It is not just technology that has been fueling the addiction to personal freedom and destabilizing society but changes in the foundation of Western thought. Throughout the twentieth century, the steady advance of the belief that morality and knowledge are not universal, that they are socially constructed rather than rooted in truth or reason or God, came to dominate popular culture. Its rise disempowered hierarchies of all kinds and provided justification for the expansion of individual freedom and personal choice on an ever-broader scale. Today, when virtually everything seems relative and nothing absolute, it is hard to grasp how profound this shift in worldview has been. It is not hard, however, to see here the double side of change: the very rationale that, for example, delegitimized colonialism and segregation has ultimately disempowered family norms and community institutions.

The most salient examples of this disempowerment include the liberation movements that have transformed the United States. These began with the American civil rights movement in the 1960s and have included the sexual revolution, the feminist movement, and the gay and lesbian rights movement. Each has fought to free individuals from the dictates of traditional social norms and moral rules that were seen as unfairly limiting their options and opportunities.[11] From a marriage and family perspective, the sexual revolution and the feminist movement have been the most important of these. Both have brought obvious benefits to women, increasing their freedom, opportunity, and dignity, and the respect accorded them. They have permanently changed our society. But both have also turned out to be riddled with irony and in important ways damaging to women themselves and to children and families, and hence to schools. Although the trend toward liberation (sexual permissiveness, women working outside the home, and so on) was not new, its rapid acceleration helped to devalue marriage and parenting, and ultimately to increase the number of single mothers struggling to make ends meet. People began to marry less, cohabit more, and split up more. As the birth-control pill freed women to have sex without worrying about the consequences, men began feeling less responsible for women they impregnated. Beginning in the 1970s, the rate of birth-control use grew—but so did the rates of abortion and out-of-wedlock births, largely because the number of shotgun marriages began to drop significantly. Premarital sex was by no means uncommon in the 1950s and '60s, but strong norms of male responsibility for children led to weddings that held down the frequency of illegitimate (as they were then called) births.[12] As career opportunities opened up for women, divorce increased (a trend observed in all developed nations) and ex-husbands became less likely to pay alimony and child support.[13] In all sorts of families, whether divorced or intact, parents began to involve themselves less directly in child care.

As a psychologist, I can't help noting the unhealthy contribution to these changes by what has come to be called "pop psychology." Over the past thirty-five years, psychologists, psychiatrists, and others have advocated forms of self-fulfillment (*self-absorption* would often be a more accurate term) that encourage people to pursue their own pleasures and define themselves apart from—or in opposition to— the expectations of family and community. The "human potential movement" of the 1960s began what turned out to be a series of self-improvement and liberation fads—self-esteem, self-actualization, assertiveness training, Mars-and-Venus, and so on—that have glorified self-realization and belittled external obligation. The primary duty prescribed by many self-help writers is to oneself, to become "your own person," to throw off the shackles of family and society in the name of self-fulfillment. This kind of quasi-therapeutic narcissism is now so prevalent that it has turned upside down the "giving-getting compact"—the shared cultural understanding about what we should contribute to our marriages, spouses, children, and jobs and what we should expect to get back from them. In the 1950s, says Sylvia Ann Hewlitt, the compact, oversimplified, was:

I give the fruits of my labors to my family. I give loyalty and stead-fastness. I swallow my frustrations and suppress any impulse to do what I would enjoy; instead, I do what is expected of me. In return, I get the respect of my family because I bring home the bacon or keep up the house. The respect of the community because I strive to live up to the ideal of breadwinner husband or home-maker wife.

Now, however, delayed gratification, self-denial, sacrifice, responsibility to others and "other *mensch*-like behavior patterns [are all] out of style." The new compact puts getting first and giving second. Its summary, oversimplified, is: "I give time, energy, re-sources to a relationship as long as my needs are fulfilled, as long as I am stroked. If I become unhappy (or just plain bored), I have every right to move on to seek what I need elsewhere."[14]

In truth, the old version of the compact wasn't so purely altruis-tic and the new one isn't so purely selfish, but these summaries cap-ture the direction of the cultural shift in expectations about giving and getting fostered by the quasi-therapeutic, narcissistic mentality.

Even without the excesses of pop psychology, a dynamic, demo-cratic society like ours that maximizes technological innovation and individual freedom is, in key respects, innately unstable; by its very nature, it keeps upsetting its own taken-for-granted assump-tions and values. The more it rewards entrepreneurship and out-of-the-box thinking, the more it fosters personal freedom, the greater its difficulty in maintaining shared values and cohesion—especially when, like ours, it comes to foster a radical individual-ism that celebrates the breaking of rules. A society built on *breaking out* (of norms, traditions, and customs) so as to enhance individual freedom of choice will inevitably tend toward *breaking up*—frag-mentation, isolation, and family disruption. The very same em-phasis on self-determination that fosters innovation and undermines authority in the workplace subverts the ties of family and neighborhood (and nation, for that matter). A break-the-rules attitude toward entrepreneurship breeds a break-the-rules attitude toward personal behavior and helps to spawn, among other consequences, "broken families, parents' failure to fulfill obligations to children, neighbors' refusal to take responsibility for one another, and citizens' opting out of public life."[15]

Freedom, it turns out, is never free. It always exacts a price in lost relatedness and togetherness, lost predictability and stability. When adults free themselves from commitments to spouses, children, neighborhoods, civic associations, faith communities, and the like, they lose their connectedness. Families and communities, after all, are built upon shared values and norms, mutual obligations and responsibilities. These are all burdens and limitations, but they are the very stuff of connection and relationship that make life meaningful.

Trading-Off Children

We all pay a price for the extravagant pursuit of individual freedom, but the cost falls heavily on children and families. In this chapter, as in the last, we have seen how parents' priorities have shifted in ways that make them less ready to provide the developmental essentials. The new me-first version of the giving-getting compact, for instance, is definitely not good for children. Nurture, structure, and latitude all require a parent to be patient and to concentrate on the needs of the child. We need not advocate a return to the giving-getting compact of the 1950s to realize that sacrifice, obligation, and commitment to others are vital to raising children. There are, as Hewlitt insists, unavoidable trade-offs between adult freedom and child development: "Well-developing children dramatically limit personal freedom and seriously interfere with the pursuit of an ambitious career. . . . To become a parent is to relinquish part—often, for a while, a significant part—of one's own *direct* claim on the world and one's impact on the future and to invest oneself in helping one's offspring prepare to make their own claim and impact."[16]

From an adult point of view, it is fully understandable that one should not wish to relinquish one's own direct claim, that personal and professional interests have powerful appeal and palpable rewards, while parenting can be draining and discomforting. But from a child development point of view, it is equally clear that children need direct parenting—more of it than many are receiving—and that no time management or communication techniques can compensate for its absence (see Appendix). And since parents are transmitters of culture, passing it on as they raise their children, we should not wonder at seeing so much self-centered, me-first, behavior by young people.

The idea that children need parents to choose family more than they are doing applies to fathers and mothers both, but from my perspective it is fathering that is most lacking in the lives of American children. Forty percent are growing up apart from their biological fathers and many of these don't see their fathers on any regular basis. Among intact families, fathers are not only spending far more time at work than their fathers did, they are spending far more time just commuting to and from work each day than being with their children. If we were to adopt a national priority on better childrearing, it would begin with a campaign to improve fathering.

This said, it is hard to imagine any realistic scenario in which men, on a broad scale, would become children's primary caregivers. In fact, historically in human childrearing the balance between providing for a family and direct care for its children has been achieved through shared but differentiated roles, with fathers primarily involved in the former and mothers primarily involved in the latter. In our society, mothers' movement, by necessity and by choice, out of the home into workplace, though it has brought definite benefits to our national economy, to family incomes, and to women themselves, has seriously compounded our society's childrearing problems. The point is not that mothers should return to housewifery—school-age children unquestionably can develop healthily with mothers who have careers—but that a family without "home making" offers a developmentally impoverished context for living and for raising children.*

What's missing from too many American households is, as journalist Caitlin Flanagan puts it, "the one thing you can't buy—the presence of someone who cares deeply and principally about that home and the people who live in it; who is willing to spend [time] thinking about what those people are going to eat and what clothes they will need for which occasions."[17] Flanagan adds that because she does not wish to be burned in effigy by the National Organization for Women, she must say this work can be done by fathers as well as mothers, but that mothers seem more willing and able to do it.

I, too, have no desire to be burned in effigy by N.O.W., but I do think that feminism's devaluation of domesticity and of maternal childrearing has exacted a real price from children. If the emphasis on women's having the same rights as men to interesting, rewarding careers has given many children a broader idea about what women can do with their lives, it has also left many without an at-home parent. If there is an obvious logic to granting women equal access to the career opportunities, rewards, and power that men enjoy, it is also true that a society concerned about the development of its young would not be fostering a care gap, seeking to perpetually enlarge adult freedom at the expense of parental commitment. For my part, I don't care whether a mother or a father assumes a primary home-making role or both contribute enough so that the full home-making job gets done. But it seems incontrovertible to me that children grow up best in homes, not just houses, and that without home-making houses are not homes.

*The two words quoted are deliberate; I only wish there were an even clearer way to remove from the term *homemaking* its 1950s, home ec, Ozzie-and-Harriet stereotype and use it literally to mean "making a home life."

Ambivalence: Nostalgia and Necessity

It's not that people don't want to live in a home as opposed to a house, or be part of a real community, or have their children grow up well; they do. In fact, people long for these things. It's just that too few are ready for the necessary sacrifices. These sacrifices require making choices and limiting personal freedom, which is precisely what most Americans don't want to do; they want it all. In surveys and interviews with people across the country, Boston University political scientist Alan Wolfe found nearly universal ambivalence about the family because so many people simultaneously carry two contrasting visions of it in their heads: "One that longs nostalgically for a world in which families stayed together, three generations lived in proximity to each other, children obeyed their parents, women remained at home, and everyone believed in God; and another in which both parents are free to pursue careers, children are anxious to escape the home and give themselves over to the attractions of a consumer and entertainment culture, grandparents try to avoid either being burdened by or dependent on their grown children, and the language of rights and self-fulfillment comes to play as much a role as the language of obligation and duty." Americans want the advantages of both. "Longing for a world that no longer exists," says Wolfe, "but having no intention of giving up the one that does, they are torn between nostalgia and necessity."[18]

This ambivalence is deeply embedded and eminently understandable. Most Americans Wolfe has interviewed know "better than conservatives the positive benefits of having women work [but] better than feminists how the family is weakened by it." They find it "simple common sense that if both parents are out of the house most of the day, children will suffer," but they are wedded to their freedom (and their material well-being).[19] They are not returning to what journalist David Brooks calls "the world of deference and obedience" that once characterized the nation.

To be sure, some people and organizations are trying to restore commitment to family and community. Groups across the political and ideological spectrum are attempting (in very different ways) to strengthen marriage, for example. To make divorce less likely they try to educate the public, provide support for couples, and promote legal change. Now and then, one meets parents who have chosen to "downshift," opting out of the 24/7 career rat race, living modestly so as to spend time together as a family. Recently, some municipalities have scheduled family nights during which no organization meets so parents and children can be at home together. These and other kinds of efforts may catch on and ultimately coalesce into a broad movement to restore a more family-friendly balance in the lives of parents and children. But they face an uphill struggle because we lack a national consensus about their necessity and especially because we are wedded to our personal freedom.

Most ideas for improving the lives of children quickly become fodder for the culture wars. People everywhere agree that marriage, family, and parenting are in trouble, but not about what should be done—whether, say, changing social and economic policy will be effective, and if so, whether the change should foster self-reliance and moral renewal or government support and social reform. Does expanding day care weaken family responsibility, or does opposing it promote sexism? Would eliminating no-fault divorce keep families intact and improve children's lives, or leave women trapped and dependent? Our cultural divide makes it difficult to approach, in any consistent way, questions about the future of the family and childrearing.

Underneath this public rift lies a deeper and more important fault line: people everywhere, even as they long for closer connection and greater continuity, cling to their freedom. Even Americans who bemoan the country's moral vacuum and blame it on the permissiveness that began in the upheaval of the 1960s embrace the priorities of that upheaval, such as civil rights. Even those who lament the loss of community resist any effort to limit individual choice in public or private behavior. Even those who decry the decline of the family and the rise of divorce do little to increase their own parental commitment, especially if this would intrude upon their individual freedoms, and most people uphold the right to end not only a bad marriage but a disappointing one. Americans, particularly educated Americans, are seeking a kind of hybrid life— trying, as Brooks says, "to build a house of obligation on a foundation of choice."[20]

It's hard to foresee a resolution to this national ambivalence: a renewed embrace of the kind of limits on personal freedom that helped give marriage and family their permanence and authority; a speedy return to the belief that an adult's life can be meaningfully defined by the sacrifice made for spouse or children; a broad agreement that our way of life, for all the instant gratification and material wonders it offers our youth, has grown increasingly unfriendly—and in some ways toxic—to their development. Such changes in perception and behavior would require decisions by large numbers of parents (and their employers) to moderate their focus on self-fulfillment and work-and-spend and to reinvest their time in children and family, in quality of life instead of quantity of possessions and arc of career. Absent such shifts in priority, many of the common proposals for pro-family social change seem unlikely to build momentum. And so long as large numbers of parents don't resolve their ambivalence in favor of a more direct investment in the raising of children, schools are likely to remain at a disadvantage, the focus of displaced anxiety, unrealistic wishes, and excessive blame.

Part Two

. . . .

Limits and Leverage

Real-Life Coping for Schools

10

. . . .

Rethinking Accountability

"So much for the challenges," the principal said. "We want to know what we can do about them." Her faculty, a group of forty elementary teachers, nodded vigorously. Several had already asked this question, and I had put them off, insisting that we needed to grasp the full context of the challenges before tackling them. But educators are practical problem solvers; they could wait no longer. They were convinced they should be doing something, and if I had ideas about what would be helpful, they wanted to hear them.

In these pages, as in that school, I have so far dwelt on the dilemmas in childrearing because they are truly reaching crisis proportions. The threat they pose—not just to our schools but to our children and ultimately our nation—is real and deep. They will not yield to quick fixes. We can't graft naive, utopian solutions onto grave, intractable problems. At the same time, we do need to act and the looming crisis does offer an opportunity, a chance to face issues we have been trying to fudge and rethink fundamental choices both about how we school children and about how we raise them. In the rest of this book I suggest some major revisions to the ways schools have been trying to cope.

These revisions, however, do not begin *at* school but with our expectations *for* school. The problems I have here reviewed are not caused by school, though some are intensified there. They begin before school and lie largely beyond its direct influence. It would be misleading to suggest that if teachers and principals just handled students and parents differently, they could reverse the developmental decline of the family, improve children's readiness to learn, and turn mountains (the pyramids of problems outlined in Chapter One) into molehills.

In the remaining chapters, I have lots to propose in the way of practical steps educators can take to be helpful, not only to their academic mission but to the lives of parents and students directly. I argue that they need to think more strategically about structuring the entire experience of membership in the school community; that as part of this effort they need to redefine the home-school relationship, and that they need to better prepare teachers for dealing with parents and also moderate their expectations for changing parents through educational programs. But before any of this comes the matter of school accountability—specifically, a need for much greater realism about what the nation should expect of its educators and what they should expect of themselves.

For several decades now, as families' developmental functioning has declined, we have turned to schools to pick up the slack, delegating to them responsibility for a growing array of students' nonacademic needs. We haven't declared this as a national policy (although there are those who, in effect, urge us to do so)[1] but we have steadily moved in this direction, both by assigning to schools former family functions (from breakfast, lunch, and medical checkups to the prevention of complex social and behavioral problems) and by tolerating conditions in which the schools cannot function unless they undertake these tasks. This inexorable burden-shift is now taken for granted, thoroughly entrenched in our collective understanding of *school*. Even many educators embrace it. But it is stretching schools to the breaking point. It demands far more than they can manage.

The crisis in childrearing requires that we stop expecting educators to accomplish what they can't and start empowering them to accomplish what they can. We must stop blaming them for problems they didn't cause and can't cure and start broadening our notion of accountability—indeed, of education itself.

Disconnect: The View from the Conference Center

If the world of the family has been transformed over the past forty years, so has that of the school. Well into the 1960s schools were what management consultants used to call "high slack" organizations: they had lots of unused capacity. The pace of innovation was slow. Institutional authority was strong—the school's word was generally law. Educators could confidently assume that the best way to prepare students for the future (the unknown) was to teach them about the past (the known), in ways that were broadly agreed upon, and that included everything from a curricular emphasis on the literature and history of Western Civilization to a student dress code. All this has changed. Schools have seen a phenomenal expansion of their scope.

I think about this expansion often, but it loomed especially large one day not long ago as I contemplated the scene at a conference center where I was speaking. Outside the air was crisp and clear, the vistas long and lovely. Inside, the atmosphere was thick with frustration, the views bleak and bitter. Executives and staff members from foundations that underwrite educational reform had gathered with consultants and trainers funded by their grants to assess progress in the participating schools. The results were deeply discouraging. Test scores weren't rising; the achievement gap between minority and white students wasn't closing. Almost unanimously, those attending blamed the educators who were the beneficiaries (and targets) of their generosity and expertise. Principals were out of their depth and lacked vision; how could we improve their "skill sets"? Teachers were resistant and didn't care about kids; how could we get them to "reinvest"?

Listening, I thought of the educators I had met earlier that week: a fourth-grade teacher whose urban school has 60 percent turnover among students each year and whose class of twenty-seven contained only five students with fathers in the home; a suburban middle school guidance counselor coping with an outbreak of oral sex—both at school and at weekend parties—among seventh-graders; a rural high school principal berated and sued by parents whose son he had expelled for selling drugs at school. I had a palpable sense of the disconnect between those outside schools who press accountability and innovation and those inside who must deliver results, and I realized yet again that this disconnect—and the core dilemmas of school improvement—begin not at school but at home.

When it was my turn to speak, I asked how many of us in the room were former teachers. Barely half, including me. How many would want to be a career teacher or administrator right now? None, including me. Why not? The answers were predictable. They were the same ones educators give when asked why they're leaving the field, retiring early, or not applying for principalships and super-intendencies; the same ones the conference participants had dismissed earlier as "excuses for inaction": the endless parade of changes that don't last; the constant criticism by politicians, policy-makers, and the press; the relentless focus on test scores; the excesses of special education; and—repeatedly as we went around the room—the changes in the behavior, attitudes, and values of students and parents.

Whenever I hear this list, I marvel that the criticism for failed innovation always falls almost entirely on practitioners and is never shared by outsiders, even the most naive and arrogant, or by parents. Again and again, the outsiders have promoted unreasonable expectations for schools and, when their prescriptions have failed, attacked the patient for refusing to get better. The behavioral challenges educators face, though enormously complex, are only part of a larger wave of change that threatens to overwhelm them. Even as they try to address the shifts among students and parents, their plates are overfull: they have been struggling to implement a range of complex academic innovations, changes more vast and far-reaching than at any time in their history. Academically, the sheer volume of curriculum teachers must try to cover as students move from kindergarten through twelfth grade keeps rising (nothing is ever removed from the American syllabus). And this larger volume now includes content that is, in its upper reaches, vastly more sophisticated. In most schools instruction is now much more differentiated and individualized; rather than taking all students through the same material in lockstep, an elementary teacher may be effectively teaching three or four classes within the same classroom. Mathematics and science have expanded beyond anyone's imagining thirty years ago. As the decades pass teachers of history have ever more to cover. Moreover, until relatively recently most American schools weren't even using a computer, much less attempting to integrate technology into their instruction. And all this complexity is further compounded by the inclusion in regular classes of special needs students, especially when they have significant psychiatric or behavioral disabilities.

Special education (SPED) deserves a special digression here because it offers a classic example of well-meant school improvement whose unintended consequences have created huge burdens for schools. The original rationale for SPED reforms that began in the 1970s seemed to many of us in education and mental health full of promise. Students with disabilities would do better in their local schools than warehoused in separate institutions, and within the school they would do better if integrated into regular classes rather than kept in substantially separate "pull-out" programs. "Inclusion," as this effort came to be known, would provide better instruction and a richer, more normal social experience for these students, and would keep them from suffering the stigma of being segregated into special institutions and programs. At the same time, it would teach students without disabilities valuable life lessons. Moreover, the classroom modifications made to accommodate SPED students—more individualization, a variety of strategies and approaches to teach each given concept, and so on—would help regular students as well.

Though this all made perfect sense to me thirty years ago, not all of it does now. Schools everywhere, especially in better-performing districts and especially in the elementary grades, have made enormous strides in their ability to integrate into regular classes students with primary learning disabilities—that is, academic disabilities largely uncomplicated by other issues. But a combination of their very success, of changing expectations, and of changes outside school have made the reality of special education extremely difficult. These are some of the key problems:

- *Ever more challenging students.* The SPED population is much larger and much more difficult to teach than was ever envisioned, due to, among other factors, medical advances. Many more premature, low-birth-weight babies now survive; they are at high risk for physical, cognitive, and psychiatric disabilities, and a substantial proportion of them require more attention throughout their childhood than age-mates who were full-term infants. Meanwhile, the decline in parental nurture and structure has increased the number of students— regardless of their status as infants—presenting with primary behavior and psychiatric problems.

- *Classroom complexity.* Even as districts now include students with much more serious disabilities than in the past, they are pressed to raise academic standards, challenging precisely the areas where many SPED students are weakest.

- *Regulatory nightmares.* Procedural requirements for documentation, testing, and meetings have reached mind-boggling proportions.

- *Funding shortfalls*. Even if there were a proven educational technology for every disability, schools couldn't begin to afford the expense; they can't even meet current costs. As a result, in districts everywhere regular education budgets are being cut to preserve SPED services, which are mandated by law. For example, the treatment of just one autistic child—their numbers are growing rapidly—can cost a school district the entire salary of a teacher who would teach a full roster of regular students.[2]

No one—I emphasize this—seeks a return to the dismal past; children with significant medical and other disabilities deserve help. But where and at whose expense? Many thoughtful observers have come to question whether schools should be responsible for treatment as well as education. In any case, it is undeniable that special education represents a vast expansion of the school's role and dishonest to pretend that regular education is not suffering as a result.

SPED students' rights are but one of many factors enlarging schools' responsibilities. Others stem from research into the human brain and the different learning styles of students and from a concern to prepare students for a global, fast-changing economy in an ever more diverse world. Both of these have led to innovations in curriculum and in instructional methods, making classrooms much more complex. Over the past twenty years, we seem to have reached a national consensus that our schools need "change" on many fronts—but no agreement about which changes in which order of priority. Should schools focus more on basic skills, the amassing of facts and "content" and mastery of the traditional disciplines, or should they emphasize "constructivism," higher-order thinking, and interdisciplinary learning? Should they confine themselves to academic excellence or also emphasize character and values—and if the latter, which traits and values and by which methods? How far should their diversity programming extend? How thoroughly should they integrate technology into classroom instruction?

Each of these choices is, in and of itself, complex, and they are by no means the only ones facing schools. To resolve them all would take more time and energy and money than any school has available. What priority, then, should each initiative receive? Most schools can't decide—or aren't allowed to decide—and end up tackling too many changes simultaneously, only to discover that it is easy to overdose on good ideas (not to mention on bad ones). Even if each individual venture is worthwhile, when a school has more than one or two intricate, costly, and time-consuming initiatives in progress, they end up fragmenting energy and competing with one another for a faculty's time and allegiance and a school's budget. And, as I noted earlier, schools are not simply victims of externally driven rising expectations. In many faculty contribute to students' burdens (and their own) by constantly looking to extend the curriculum in scope and sophistication. And now, after years of adding one new initiative after another, schools face the further challenge of high-stakes testing.

The Great Accountability Fallacy

American education has been overtaken by a frenzy for accountability and assessment. This frenzy is the extreme outcome of twenty years of conflicting efforts to restructure our schools. Its direct roots trace back to A Nation at Risk, the influential 1983 report drafted by a special commission formed by then-Secretary of Education Terrel Bell. The report famously decried "a rising tide of mediocrity" among America's schools and students, which, it predicted, would lead to an inevitable economic decline for our nation, while Asian countries, thanks to their excellent schools, would flourish. This prediction proved dead wrong (our economy boomed; Asian economies tanked), but by then it had become the conventional wisdom. It paved the way for twenty years of school-bashing, for an endless stream of conflicting and contradictory reform proposals, and for a simplistic, corporate-style, bottom-line approach to measuring progress.

Of all the negative legacies of A Nation at Risk, the most misguided may be an emphasis on a narrow view of "accountability," on treating schools as factories that turn raw material into products for which they alone are to be held responsible. Six years after the report was published, our first President Bush (with help from then-Governor Bill Clinton), oversaw the birth of Goals 2000, an initiative full of impossible objectives (within eleven years, U.S. students would outscore the world in math and science, and so on). Schools, predictably, failed to meet these absurd targets, thus confirming for many the rising tide of mediocrity. From there, it was a slippery slope to the test-based accountability mania that is now peaking under our second President Bush and his No Child Left Behind Act of 2002. The legislation would more accurately be phrased "No Child Left Untested," since the plan relies so heavily on a barrage of annual exams—many highly suspect—to improve school performance and student achievement.[3] And like his father, George W. Bush has his own impossible goal: within twelve years all the nation's children are to score at the "proficient" level or higher. Nothing could be less likely.*[4]

Although the Bush plan is especially unrealistic and unfair, the problem about accountability is much larger and involves not just the advocates of high-stakes testing but their opponents. They, too,

*There is a sharp, painful irony about the pressure and criticism heaped on America's schools as a result of A Nation at Risk and Goals 2000. In 1993, looking back, Bell had real regret. About the former, he claimed that the report had intended to inspire the nation to *support* schools, not blame them, precisely because they were struggling with the kind of issues I outline in this book. "No school," he wrote, "no matter how effective, can fully compensate for failure in the home." He pointed to a "cataclysmic change in the quality of students' lives outside of school," which, along with other factors, "made it almost impossible for schools to succeed" despite teachers' "heroic efforts." And, he acknowledged, the report counted too heavily on school improvements "that affected only six hours of a child's life and ignored the other 18 hours each weekday plus the hours on weekends and holidays." He ended by saying, "We have foolishly concluded that any problems with share the accountability fallacy. The original proponents of school reform and the current supporters of testing disagree sharply about the kind of schooling and assessment that will best drive improvement. The former, mostly liberals, have generally aimed at in-depth learning based on "authentic instruction" and "authentic assessment"; for them accountability means having students demonstrate their ability to apply what they learn. Often, they also see schools as instruments of social change that should promote equity and diversity as well as high academic standards. The latter, mostly conservatives, insist on a narrower, shallower, one-size-fits-all approach to improvement and scorn the promotion of what they see as political correctness. They tend to view public schools as inadequate, irresponsible, and oppressed by teacher unions, and insist that testing is key to promoting higher standards because it will dramatize schools' profound weaknesses and motivate improved results by teachers and pupils. Liberals respond by agreeing that there are serious performance problems in schools, but attribute these to the very kinds of instruction and assessment conservatives want to reinforce—the rote recall of facts, figures, and formulas. The disagreements go on.

These differences are serious and substantive, but they are mostly about goals and methods. The rancor between the two camps masks a shared underlying assumption. As I suggested at the outset, both view schooling as *the* critical—indeed, as virtually the sole—factor in improving student performance, and largely overlook or discount the realities explored in these pages. Both promote what I call the Great Accountability Fallacy: they see education narrowly as

the levels of academic achievement have been caused by faulty schools staffed by inept teachers—and that by fixing the schools we can attain the levels of success we do desperately need." Though much too late, he was right on target. And though he wrote of A Nation at Risk, his words apply, with some exceptions, to most of the reform efforts of recent years (Bell, 1993, pp. 593–595). Goals 2000 began on just the right note; its first goal was all children would arrive at school ready to learn. Imagine how this, by itself, would affect students' learning and test scores, not to mention their civility and values! Of course, Goals 2000 assumed that this, too, would mostly be up to the school.

schooling and schooling as much more influential than it is.[5] Formal schooling is a vital part of a child's education, but only a part, and not the most influential. As the psychologist Mihaly Csikszentmihalyi says: "Whether or not children will learn does not depend primarily on what happens in school, but on the experiences, habits, values, and ideas they acquire from the environment in which they live."[6] Schooling is a part of that environment, but only a part. By the time seniors graduate at age eighteen they have spent 90 percent of their lives, including their earliest early years, outside school.[7] The adequacy and content of the formal schooling they receive, though vital, is not nearly as important as the adequacy and content of the nurture, structure, and latitude in their families—or as their socioeconomic status, or as the media culture that holds them in thrall.

The data about the limits of schooling's impact have been available for decades. Nearly forty years ago, James Coleman made a powerful case that parents' involvement in their children's lives has a much greater effect on their ultimate achievement than the school itself.[8] This caused considerable controversy and led to a thorough reanalysis of Coleman's data by Christopher Jencks and a team at Harvard. Their conclusion was even sharper. The data, they said, showed that schools' influence was "marginal," that children were indeed influenced far more by "what happens at home [and] on the streets and by what they see on television." A school's output, they said, depends almost entirely on "the characteristics of the entering children. Everything else—the school budget, its policies, the characteristics of the teachers—is either secondary or completely irrelevant."[9]

Strong stuff—and very unwelcome, to say the least. It helped provoke a powerful counterattack. This was already the heyday of the so-called "romantic" critics of education. Writers like John Holt (*How Children Fail*), Charles Silberman (*Crisis in the Classroom*), and later Jonathon Kozol (*Death at an Early Age*) and others were skewering the shortcomings of urban public schools and traditional education approaches in general as stifling children instead of inspiring them.[10] The most dramatic and dogmatic opposition to the Coleman-Jencks line of thought came from Ron Edmonds, the founder of the effective schools movement. Edmonds famously said, "We can, whenever and wherever we choose, successfully teach all children whose schooling is of interest to us. We already know more than we need to do that. Whether or not we do it must finally depend on how we feel about the fact we haven't so far."[11] Schools, he insisted, can be powerfully influential in students' lives; and the failures of students, particularly minority students, were really failures of educators. His followers could point to Robert Rosenthal's *Pygmalion in the Classroom* study, which showed that students performed better simply when teachers were led to expect that they would do well.[12] Other research into what came to be called "efficacy" supported the idea that when a teacher has high expectations for students and provides high levels of support, learning improves. In the end, these arguments trounced those of Coleman and Jencks and became the dominant orthodoxy in education. They lie at the core of both *A Nation at Risk* and its descendant, No Child Left Behind.

Though Coleman and Jencks didn't prevail, there has always been much to confirm that they were on to something really important. Indeed, over the past thirty years evidence that schools have much less impact on student outcomes than commonly thought has continued to accumulate, confirmed in research that school improvement advocates have largely minimized and ignored. In 1992, for instance, in an aptly titled monograph, *America's Smallest School: The Family*, educational researchers Paul Barton and Richard Coley summarized a range of studies confirming that the family is truly the cradle of learning, the essential socializing institution, and that student achievement improves when there are two parents in the home, when children are well cared for and feel secure, when the family environment is intellectually stimulating, when parents encourage self-regulation and perseverance, when they limit TV, monitor homework, and ensure regular school attendance—when, in short, they are authoritative.[13]

This same evidence shows that schooling, by contrast, is a "weak treatment," responsible, some observers think, for less than 25 percent of a student's total outcome in academic achievement and social behavior.[14] Even 25 percent may be too generous. On some tests we can account for almost 90 percent of the difference among students' math scores by knowing only the number of parents in the home, the level of their education, the type of community in which they live, and the state's poverty rate.[15] Now that states are testing students en masse, the strong correlation between scores and socio-economic status is recurring everywhere. As Howard Gardner, the nation's leading authority on multiple intelligences, points out, we can predict a child's chances of completing college and her likely income simply by knowing her ZIP Code, and can do so with particular confidence if we also know how much family support she has and her family's ethnic and religious values.[16] Of the experiential factors that have been shown to have an enduring effect on a child's IQ, all stem from the family environment (such things as parents' cognitive stimulation and nurturance of the child, the presence of two parents in the home, their income and education levels, and so on); none stem from school.[17]

Downplaying and often flatly dismissing this evidence, reformers on both the right and the left treat schooling as a strong treatment and dwell heavily on its responsibility (and failure) to engage students, while virtually ignoring any obligation of students to be "engageable" or parents to foster "engageability." But, as described in Part One (especially in Chapters Five, Six, and Seven), what ails America's youth most is not the way they're being schooled but the way they're being raised. It is the lives of our children more than the skills of our teachers that have deteriorated over the past thirty years. The supports vital to good development (and hence to schooling) are in free fall. Schools truly are victims of the crisis in childrearing more than its perpetrators. A great many need to improve and a great many of those need to improve a great deal, but their improvement will, by itself, never overcome fundamental problems that start at home.

Neither Excused Nor Diminished

To argue this way may seem to minimize the concerns and efforts of those who have devoted themselves to improving American education; it doesn't. Thousands of teachers and administrators have embraced a mission of dramatically raising achievement for all students. They have committed themselves to serious, in-depth school change that is not defined narrowly by test scores, have worked to make schools free from prejudice, and have invested years of hard and successful work changing old schools and founding new ones. They often grow angry when they hear older teachers complain that students are harder to teach and parents harder to deal with. They see this as a cop-out, a cover for indifference and incompetence, and as bashing students and parents. Or they acknowledge some of the negative influences on students' out-of-school lives but look to the school to overcome them. "These are the kids and families we have," is their message. "We can't control what happens out there. It's up to us to teach them. No blaming, no excuses." They might object that I am, first, giving aid and comfort to the uncaring and inept and, second, demeaning their own mission and commitment.

To the second, I can answer unequivocally, "Not so." Nothing in this chapter trivializes the work of teachers. School is not the most important influence on a child, but it is a very important one and it can matter hugely. Even if it accounts for, on average, 10 percent to 25 percent of a student's outcomes, this is a key contribution: it can be decisive in the shaping of lives and careers. In my life as in countless others, the impact of individual teachers and of the school as a whole were profound. There are surely students everywhere for whom the schools' influence is greater than 25 percent, whose lives are transformed—literally even saved—by teachers. But it is futile and unfair to expect these stirring examples to be the national norm.

To the charge of defending those who don't care and don't deliver, I would like to answer just as unequivocally, but an honest answer is, "Not entirely so." The developmental decline of the family can indeed be misused by educators who cop out. However, none of what I say here—*none of it*—defends such misuse. None of it denies that many schools are in great difficulty and many others are sub par. Having visited hundreds of schools, I have seen convincing evidence of the need for improvement. The worst are truly appalling, from their facilities to their faculty. Some of the so-called best get by because their students are, as a former independent school headmaster says, "teacher-proof: they're so bright and gung-ho you can't keep them from learning no matter who's at the front of the room." In my experience, more than a few elite secondary schools survive with pedestrian pedagogy because they enroll high-performing students and put them in small classes.

When I visit a bad school where faculty are plainly incompetent or a boring school where faculty are adequate but uninspiring, the reformers' commitment is easy to understand. I have no interest in excusing bad teachers, apologizing for those who disregard all that we have learned in recent years about curriculum and instruction, or defending those who use the changes in families as an excuse for not trying. But even if the crisis in childrearing can be misused, it is nonetheless real. To expect schools to overcome it is just as unfair as it is for cynical or self-indulgent teachers to sell out their students.

We have every right to expect educators to do the absolute best job possible with the resources we give them. We don't have the right to expect them, by themselves, to master the forces that are shaping today's students. More than twenty years of exaggerating the schools' potential for influence has resulted in their being blamed not merely for their legitimate faults but for problems they didn't create and can't fix.[18] It has led to their undertaking, by fiat and by choice, academic goals that discount the crisis in child-rearing and to a near-universal assumption that they should accelerate achievement despite student deficits they are, in truth, helpless to remedy.

If we are genuinely serious about helping our students prepare for the future, about leaving no child behind, we must broaden our notion of accountability, accepting that the school's impact is more modest than we wish, the family's more robust than we have acknowledged. Barton and Coley concluded that meaningful progress in schools would require a change in the fundamental attitude of American society, beginning with a national commitment to "improve the family as an educational institution."[19]

This, of course, vastly enlarges the task. It is hard enough to envisage changing schools, but the family, too? No wonder reformers rarely look beyond the classroom. But there is no avoiding this need, as Coleman saw when he criticized the folly of treating school as "a complete environment," and as Harold Howe also saw when he noted: "It sounds simpler to focus narrowly on fixing the schools so the schools can fix the children. But no amount of school reform will turn children into enthusiastic and successful young scholars if they come to school already . . . damaged by family circumstances."[20] How can we truly imagine any *broad, significant, enduring* improvement in school outcomes without a corresponding improvement in the family as a "readier" and "sustainer" of students?

11

. . . .

What Makes Us, Us

Clarifying Purpose and Conduct

I f it is true that we need to moderate our expectations for schools
and that they cannot, on their own, reverse the decline in family
functioning, it is also true that they cannot simply wait for families
and the larger society to change. And they haven't been idle.
They've been trying a host of efforts to restore and improve the climate for learning and their relationships with students and parents.

Unfortunately, the outcomes of these efforts are not often encouraging, at least not for very long. How can schools not only
restore and renew their institutional strength but offer meaningful
help to their families? The answer, I am convinced, begins with perspective, not programs, and with strategy, not tactics. The shifts in
student and parent behavior must be seen not as a temporary aberration but a pronounced trend; simply intensifying traditional efforts
to improve communication and the home-school relationship in
the usual ways will be inadequate. Instead, educators must think
strategically and restructure their relationships with families. This
means no longer expecting the broad range of students to show the
attention, courtesy, industry, and motivation schools once took for
granted, and no longer expecting the broad range of parents to show
the patience, cooperation, confidence, and trust schools once depended on. It requires a systematic effort to build and sustain consensus throughout the school community about two key facets of

school life: purpose and conduct—core values and basic responsibilities. And it means redefining the home-school partnership less as one of equally prepared, equally informed parties and more as one in which schools need to be more parental vis à vis parents.

Traditional Problem Solving

For many schools the focal point in coping with the challenges this book explores is the increase in discipline and behavior problems students present. Typically, schools respond in ways that move from situational to systemic. The former are largely reactive; the latter aim to be preventive. Schools begin by attending to each case as it arises, using a combination of explanation, discipline, and counseling or other interventions. There is now a large literature recommending a variety of disciplinary philosophies and approaches to managing student behavior both in the classroom and schoolwide. A school's preferred strategy depends largely on the beliefs and training of its administrators and teachers. Whatever their predominant modus operandi, their aim is generally to reassert the school's expectations and norms, and ideally to turn problems into teachable moments, to help students reflect on their behavior and appreciate its consequences for others or themselves, and so on. If the behavior suggests a psychological problem or a condition that would benefit from professional assistance, the school may also recommend or insist on counseling or some other treatment.

When similar incidents recur among a number of students and thus begin to appear as symptoms of an underlying issue, teachers and administrators start looking for ways to be proactive, figuring that if they just keep responding to each event—imposing the same punishments, referring one student after another to the psychologist—they'll never get to the root causes. Often a first step is to consider some kind of informational outreach to parents. Educators see parents alternately as part of the problem (especially when they ignore the school's concerns and defend their children's misbehavior or when they attack the school and themselves say or do outrageous things), and part of the solution (allies who can provide a positive influence at home). They hope information and guidance will inspire and enable parents to improve their connection to and oversight of their children (providing stronger nurture and structure, as discussed in Chapters Five and Six), their willingness to let students learn from the consequences of their actions (latitude, Chapter Seven), and their own relationship with the school. The outreach generally consists of lectures or workshops, sometimes in a series, more often on an occasional basis; sometimes presented by school staff, other times by an outside expert. I have participated in and observed these kinds of programs for nearly thirty years; they have improved markedly, thanks in part to the growth in our knowledge base about child development and to the increase in the number of guidance counselors and school psychologists who have advanced training, but their impact has not. Almost without exception, educators are dissatisfied with the results.

The obstacles to successful parent education begin at the most basic level, with attendance. As parents' lives grow busier and their work days longer, they are less able and willing to come to evening programs, especially a series of them; schools everywhere report that their audiences are shrinking. Worse, the parents who need the programs most attend them least. In fact, the audiences tend to consist overwhelmingly of the school's most supportive mothers. Says a guidance counselor, "We're always preaching to the choir, and mainly the sopranos and altos. I'd like to send a special notice to our most difficult and most ineffective parents, including the dads: *We planned this evening specifically for you. Be here or else!* I keep hoping but they rarely come."

A more substantive problem is readiness: many parents these days are less knowledgeable about aspects of childrearing than in the past. They need more of the most basic kind of information and assistance, the essential insights described in Chapters Two and Three, which makes it hard to cover an adequate amount of information in a few evenings.

The fundamental underlying challenge has to do not with availability or sophistication but with the nature of parenting itself: it lends itself badly to advice. It is so involving, it touches so many parts of a person with such immediacy, that it is hard to do planfully. Schools have no reason to stop offering programs for parents, but they should moderate their expectations about the impact of this effort—seeing it primarily as a series of booster shots for the choir, not as a means of significantly changing parents' behavior. (The Appendix explores these issues and outlines an approach to educating parents that emphasizes practical, doable improvements in nurture, structure, and latitude.)

Along with parent outreach, schools have undertaken preventive programs for students. They have tried to target not just discipline infractions but a whole range of behavioral issues—including, among others, drug and alcohol abuse, stress, bullying, hazing—using a variety of methods such as mini-courses, curriculum units, all-school assemblies, and the like. As students' problem behaviors have multiplied in number and severity, this has led to a corresponding increase in the number and range of preventive programs. The chief reward for this expansion has been, in large part, to attract ever more demand for ever more programs.

As organizations dedicated to preventing and remediating various public health and social problems have grown, and as families and other social institutions have abandoned their traditional responsibilities, schools have come to be seen as the ideal place to treat issues of all sorts, from eating disorders and suicide to pregnancy and AIDS, and from harassment and date rape to racism and sexism.[1] Among the most prominent of these efforts are those aimed at preventing drug and alcohol abuse and sex abuse. Without question, these programs mean well, but their effectiveness is a matter of real doubt. They are often brief (a few sessions—sometimes only one—squeezed into the school's already crowded schedule) and simplistic, and they often deliver too little too late or, sometimes, too early, before students are even ready to grasp the relevant concepts.

A notable example of these well-meant but weak preventive programs is D.A.R.E. (Drug Abuse Resistance Education), which brings police officers into schools to inoculate elementary school children, as it were, against drug abuse. Despite its popularity, the program has shown no measurable success in reducing eventual substance abuse among students when they reach middle and high school. D.A.R.E.'s naive curriculum and methods reduce the question to a simple dichotomy—use is bad, abstinence is good—which may appeal to elementary children, who are relatively concrete, black-and-white thinkers, but which is quickly dismissed by the same children when, as adolescents, their thinking grows more sophisticated and their opportunities to experiment with substances increase.

Dissatisfied with (and sometimes overwhelmed by the number of) programs targeted to specific risks, many educators and academics have proposed deeper, more fundamental approaches to the whole composite of behavioral, social, and moral issues presented by students. One of the best known is character education. Comprising a wide range of activities that are a center of some controversy, it aims to help children develop ethical values (honesty, fairness, respect for others, personal responsibility) and to act on these values in their lives at school and at home. Broadly defined, character education can apply to almost any program that promotes these goals and tries to help children develop into ethical adults. Narrowly defined, it consists of direct indoctrination in specific values.

The broader approaches appeal to social liberals; they favor encouraging students to become autonomous, questioning thinkers who consider the ethical implications and consequences of their behavior and who, over time, construct their own code of values. The stricter approaches find their strongest support among social conservatives, many of whom believe that the school should unhesitatingly espouse, teach, demand, and enforce particular values—often including specific religious principles.[2] For all the controversy it has stirred, however, I have encountered few schools that are teaching character in a primary, sustained way. I have, though, visited a great many that are doing things they call character education, such as promoting a series of schoolwide themes (a month's focus on, say, honesty, followed by a month's focus on fairness, and so on). When I ask faculty in these schools about the actual impact of these themes, they rarely point to anything permanent.

The other major approach with students is known as social-emotional learning (SEL). Its advocates believe that how children learn is as important as what they learn; that to succeed academically and socially they must learn cooperation, responsibility, empathy, and self-control; and that when schools teach these skills, students' achievement rises, their misbehavior diminishes, and the overall climate of the school improves.[3] Found primarily in elementary schools, SEL promotes pro-social values and habits such as responsibility and fairness, as well as interpersonal skills (how to express feelings, how to resolve conflicts, and so on). Like character education, it comes in different levels of intensity, but it tends to rely on active learning techniques much more than on direct instruction. Its overall aim is to foster what Daniel Goleman has called "emotional intelligence" and what some educators call "social competency"—the ability to be aware of one's feelings and of the feelings of others, to regulate one's behavior, and to solve conflicts constructively.

I look forward to seeing what longer-term experience will tell us about the impact of character education and SEL programs—especially the latter, because so many of the teachers I've met who use them value them so highly. Since the lives of children outside school include so few pro-social influences, we can only welcome educators' efforts to right the balance. At the same time, I am ambivalent about the larger questions raised by having schools undertake the kinds of efforts summarized so far. As I have already said, I worry about overburdening schools by *expecting* them to fill gaps in children's basic development. And however skillfully implemented, programs like these, though they can be strong positive influences, aren't sufficient to help schools cope with the changes in student and parent behavior.

In my experience, the schools that encounter the fewest boundary-breaking problems and preserve the best relationships with their families are those that are the clearest about what they stand for (purpose) and what it means to be a part of their school community (conduct). In these schools the faculty, led by their principal, clarify, assert, and defend the school's core values and the essential requirements of participation in the school. In independent schools and in some public school districts, board members must be included in this process, as well. Although "school community" is a phrase widely used in educational circles, true community cannot exist without these kinds of shared understandings. They have always been important to successful schooling, but they can no longer be taken for granted and must be more actively structured.

Purpose: What We're All About

Understanding purpose begins with a clarification of what purpose *isn't*. It specifically does not refer to the school's mission statement, or at least not to the typical mission statement. I have argued elsewhere that far too much of the vision in schools is dull and blurred instead of clear and inspiring. Most school mission and vision statements proclaim identical commitments and goals, even when the schools themselves differ sharply. Most are typically too long, full of pledges the school can't possibly fulfill, and riddled with clichés.[4] They are essentially wish lists. There is nothing wrong with a wish list—its contents may be quite worthy—but it rarely captures the imagination in a serious way that shapes behavior and choices on a sustained basis.

By *purpose*, I mean guiding principles: the school's core defining beliefs that distinctively mark its approach to students and teaching. Achieving clarity of purpose requires coalescing around a few truly central values, not a long list of platitudes. These values are much closer to a motto than to a typical mission statement. A motto is simple, easy to remember; clear, yet adaptable; direct, yet general enough to be applied with some flexibility. It provides both focus and room for interpretation. In talking with administrators at schools where a motto really matters, I have heard it described variously as an anchor, an umbrella, and a touchstone. The point is not that every school should have a motto, but that every school should have a defined, sustained sense of meaning and direction. I always remember a teacher in James Comer's network of community schools telling me simply: "We know why we're here, what we're really doing, and what's special about how we do it."

In most schools, purpose tends to include—often to center upon—three key concepts: academic excellence, respect for others, and personal responsibility. Others do figure prominently for many schools; I am not suggesting that these must be incorporated, but in my experience, when educators concentrate on their core commitments, they often emphasize these. This makes sense for a variety of reasons. Academic excellence is an obvious primary goal for a school, and respect and responsibility are both integral to the traditional role of schools in a democracy and important to the daily functioning of a school. (A number of thoughtful observers have suggested that instead of the lengthy-list mission statement schools typically publish, they should adopt one overarching goal from which subgoals might flow: to prepare students to become productive citizens of a democracy.[5]) The particular emphasis on a particular goal will vary from school to school. What matters is clarity and consensus about it. Here are some examples of schools that are clear about purpose:

At the Town School, an independent school in New York City serving students from pre-kindergarten through eighth grade, Joyce Evans (no relation), who recently retired as head, used to meet with parents whose children were applying to the school. After a tour, she would sit down with them and tell them, as she put it, "What you just saw is what you would get, and if this is right for your child, we'd love to have you apply. If not, there are many excellent schools in New York to consider. Your children may thrive in many school environments but you may not. You need to trust the school, its philosophy, and those who lead." If parents were seeking a quiet school, she would explain, "this may not be the school for you. As you can see, we have a hum." (The school, when I visited, did indeed have a hum; not a disorganized, chaotic noisiness but a lively, purposeful hum.) "If you want your child always reading *at* a desk and never *under* a desk," she would add, "don't apply here. As you can see, some of our children read under the desk." By this Joyce didn't mean that a hum and reading under the desk were themselves core values at Town, but that they exemplified the school's approach to education and its beliefs that young children learn best in a thoughtful but flexible, creative environment. Her message on the school's Web site pointed to Town's motto, *Gaudeant Discentes* ("let there be joy in learning"), and described teachers at Town as "facilitators [who] orchestrate the productive 'hum' as students interact with one another, engage in discussions, use a myriad of resources and become involved in their own learning."

All this is impressive, as are the school's reputation and the list of secondary schools to which its graduates are admitted, so most visiting parents would assure Joyce that Town was perfect for their child. But when occasionally a parent whose child was admitted would call her later to complain that the child's classroom was noisy or the child was reading under the desk, Joyce would not immediately say, "Let me see what I can do," but in essence, "Yes, that's us. That's what you bought." Of course, she was doubtless more diplomatic in her phrasing, but she was nonetheless clear with parents about what Town stood for; what the school was—and wasn't.

Town is an independent school. Unlike Town, public schools don't get to select their families. But they are not helpless:

> In Winnetka, Illinois, a nationally renowned, high-performing public school district, there has been a conscious, deliberate, and successful effort to sustain a strong progressive tradition and keep the elementary schools truly child-centered and developmentally appropriate. The district has a distinctive Dewey-inspired philosophy that dates back to the 1920s, and at this writing it has not succumbed to the high-stakes-test mania that has swept America. The tests do not drive its curriculum and teaching. But Winnetka doesn't simply assume that its priorities and practices will be automatically understood by its parents, even though they tend to be highly educated. In fact, its superintendent, Dr. Rebecca van der Bogert, conducts orientation sessions for parents of new students to explain the philosophy and history that undergird the district's values, beliefs, and pedagogy. These are not just show-and-tell overviews but a real introduction to the theory and practice of a rich, developmentally focussed approach to instruction. The district has produced a video about its core values and trains a group of parents in each school to be "philosophy docents" who can convey the values to fellow parents. Individual schools also do extensive outreach, not only to keep parents informed about current activities but to remind them of the underlying rationale and purpose of these activities. Because so much of Winnetka's instruction involves project-based learning there is always much to show parents, who are readily welcome in the schools. Despite its impressive results and its parents' sophistication, the district does not take for granted that its core purposes will speak for themselves. It helps parents—early and often—to understand.

Some might object that Winnetka is virtually a set of private schools: the district's resources and budget are substantial, its families mostly white, wealthy, and educated. True, the Winnetkas of

America do not suffer all the challenges that other districts do and are not under the same pressure to raise test scores, in part because their students come from backgrounds that make good results highly likely. Consider, then, Fenway High School in Boston:

> Fenway is an alternative public school, not a neighborhood school, and students must apply—but admission is by lottery, with no entrance tests, no preference for better performers. A pioneer in the movement to create new, small urban public schools and a member of the Coalition of Essential Schools, Fenway serves primarily minority students (80 percent), including many whose prior academic records are not strong. Its own record with these students is impressive, in part because Fenway is clear about purpose and conduct. It captures its values in a phrase: *work hard; be yourself; do the right thing.* Those new to the school receive a jersey with the school's name and logo and the phrase written across the front. Working hard is important as a virtue in its own right and a habit for learners everywhere, but it is particularly key for students who have not previously done well in school and who might be more prone to give up and drop out. *Be yourself* doesn't mean simply doing whatever you please but being true to yourself, knowing what you stand for. *Do the right thing* provides a framework for issues of responsibility and community. Fenway doesn't spell out in detail what the right things are, but when there is a disciplinary infraction or a dispute between students, administrators ask, "Was that the right thing to do? Did you do what was right?" Fenway's values are focussed and clear and emphasized in a variety of very concrete ways.

With their alternative status and small size, schools like Fenway, though they are not private, have more freedom to shape their purposes than other public schools. There is no doubt that building a consensus about purpose is hardest of all in a traditional public school, especially a large one that serves a diverse population. Faculty and administrators in many of these schools have been disempowered over the past twenty years, hemmed in by laws and regulations that give control over their curriculum to the state and at the same time force them to share their decision making with advisory councils that include parents and community representatives. The former is not only demeaning, it intrudes on the heart of purpose, a school's academic priorities; the latter, in addition to keeping principals out another ten nights per year, leads to the sort of mission statements and policies that promise everything to everyone (see Chapter Twelve).

No wonder the movement toward dividing large high schools into smaller, self-contained ones is spreading. Although we have yet to see how this effort will develop, it could be among the most promising reform initiatives undertaken in many years. From virtually every point of view, large schools are problematic. This is not just, as has often been noted, because they are complex to manage, but because it is so hard for them to clarify purpose and conduct and organize themselves around a clear, focussed set of core values.

Despite the obstacles facing them, however, traditional public schools are not helpless. More have begun using their advisory councils to participate along with the faculty in building greater shared understanding about the school's central focus. More have been experimenting with something like a Winnetka-style orientation for new parents. (The message: "Welcome. We want to share with you our priorities as a school and tell you how you can best help your child succeed here.") More have redesigned back-to-school nights and the publications they send home to reiterate their "purpose message." And more have been taking this message directly—and repeatedly—to students in handbooks, assemblies, and class discussions, spelling out how the school's purpose translates into conduct.

Conduct: What It Means to Belong Here

Conduct refers to the way the school's core values are enacted, to the conditions of membership in the school community, the essential responsibilities of belonging to the school. By essential I mean "minimum, nonnegotiable." Schools have no right to tell families how to live their lives or what to believe, but schools cannot function without shared agreements about basic norms for behavior within the school and about education itself. Like families, schools need structure: a box around behavior and expectations, not just for students but for everyone. Clarity regarding conduct is, at its heart, a commitment that a school's central values apply to the entire school, students, faculty, other staff, administration—and parents. And in independent schools and in those public school districts with a systemwide emphasis on purpose and conduct, this commitment would need to include board members as well. Many schools have expectations for student behavior and a formal disciplinary code. The best have expectations for all their participants. Thus, if respect for others, say, is truly one of a school's core values, simply teaching this to students, expecting them to demonstrate it, and acknowledging them when they do and correcting them when they don't is inadequate. The adults in the community—faculty and parents alike—must also model respect and hold one another accountable for doing so.

I first encountered an example of clarifying conduct at a gathering of what is perhaps American education's most whimsically named organization: The Headmistresses of The East. Every autumn, this group gathers in Princeton, New Jersey. Its members are not, as their title might suggest, old-fashioned female administrators with a whimsical devotion to the Wizard of Oz. Almost none of them are actually called "Headmistress," and men are allowed to belong. They are a group of talented, thoughtful, engaging heads of independent schools.

It was after discussing with them some of the ideas that ultimately led to this book that I first began to consider the importance of conduct. One of the members described for the group the implementation of a "values contract" at his school. This contract, signed by parents, included three sections: "What the School Stands For,"

"What You Can Expect from the School," and "What the School Can Expect from You." A significant violation of its provisions by a student *or a parent* were grounds for not inviting the student back for the next school year. Around the room, surprised administrators sat up. "As a matter of fact," said this headmaster, "I have three first-grade mothers on probation right now." They had been so outrageous toward teachers at the fall conference that he had written letters reminding them that they had signed the contract. They were free to disagree with faculty, he told them, but not to do so disrespectfully; they couldn't call names, swear, point fingers, threaten, and the like.

Later that same year, I visited a public school that had also worked to define its values and expectations and where a teacher, annoyed by a parent's question at back-to-school night, unexpectedly launched into a sarcastic personal attack on the parent. When the principal found out, he talked separately with the parent and the teacher, and then, in private, reminded the teacher in no uncertain terms of the school's commitment to mutual respect, demanded that he apologize to the parent, and warned him of serious disciplinary action if another such outburst were to occur.

In neither of these cases were the administrators attacking people; they were defending values. Of course the parents in the first instance and the teacher in the second both felt criticized, and they were indeed being confronted, but the confrontations were not ad hominem and they didn't reflect mere personal pique; they were undertaken in the name of agreed-upon community norms. The lesson these episodes teach about values is direct: *You can't defend what you haven't proclaimed and there is no point proclaiming what you won't defend.* No task is more important for a school leader than to be what a superintendent I know calls "the voice of the covenant"—to take primary responsibility for nourishing, celebrating, and protecting the core values and behavioral norms of the school community.

In the past few years I have visited a small but growing number of schools, public and private, that have made strong efforts to confirm their covenants by having parents and students sign on to what we might call codes of conduct. Some of these documents contain explicit provisions, such as "I will abide by school rules and policies and will support the mission of the school," and "I will model appropriate ethical behavior for my children and others." Many schools don't go so far in this direction but do require parents and students to at least acknowledge in writing that they have read the school's handbook and the policies it contains. I have also visited many others that have revised their communications to parents to be much more specific about what the school views as essentials. At one middle school, for instance, faculty, in some desperation, held an evening for parents because of an epidemic of problems having to do with structure and latitude (issues discussed in detail in Chapter Six and Chapter Seven, respectively). "There were just so many examples," a guidance counselor said, "of parents not knowing what to do about the simplest elements of sending a kid through middle school." Privately, among themselves, teachers called the event "belaboring the obvious" and worried that parents, mostly upper-middle-class college graduates, would find it condescending because the topics were so basic. The evening covered such fundamentals as homework. "We told them," the counselor said, "'Don't do your child's homework if he or she is having trouble with it; you'll only disguise the problem they're having. Tell us about it or have your child tell us. We'll work with them. In seventh grade there is no risk or penalty—nothing that shows on a college application—for needing help with a concept.'" Other topics included behavior, discipline, and an outline of the process for raising a concern or a complaint ("Call the teacher first. Call the administrator only if the matter is not resolved," and so on). To the faculty's surprise and relief, the evening was a smash success. Parents loved it. Many said it was the best such event they'd ever attended.

A key part of clarifying conduct involves belaboring the obvious (or what used to be obvious), no longer taking for granted basic understandings about values and behavior that schools used to be able to rely upon. More and more schools now reduce key guidelines and policies to one-page summaries and send them home several times a year. (They have handouts with titles such as "Guidelines for Homework" and "How to Register a Concern.") More have begun to use assemblies and other gatherings to remind students explicitly about norms for behavior and, in a similar fashion, to emphasize these for parents at back-to-school nights. The message to parents: "To help your children grow up to be successful people and good citizens, these are the values and expectations we're teaching them. We need you to help us help them succeed by joining us as models of these values and behaviors."

Ideally, this message should begin early: a prospective family needs to know what kind of school it is joining and the school needs to remember that it is welcoming a family, not just a student. Too many schools have decided that true excellence means being all things to all people. They neglect to prepare students and parents for what the school expects. Having failed to establish guidelines about community membership, they risk having their decisions, notably those about discipline, seen as arbitrary and capricious. By contrast, the more clearly and energetically a school stands for something, the more attractive it proves—and the better prepared it is to hold all its members to its standards. This calls for a vigorous, informative welcome and orientation for new parents, much as is done in Winnetka. (In independent schools, it calls for exploring the goodness of fit between a family's values and the school's before admitting even the most promising student.) Orientation programs should include not just an effort to make newcomers feel comfortable but also to be sure they are informed about "what it means to be part of us," about "what makes us, us."

Coherence, Not Rigidity

Pushed to an extreme, a focus on purpose and conduct could be narrow and suffocating, so I want to emphasize that none of this calls for turning schools into academies of conformity. The aim is to renew schools' basic institutional authority and organizational coherence, not to straitjacket students and parents. Without authority and coherence, schools' efforts to foster citizenship, character, and academic competence cannot succeed, especially given the forces that are splintering American society and disabling American families. But our schools serve the most diverse population of students in the world, and the assertion of purpose and conduct do not argue against respect for this diversity in a school.

To be sure, it is harder to clarify expectations for a heterogeneous group than for a homogeneous one, but public schools cannot control their demographics, and many educators would never forgo the richness and vitality that a diverse school can offer. Those truly committed to diversity need to think especially hard about what this actually means—that is, not just about the ways a school will adapt to the values and traditions of different families who join it but about the common expectations (remember, these are the *minimum* nonnegotiables) it must require of all participants in order to remain a coherent community. Purpose and conduct call for schools to hold fast to their values *and* reach out to their constituents.

Having clarified purpose for itself, a school that wishes to be truly diverse needs to work extra hard to disseminate its values and expectations throughout the school community. I recall in this regard a school board member who had also served as a college trustee. Describing the college's struggles with diversity, he said, "First we were a community, but not at all diverse. Then for ten years we pursued diversity and we became much more diverse, but it totally fractured our community. Now, in these last five years, we have started to put the two together—what can be different, what must be shared—and we're slowly becoming a diverse community." Diversity without coherence and community is self-destructive; diversity within coherence and community can help a school bring out the best in all its participants.

12

Redefining the Home-School Partnership

I mplicit in the defining of purpose and conduct is a redefinition of the partnership between parents and schools. Thus far, I have omitted parents from the shaping of the school's values and norms and had little to say about their role in general. This may seem surprising, since it is almost impossible to find an American school that doesn't proclaim its partnership with parents and since in most schools the overall home-school relationship is constructive and there are parents who play a variety of helpful—sometimes vital—roles, from volunteering to raising money and advocating for the school.

Many policymakers and some educators are convinced that vigorous parent participation both in the life of the school and in its governance is not only morally and politically right but improves the quality of the school's decision making and contributes to higher student achievement. This view is on its way to becoming an orthodoxy. A number of organizations and coalitions encourage the growth of partnerships between schools, parents, and community members.[1] They offer books, videos, seminars, and other resources for parents who want to become more engaged in schools, and they conduct and cite research that supports the impact of parent involvement on student outcomes.

Many states now require each public school to have an advisory council composed of parents and community members (and, usually, teacher and staff representatives, as well) to advise the principal and shape the school's plans for improvement. The No Child Left Behind Act subscribes to this orthodoxy: it is all about parental rights (and almost mute about parental responsibilities). For these and other reasons, most schools have become, at least in their public posture, extremely deferential to parents as coequals in the enterprise of schooling. "Parents know their children best" is the line one often hears from principals at back-to-school nights.

Well, yes and no. Parents certainly know their children more intimately than teachers do. But what matters is not just knowing a child best but knowing what's best for a child. And here, the concept of partnership, as it is traditionally understood, falters. As I have noted, parents' competence and confidence are both diminishing (see Chapters Four and Eight); so is the time they spend with their children and their direct engagement in their children's lives (Chapters Five and Nine). An equal partnership between home and school still makes sense in terms of, say, aspiration and commitment (wanting the very best outcome for a child), but not in terms of developmental and educational savvy. The loss of savvy among parents is understandable, as I have tried to make clear, but mothers and fathers who are unable to provide essential levels of nurture, structure, and latitude are not well suited to be full partners with educators when it comes to making decisions at school about purpose, conduct, and governance.

Educators need to recast the idea of partnership more as one in which they parent parents. As growing numbers of teachers and principals have discovered, parents are desperate to have reliable, knowledgeable professionals tell them what's good for children—often, to tell them specifically what to do. (Recall from Chapter One the mother asking a principal to tell her daughter to stop dating older boys; the father asking him to make a rule against drinking at home; the mother asking her child's first-grade teacher whether 10 P.M. is an appropriate bedtime, and so on.) Parenting parents does not in any way imply condescending to them, ordering them about, demeaning them, failing to listen to them, or discounting their concerns. It means being appropriately clear and assertive about the school's values and expectations, about what's good for students, and about the role of parents in the school. It means not withholding professional judgment when a question arises about how a student can be best served (more on this in Chapter Fourteen) or how the school itself can best function. It begins by distinguishing three different forms of parental involvement: in governance, in helping out, and in the lives and learning of their children. These are often lumped together in discussions of partnership and parent participation, but they are different. The first is at best a mixed blessing; the second can be very helpful; the third is far and away the most important.

Reconsidering Parental Involvement in Governance

The ideal of a school that successfully involves parents in fundamental matters of policy and decision making and maintains this involvement over time may be inspiring to some, but in reality, such schools are hard to find; there are very few of them. This is no accident. Parent participation in governance and in shaping mission and direction is not nearly so simple or straightforward as it seems. In fact, it presents a series of obstacles that are at once ordinary and obvious yet complex and frustrating.

To begin with, parents come to school governance and policy with an inherent conflict of interest; they may be invested in their children's school and want what's best for it, but within the school they also want what's best for their own children. This doesn't mean they can't be objective or contribute effectively to decisions—they have useful perspectives to offer—but that there is always a potential for their own self-interest to intrude, even on apparently simple issues. When the need is for advocacy on the school's behalf, competing individual interests are unlikely and parents can often provide skills and stature that serve the school well. I think of an elementary school that had been promised renovation for years but had never received funding by the district's school board. The superintendent and principal gathered an "advisory committee" of parents that included an architect, a builder, an advertising executive, two former school board members, and the leadership of the school's PTA. Together, they mounted a campaign that made the case and mobilized pressure for the renovation; the board ultimately funded the project. But I also think of a faculty-parent committee empowered to plan the timetable for the renovation of a high school. The project was technically complex and was to occur in stages, which the committee was to schedule. Parents of juniors and seniors argued fiercely for reconstructing the wing housing freshmen first. This would add to the cost of the renovation and delay its eventual completion, but it would also let their own children graduate with the least disruption. After weeks of debate, the district's superintendent and board finally had to step in and decide the timetable.

In this regard, a related problem with parental empowerment in schools is the growing tendency, also noted in Chapter One, for parents to see school through the eyes of their offspring, to take literally their sons' and daughters' complaints about teachers, coaches, and administrators, and to use committees, task forces, and councils as forums for airing these grievances. Those who don't work in schools would not believe how often principals now hear parents say things like, "I know my daughter didn't start that fight; she told me so," or, "Mrs. Smith is being unfair to my son; you should hear the stories he tells me." I have talked with dozens of principals whose lives have been made miserable by a small group of parents (sometimes by just one) who join the school's advisory council to settle a personal score or press a single issue.

A different kind of challenge is that parents, even the best educated, are generally not well informed about current educational realities. Their memories from their own school years lead them to underestimate how much more difficult some students and parents are to work with. They are thus not always helpful contributors to school governance. Having parents truly grasp these and other issues presents a formidable burden for principals and teachers. It requires lots of time, something educators have little of, given everything else that is now expected of them. For those who can make and take the time, this burden can also offer a real opportunity. The mandatory creation of advisory councils in public schools has not, in my experience, improved decision making, but it has increased the number of parents who have learned much more about the school's needs and have as a result become better advocates for the school. Many principals describe this as the best outcome (when they speak confidentially among themselves, they often describe it as the *only* good outcome) of having to have an advisory council. Unfortunately, the challenge of orienting and informing parents is perpetual. Almost as soon as a school develops a cadre of informed, knowledgeable parents, it begins to lose them as their children move up through the grades and on to other schools; the process has to start all over again.

A final complication lies in the procedural complexities of melding multiple constituencies. The more diverse the school community, the more likely the school is to encounter differences among families in behavior, values, and expectations. As parents have grown more contentious and more willing to assert their points of view, managing their involvement has come to demand more expertise and more time—often, much more of both than principals have available. In such cases, early and broad involvement of parents in crafting a school's purpose and conduct can paralyze the enterprise. It typically leads to an exhausting, procedure-riddled process—and to a mission statement full of compromises that promises the world to everyone and inspires no one.

A New Kind of Partnership

The problem here is not what it may seem. It is not to devise better ways to engage parents more fully in school decision making. The conventional wisdom about parent involvement in policy and governance rests on a thin reed. It has emerged mostly from stories of heroic turnarounds in low-performing urban schools where families feel disenfranchised and are detached from their children's schooling and where the challenge is to master the most basic organizational and educational tasks (attendance, homework, and so on). These communities often include a high proportion of parents who have dropped out of their children's learning. This is a serious problem in American education, but it is not fixed by having parents sit on advisory councils or mission committees. In fact, in my experience the heroic turnarounds are always led by exceptional principals who take initiative in virtually every aspect of the school's life—including the mobilization of parents. And contrary to the conventional wisdom, research has not shown a strong relationship between parental input in school governance and student outcomes. What it has shown is that student outcomes are likely to improve when parents participate in school events and especially when they involve themselves in the life and learning of their children.[2]

Years of consulting in schools of all kinds, from the most participatory to the most authoritarian, have taught me that what is crucial is that parents understand and respect a school's values and norms, not that they participate in creating them. This understanding and respect certainly permit a role for them in the creation or the revision of a school's priorities, but they do not require this. In parochial and other religious schools, for example, parents often have little say about what the school stands for and its behavioral standards, but typically embrace them. At the other extreme, in some public schools and many small independent and charter schools it would be unthinkable to adopt the kind of purpose and conduct effort I have recommended without a wide-open, inclusive process that invites parents to participate along with faculty. But even if a school's current parents play an active role in defining values and norms, the decisions they help frame cannot be revisited several years later when their children graduate and they leave the school and then again several years after that when another cohort of students and parents leave. No school can engage in an every-few-years revision of its core priorities and conditions of member-ship. Once adopted, a school's values and expectations are in the hands of its principal and faculty; it is they who are the key shapers, keepers, transmitters, and exemplars of the school's covenant on a daily basis and over time. The covenant must be truly meaningful to them so that they can commit themselves to making it come alive and stay alive in the school, introducing it to new parents and colleagues who join the school and embedding it over the years into the school's culture. This suggests that the formula for parent par-ticipation during the defining of purpose and conduct should be "as much as this school needs."

Whether a school's process is largely faculty-driven or not, once those charged with formulating purpose and conduct reach a con-sensus and commit themselves to it, they need to think in broad structural terms about how to bring students and parents into the fold. It is vital to build a broad, shared understanding of the con-sensus among the larger school community. Student assemblies and all-school meetings, back-to-school nights and parent conferences, newsletters and PTA bulletins—all provide opportunities to under-score and reinforce core values. A start-up initiative to increase awareness is not enough; there must be a continuing effort that includes orientation for new members and reminders and refreshers for everyone. For students these efforts can concentrate on values and behavior. Parents will also need this information, but it is often necessary to publish and reiterate very concrete guidelines for them about such things as how to communicate with the school. As de-scribed in Chapter Eleven, schools often find that an investment in parent understanding pays off, even when it involves information educators regard as "belaboring the obvious." It isn't obvious any-more, and teachers and administrators must face up to this reality.

Much of this work must be initiated by school staff, but here is where parent assistance can be vital. A school can turn to its strong, supportive parents and stewards for advice about and help in spread-ing the word among parents at large. The principal, perhaps together with a few teachers, can present the faculty's work on purpose and conduct to the cadre of engaged parents who play key positive roles in volunteering, fundraising, advocacy. In public schools this might well be the advisory council and PTA members; in independent and charter schools it would be the school's board. This presentation provides an occasion both to road-test the purpose and conduct provisions as drafted; to get input about their substance, clarity, and fit for the eventual audience; and to seek advice and help about how to spread the word, how to begin building a broad consensus about it throughout the school community.

Parental Involvement in the Life of the School

If redefining the home-school partnership does not assign parents a primary role in devising purpose and conduct, or, more generally, in governance and policy, it does place real importance on parents' involvement in the life of the school and in the lives and learning of their children. Here again, schools need to take a more assertive, parental stance with parents, encouraging them to engage themselves appropriately in these ways. Many principals would object that they already have high levels of parent participation in their school: as "room parents" in elementary schools; as volunteer teaching assistants in classrooms up through middle school; as extra librarians, cafeteria monitors, advisers to clubs, chaperones on field trips, and so forth. Indeed, in many suburban schools I visit, administrators say they have more volunteers than they need. "Parent involvement? We're choking on it here," a principal laughed when I asked about this. "We can't find enough things for our mothers to do."

Though it's always possible to have too much of a good thing, in many schools parent involvement makes a palpable difference in the school's functioning. Parents in many communities have become volunteer fundraisers. In the nation's poorest cities, schools often rely on parents to supplement inadequate staffing and maintain basic order and deliver services (tutoring) that would otherwise be unavailable. In the nation's wealthiest suburbs, some enrichment programs are sustained in part through parent volunteers coming into classrooms. And as school budgets have failed to keep pace with rising performance expectations, these districts often rely on parents to help them raise money from private donors to fund special projects and preserve key programs.

The actual help parents provide to a school's educational program is only part of the benefit of their volunteering. Many administrators would agree with a headmaster I know who says candidly to his parents, "If truth be told, there are sometimes more opportunities to be active here at school than we technically need, but we're delighted to have them—and you—not just because it helps our school but because it sends a very positive message about school to your children." Of course, even in schools that encourage high levels of participation, the range of opportunities for active volunteering is limited. The larger way parents participate in the life of the school is by attending programs, plays, performances, games, back-to-school nights, and the like. These ordinary events are opportunities for parents, through their actions, not just to communicate with the school but to send a message to their children: *We're interested; we care about your school; we follow what's happening; we know the teachers; we hear about you; we catch sight of you; we're all in this together.* Needless to say, many parents are drawn to events where they can meet their children's teachers and see their children in action. But as parents' lives grow ever busier, their attendance at school events (except for athletic contests) seems to be dwindling, especially when their children reach high school.

Of all the ways parents can involve themselves at school, one looms particularly large, I believe, and it is one that is in decline even in schools with lots of eager volunteers: it is for both parents to attend parent-teacher conferences. Often, this is left to mothers, who must then translate to the child's father what the teacher reported. Meeting with the teacher is not merely the best way for parents to learn about their child's progress, it is a key way for them to show the child how much school matters. Young children and teenagers always notice whenever both parents pay attention to them together. Not surprisingly, students tend to perform better when their fathers as well as their mothers are involved—even when the father doesn't live with the student.[3] Even if—especially if—parents are separated or divorced, when they demonstrate to a child that they both care enough to meet together with the teacher, they confirm something very important about their commitment to their child and their child's education. A school can help by sending all its parents a strong message: *We expect you both to attend; doing so will help your child.* Here's one example of how a school did this:

> Principal Jane Green grew concerned that while some parents in her middle school were coming to their children's sporting events and music and drama performances, most were not coming to back-to-school night and curriculum evenings, and many couples were not attending parent-teacher conferences together. She decided to see if she could improve things. She began to remind parents that their attendance at these events, especially their joint attendance at conferences, would both help them support their children's learning and underscore for their children the importance of education itself. She began repeating this message in every forum she could: in mailings home, in brief announcements before the start of student plays and music performances, in conversations with parents at games. She mobilized the faculty and the PTA to spread the word. She arranged to have eighth-grade students volunteer to provide free child care in the afternoons of conference week for the benefit of parents with young children. She began calling parents who missed the fall conference, expressing her regret, listening to their excuses but politely hoping they would make it to the next one. Attendance improved, but not enough. "Finally, she says, "I got firm."
>
> Jane decided to mobilize students, asking them at all-school assemblies to remind their parents about conferences. She worked with her faculty to publish sign-up sheets months in advance, with

the dates and times for conferences. And she began saying to parents, "I know you're busy, but I'm sure that with this much notice you can arrange your schedule to come in on two afternoons a year for a half-hour each. It's very important. It will matter to your child and it will make this a better school." By the second year of this effort, parents were showing up in noticeably greater numbers, not only at the conferences but at the academic evenings, as well.

Parental Involvement in Children's Lives and Learning

Of all the ways for parents to contribute at school, by far the most significant is to be engaged in their children's lives and learning. This is what authoritative parents do. The greatest influence parents exert on their children's achievement and behavior lies in providing sufficient nurture, structure, and latitude. This, as Chapter Three pointed out, is strongly associated with the development in children of the self-regulation, motivation, and perseverance vital to academic success. It also contributes to a productive school climate that facilitates teaching and learning. Authoritative parents are likely to ask their children about their classes, to make sure they do their homework and manage their time. They are likely to underscore the importance of schooling by attending school conferences and programs. And they are, in my experience, likely to model the importance of learning by reading newspapers and books, being interested in ideas, discussing current events at the dinner table, and so on. Many schools, as I have noted, seek to foster more authoritative parenting through educational presentations, efforts whose outcomes, as I also noted, are generally disappointing. For a variety of reasons, beginning with the very nature of childrearing itself, schools cannot, through outreach and education, make parents become fully authoritative. (See Appendix.) What they can do is keep urging parents to engage themselves in their children's daily lives and schoolwork.

Schools can recommend a whole range of specific steps to parents depending on the issues they see as affecting students' performance and behavior. It is ideal to concentrate, where possible, on matters that parents themselves are struggling with and about which they need encouragement to assert themselves. It is also ideal to focus on only one or two issues at a time, so as to avoid overtaxing faculty and overloading parents, to stay with the chosen issues for an extended period (for two years, say, not just for a month), and to undertake these as a matter of collective school policy rather than a series of individual initiatives by separate teachers. For example, a principal and faculty could take on an effort to limit television and promote reading and literacy. They could remind parents of the strong correlation between high TV-watching levels and low reading achievement and of the evidence that conversing with children at dinner (instead of eating in front of the TV) helps them develop larger vocabularies and a better knowledge of world affairs. They could, as some schools do, throw themselves into "TV turnoff week," the national program that every April encourages families to go a full seven days without television. They could urge parents to set a maximum number of hours for watching television each week (preferably not more than fifteen; ideally, ten); they could also recommend not letting students have televisions in their bedrooms. This effort need not be strident or negative but an earnest campaign by thoughtful educational professionals to foster students' academic achievement and personal development.

Some faculty object that an initiative like this, no matter what childrearing practice it targets, will be ineffectual. Surely, it is sensible to expect a modest impact. Nonetheless, one of the ways to change people is simply to make it harder for them to keep unthinkingly doing what they've been doing and to make it easier for them to try something new. Parents can always ignore a school's message, but faculty can make it more difficult for them to do so. In the course of a conference, for instance, a teacher can ask parents how much television time they allow and whether there is a TV in the student's bedroom. In cases where a student is in academic difficulty and is apparently watching lots of television, a teacher can express an earnest concern, urge the parents to take action, and, if they seem at a loss as to how to proceed, refer them to the school counselor or psychologist for guidance about how to limit TV time. And of course, whenever there is evidence of parents' responding, school staff can congratulate and celebrate them. Throughout, the goal is to help parents engage with their children in constructive ways. Jane Green's approach is worth remembering: "My teachers and I," she says, "have a clear and simple message, and we use four P's: we're pleasant, patient, and positive—and we persevere. We're helping some of our parents do more of the things that good parents do, and it's made us a better school."

13

Resistance and Leadership

Building Faculty Will

Defining purpose and conduct and redefining partnership promise long-term benefits—at a near-term price. Although the schools that ultimately do best with their families are likely to be the ones that are clear about what they stand for, what it means to belong to their community, and about their guidelines for parent involvement, reaching this clarity requires extra work for educators. Once established, it helps reduce and prevent the kinds of problems that have been consuming ever more of their time and energy, but crafting it, building a consensus about it, and then sustaining this consensus are not small tasks. They can provoke immediate resistance among some faculty and later resistance among others as real implementation begins. Much of this resistance is quite natural. School leaders need to address it. They need to help teachers develop the necessary will and skill—in that order: first the motivation, which this chapter addresses, to invest themselves in the development of purpose and conduct, then the competence and courage, which Chapter Fourteen takes up, to assume a more parental role vis à vis parents in face-to-face interaction.

The Roots of Resistance

In *The Human Side of School Change*, I explored at length the complexities of leading innovation—and managing resistance to it—in schools.[1] I argued that implementing planned innovation is almost always harder than expected in any organization due to the natural human tendency to resist change, and I argued further that innovation is almost always especially hard in schools because of the particular characteristics of educators as people and of schools as institutions. School leaders who hope to address purpose, conduct, and partnership issues will need to anticipate and understand the resistance of faculty who, even if they are unhappy with the status quo, may be at best reluctant about trying to change it.

In my earlier book, I noted that the way anyone responds to virtually any change depends primarily on what it means to that person, and that any change almost always causes ambivalence, in part because it means different things to different people, but mainly because it means different things to each individual. We acknowledge that change is inevitable in life, we often yearn for our own circumstances to change, and yet a fundamental conservatism dominates our psychology, making us naturally resistant to change when it occurs. This conservatism is not political but a deep impulse to preserve continuity and familiarity in life. We are, as the late Harvard paleontologist Stephen Jay Gould once wrote, "pattern-seeking animals [who] must find cause and meaning in all events."[2] Pattern-seeking is a biological tendency hardwired into the human brain and we literally can't survive without it, but it leads us to cling to patterns, even ones we don't like (staying in jobs and relationships where we feel mistreated, for example) because they give our lives meaning; they let us make sense out of things, even if we don't like the sense they make. The devil we know is usually preferable to the devil we don't know, as the old adage has it. Patterns require predictability and repetition. When a change disrupts the predictability that gives our lives meaning, it requires us to adjust, which means not only extra work but often real pain. Hence, resistance.

I must underscore that this doesn't mean we never seek change; we do. We often wish that things would change; sometimes we long desperately for this. But we are usually longing for *other people* to change; and when we ourselves do wish to be different, we want to be transformed instantly, not to endure an awkward process of adjustment, mistakes, false starts, and trial-and-error. And change is always and everywhere accompanied by mixed feelings, even when it involves ending a practice we dislike. I think of two teachers in an elite independent school describing their reaction when an ancient practice of arranging itself by seniority for the annual faculty picture was abandoned one year. Instead of the longest-serving teachers standing in the front and the newest arrivals standing in the back, they gathered to pose for the photo "as a community." These teachers' reactions were classic. "The seniority arrangement was silly," one said, smiling but rueful. "I never liked it. I wanted the change. But I've been here eight years and I've moved up six rows toward the front. Now I'll never get there, or if I do, it won't mean anything."

When I suggest that our response to change depends chiefly on its meaning, I speak of two main components of meaning: *understanding* ("I see what you mean") and *attachment* to people and ideas ("you mean so much to me"; "teaching a child to read means so much to me"). The first, which is cognitive and involves the way we see the world, may be the more obvious aspect of meaning, but the second, which is affective and involves our emotional ties to people and principles, is often the more problematic when it comes to coping with an innovation. In any case, the more a change disrupts the patterns that govern people's understandings and attachments, the harder it will be for them. Viewed from this perspective, resistance is a thoroughly natural response to change of all kinds, including, in this case, my call to define purpose and conduct and redefine partnership. Successful implementation will require attending to the meanings these changes have for the educators who must implement them.

Three primary meanings of change that spark resistance can be summarized as loss, incompetence, and conflict. The synonym for change we most prefer is *progress*, but *bereavement* is every bit as accurate. We are bereaved when someone we love dies, but we are also bereaved when an assumption we take for granted—parents should respect the professional judgment of educators, say—is devalued. This kind of grief is not usually as intense as that caused by the death of a loved one (though it can be), but it provokes a similar mourning often marked by disbelief, denial, sadness, and anger. Similarly, a school promotes innovation (a new curriculum, a new teaching method) to enhance teachers' competence, to improve their ability to fulfill the school's mission, but the innovation typically threatens their *existing* competence by requiring them to abandon something they know how to do and adopt something they don't know how to do. Ultimately, if they see the project through, they may develop new skills and knowledge and the change may come to mean progress to them. But at the outset they tend to react much more to the loss it causes and the risk it poses. As for conflict, although planned innovations are usually sold as being better for everyone in the school—students, parents, teachers, and administrators alike—they never are. Every major change a school undertakes creates winners and losers, at least at the outset. Some people's beliefs and commitments will be better aligned with the new priorities than others'; some people's skills and temperament will be more relevant and useful than others'; some people's roles and status may rise while others' decline. This creates the potential for conflict at levels from the highest (educational philosophy and values) to the basest (who's where in the pecking order).

Although change may be challenging for anyone, it typically grows harder with age and experience and typically is harder for educators than for those in most other professions. Having already made this case at some length,[3] I will only summarize it here. The majority of America's teachers are in midlife and beyond and have been teaching for at least twenty years, often at the same school. These veterans are now retiring in large numbers, but they remain in most schools the dominant tone-setters. Their youthful idealism has been tempered by experience, and their energy levels and appetite for new projects are, with rare exceptions, lower than when they began. Their skepticism is higher—and in not a few schools, verges on cynicism. Their lives, inevitably, are more complicated by personal and family demands than when they were starting out. Many are seeking to limit their involvement at school rather than increase it, and to concentrate mainly on those parts of the job they find rewarding. They're not looking for more to do. This "focussing down" is a normal trend in the later stages of any career.

More generally, teachers, whatever their age and experience level, differ from those who select other professions, especially corporate careers, in ways that can make change problematic. Education attracts people with a strong security orientation and a strong service ethic, conservators, not entrepreneurs with a thirst for risk and competition. It is the only field that offers tenure, and it draws those who are willing to trade salary for stability. Teachers have traditionally tended to change employers much less frequently than corporate professionals, to look for a school that is a good home and to stay there. They also tend to be less worldly; school board members often find them naive and thin-skinned. But teachers are, after all, people who thrive in—and usually prefer—the company of children and adolescents (would we want our youth taught by people who *didn't?*) and who try to accentuate the positive. They wish to help, nurture, foster, inspire, encourage, and bring out the best in students. They generally like people and want to be liked. They take their work very personally.

All of this makes them quite sensitive to criticism and conflict. As a group, teachers, even more than many other human service professionals, tend to be highly conflict-avoidant. They may have little trouble setting limits and asserting themselves with students, but not with adults. Acknowledging this vulnerability, I sometimes tease teacher audiences that they originally planned to enter a convent or monastery, adopting a life of complete sacrificial devotion to others. At the last moment, contemplating the full list of vows they would have to take, they found the chastity too much to bear, so they turned away and chose instead the second-most-sacrificial life they could find; its door said, "School." So they ended up with most of the vows of the convent or monastery—not the chastity, but the poverty, the obedience, and the gift for guilt. Most teachers bear on their chests a latent scarlet G for "guilt." They suffer from a disorder I think of as "closet omnipotence," the conviction that they should be all things to all people and everyone should like them. Their guilt buttons illuminate at the first hint that they have disappointed someone or failed to meet someone's need (especially a student's). This stimulates high levels of conscientious dedication, but can leave teachers vulnerable to feelings of chronic inadequacy and hesitant to assert themselves in appropriate ways with other adults.

Resistance to change is not just a product of characteristics within educators as people, but within the culture of schools as institutions. Education is fundamentally a backward-looking enterprise. In a nation obsessed with innovation, this may seem a terrible condemnation; it is not. Drawing on the past is an inevitable, central feature of schooling. A school's mission is to transmit knowledge and values, to prepare children for the future, which it can only do by teaching them about the past—not just history but the assembled body of knowledge in each subject. We can only teach what we know. Moreover, much (though not all) of a school's curriculum is, if not timeless, slow-changing (fractions, the periodic table, the meanings of *Hamlet*, the causes of the American revolution, and so on) and many schools pride themselves on their devotion to enduring truths and established traditions. Good teaching is always creative, but it is not perpetually innovative; it benefits from regular refreshers and occasional overhauls, but it doesn't demand the kind of continuous updating that, say, law or medicine or high technology do. Continuity is a powerful fact of school life.

Resistance in Action

Understandably, then, proposals about purpose, conduct, and partnership may spark resistance among teachers. For starters, many
resent the necessity. Simply acknowledging the need to take action
may represent real loss for some: a backtracking, a giving in, an
acknowledgment that they can no longer assume or expect parents'
trust and esteem. Veterans especially remember a time when students and parents accorded them automatic respect and rarely questioned their authority, when getting into trouble at school meant
getting into trouble at home. Facing up to the new family-school
dynamic may confirm a palpable loss of status for them. They
resent being second-guessed and directly challenged, and they can
also resent being told they must work to do what may appear to
them as restoring the kinds of conditions they once took for
granted. "A lot of us now have a lot less tolerance for these 'high-
maintenance' families," the head of an urban teacher union told
me. "We don't want them to treat us the way they do and we don't
want to have to do extra work to learn how to manage them. We
just wish they'd shape up!" This attitude, in varying levels of intensity, is by no means uncommon. Nor is it illogical. It reflects legitimate concerns and the focussing down I mentioned earlier.
Nonetheless, it leaves administrators in a bind. They sympathize,
but they also see that this reaction can exacerbate tensions with
families, and they worry about the risk of alienating tax- and
tuition-paying parents.

Even if teachers accept the necessity of responding, they may
dislike the fact that the changes in parents and students call for
more involvement and more work—work of a kind they don't welcome. They may be concerned that the work is time-consuming,
both at first and continuously. Schools can't close for several days
during the academic year to send the faculty on a purpose-and-
conduct retreat, and most can't afford to hire the staff for a summer

session. If this means fitting the necessary meetings into the school year and grafting them onto all the school's other initiatives (in curriculum, instruction, assessment, and so forth), teachers are likely to begrudge the effort and unlikely to invest themselves in it. And even when a faculty does clarify and establish a set of core values and minimum conditions of membership, it must, as I have said, work to help students and parents understand these, to build and sustain their sense of personal connection and institutional affiliation. This puts a premium on marketing of a kind, on keeping the school's guiding themes in everyone's awareness, repeating them rather than taking them for granted.

Nor does the work end there. It's not enough to proclaim and persuade; purpose and conduct benefit from sustained steps to improve the experience of belonging to the school. For example, middle and high schools have created or upgraded advising systems so that the students each have at least one faculty member who knows them well. Some have adopted a full-scale advising curriculum that tries to address the stresses and life issues students commonly encounter before they reach problem levels. Some schools have also tried to make their report cards more informative by including more detail and more narrative description, and, as described in Chapter Twelve, they have also tried to add emphasis to parent-teacher conferences. These and other measures require teachers to develop new skills, threatening their sense of competence. Moreover, the steps a school takes to build a consensus about purpose and conduct and shape a partnership with parents must over time be preserved, renewed, and updated. Thus all who join the school in each succeeding year—staff, students, parents alike—must be properly oriented. Skill at this kind of work is likely to grow with practice, but the anticipation of having to exercise this skill year after year can loom as a real burden.

Of all the potential concerns for teachers, the greatest may well involve the changes in their relationships with parents and with each other. Improving parents' sense of personal connection and in-

stitutional affiliation usually involves making faculty more responsive and available by reaching out proactively, replying more
promptly to calls and e-mail, being more willing to discuss concerns,
and so on. This will inevitably bring teachers into more frequent
contact with parents, something that is not high on their personal
wish lists and for which there is little room in their schedules, even
if they appreciate the reality that parents who now live in a 24/7
work world need a stronger sense of responsiveness from schools
than in the past.

A more important concern about dealing with parents involves
the potential for conflict. The need to support and defend the
school's values and norms raises the prospect of engaging with parents in new and more direct ways. As many teachers correctly anticipate, creating new expectations for behavior in the school can, in
the early going, *increase* the potential for tension and disagreement
with students and parents as everyone gets used to the school's assertion of what it stands for. Handling these issues with students
may not be a source of significant concern for educators (although
it can be in large urban schools with a history of student violence).
Addressing them with parents, however, is almost always a source
of very significant concern. It presses hard on teachers' impulse to
avoid conflict. In my experience, a large majority of teachers (even
those who say most stridently, "I just wish they'd shape up") are not
confident about dealing with parents. On the contrary, they are
often quite anxious about doing so. They need encouragement and
useful training—outlined in Chapter Fourteen—to help them.

If anything could be more unwelcome to educators than the
potential for conflict with parents it would be the potential for conflict with one another. But taken seriously, purpose and conduct
require educators not simply to hold students and parents accountable for respecting and enacting the school's values, but each other,
as well. This raises the specter of having to call one another on, say,
breaches of conduct, and runs directly counter to the culture of
schools, particularly their conflict avoidance.

When I talk with a faculty about clarifying and defending purpose and conduct as these relate to students and parents, they are often enthusiastic. When I point out that the same principles apply to their relations as colleagues, that all the adults in the school community need to model the school's values for students, the room usually grows quiet. People's thoughts are already turning to colleagues who are disrespectful or daunting in some way, wishing that their misbehaviors would be confronted, doubting that this will ever happen, and sure that they themselves could never start such a confrontation. In my experience, dealing with a fellow staff member directly about a charged issue is, to most educators, nearly unthinkable. Consequently, one useful support for a faculty is training about how to be able to talk together more frankly. Teachers often need coaching about how they might make a respectful observation or pose a respectful question to a colleague who ignores or violates a shared agreement, how to respond if they find themselves on the receiving end of such an observation or question, and so on. Many of the same principles summarized in Chapter Fourteen about dealing with parents apply here.

These are some of the common resistance issues teachers may present. There can, of course, be others. Most deserve to be considered on their merits, but a wise leader will remember that at the root of most resistance lies the matter of meaning, specifically the prospect of loss, incompetence, or conflict. Unless these are addressed, resistance is not likely to abate. The question is, how to address them?

Leadership

The answer is a long one, and I have already considered it, too, in *The Human Side of School Change*. The short form is that to embrace change, people must come to understand its *why*, *what*, and *how*: why they can't simply preserve the status quo and keep doing what they've been doing, what they must start doing, and how they can accomplish this goal. Effective implementation of any innovation thus begins with candid discussion. School leaders have to make the case for the changes they propose and acknowledge the distress this can cause. This requires a clear statement outlining the current problem and the risks of continuing with the current ways of coping (why), the new measures to be implemented (what), and the concrete help that will support the implementation (how). Far too often, principals try to put a purely optimistic spin on the changes (in this case, it would be something like "We have a great opportunity to improve our communication with parents") and then race to the plan and the dates of training. To motivate change and build commitment, staff need straight talk. Candor calls on principals to spell out for faculty the genuine importance to the school of defining purpose and conduct and redefining partnership. This is often where the loss begins, but it cannot be avoided.

At the same time, an intellectual agenda for change is never, by itself, sufficient to motivate people. Staff must feel that the leader is committed to the change but also to them. Principals, then, need to expect the grief and tolerate the mourning. They need to acknowledge honestly and empathically the costs of the change. Teachers must be permitted time to complain, to wish things were different, to long for the old days, to worry that they won't be able to deal authoritatively with parents, and so on. This opportunity can't last forever, but if it is denied altogether, resistance simply goes underground and undermines the necessary change. I have seen skilled school leaders take five early steps, among others, to help reduce resistance and build commitment among teachers:

- *Join the early resistance rather than try to override it.* They have made clear that the need to assert purpose and conduct and to reshape partnership does not primarily reflect a school-caused problem. They have been sensitive to loss issues, acknowledging that the work seems both difficult and unwelcome to some.

- *Identify (rather than hide) weaknesses in the school's own functioning.* An honest approach has to include a frank look at ways school staff may be contributing to the very problems they complain about—by sending mixed or unclear messages to families, for example, or by not responding to legitimate parent complaints.

- *Refrain from demonizing students or parents or exaggerating an "us versus them" dichotomy.* "I and most of you in this room are raising kids of our own," one elementary principal told her teachers. "We all know how hard it is." They have been clear that the aim is, as another put it, "to help parents help their children be successful here."

- *Present the situation as "pay me now or pay me later."* They have agreed that extra work is involved, but have been clear that there is both a potential payoff for this investment and also a real risk in not spending the time and effort. As a high school principal told her faculty, "We need to make the atmosphere less combustible or we're going to be fighting more and more fires every year."

- *Make a strong personal commitment.* They have put themselves on the line, making clear in a direct, almost visceral way, their own investment in the project and to helping teachers succeed. "I won't be asking you to do anything I don't do and I will be out in front—and solidly behind you too" is their message.

I have had a number of chances to hear principals approach their staffs in these ways. One of the best, a middle school principal I'll call Tom Brown, opened the process by calling a special faculty meeting and zeroing right in on the why:

The world has changed. We might wish it hadn't, but it has. Our families are different. You don't need me to tell you students are coming to us less prepared. More of them have big gaps in their attitude, behavior, and work habits. Parents are less willing to set any kind of limits on them, but they're more worried about the kids' future and more demanding of us. Lots of you tell me the parents question you about all sorts of things they used to leave up to you. And as you know, we're having more crises and challenges from some of them each year.

The things we've been trying just aren't working. Over the past three years we've tried to tighten up the discipline and attendance policies, we've had special emphases on respect and responsibility, we've sent more mailings home, we've added ten minutes to the parent conferences, and we've tried ways of getting parents here to learn more about us and about raising their kids. But you all keep complaining to me about one kind of problem or inappropriate behavior after another. And some of you have gotten frustrated and said things to parents that have actually inflamed a bad situation. Everybody's stress is up: yours, mine, the kids', the parents'. We didn't cause all this, but for the students' sake and for our own—and actually to help the parents—we've got to start thinking and acting differently.

After elaborating on these themes, Tom went on to outline the steps he thought they should take (the *what*) and the supports he thought they would need to accomplish these steps (the *how*). But in that meeting, in subsequent meetings, and in follow-up conversations with individual staff members, he left lots of time for questions, which he answered frankly. Didn't he think the pendulum would swing back and families would soon go back to the ways they used to be? No, he saw no sign of that. Didn't his proposal mean more work? Yes, at least in the beginning, but it should eventually reduce stressful interactions that would otherwise occur. Could he guarantee it would succeed? No. Weren't there risks in trying this? Yes, indeed, but there were also risks in doing nothing. What about time? Would his plan be added on top of all the other projects and task forces? No, some of those would have to be put on hold or slowed down. Which ones? He had some ideas but would be glad to hear their thoughts.

The two last questions are not trivial. Schools already have overloaded improvement agendas; most principals, between their own priorities, those of their district, and state and federal mandates, are overseeing several separate change projects simultaneously. As I suggested earlier in this chapter, reshaping purpose, conduct, and partnership should ultimately simplify a school's life, but it requires an initial investment of extra time and energy. Before they plunge in, school leaders need to prioritize and to calculate the price—educational, financial, political—of delaying or abandoning an existing initiative. No matter how charismatically led, change of the kind I am recommending is unlikely to succeed if it is simply added into what a superintendent I know calls "innovation congestion."

Leading from Strength

In the face of these complexities, I see at least one straightforward, encouraging certainty: the best way to actually begin a purpose-conduct-and-partnership process itself is to start by leading from strength. It is always easier to build on a strength than to attack a weakness. This is one of the great lessons to emerge from behavioral psychology. It is simpler to keep doing something than to stop doing that thing and begin doing something else, especially if it's something you're good at. Often, strengths can be used to help address weaknesses. Teachers have daily evidence of this, particularly with special education students. The way they help SPED students is not by bashing them about what they can't do but by helping them do what they can. This approach is especially important for these students because of their disabilities, but it is valuable for all humans. Any life includes moments when attacking a weakness head-on is essential, but far too often, improvement is seen as solely a matter of doing so.

Educators spend enormous amounts of time concentrating on their weaknesses, real and imagined, and far too little thinking about how they might expand and extend their existing areas of competence. Purpose-and-conduct discussions ideally begin by asking, "What are we really good at?" "As a school, what do we do best with students?" "What do we really value and how do our actions show our values?" Questions like these can lead in many directions. They can stimulate lively and constructive disagreement, especially in schools that have paid little attention to values and expectations. They can also make it easier for faculty to tolerate looking at their shortcomings and considering how they might improve. Though there is no denying the effort required, leading from strength is an excellent route to empowering the school and renewing its faculty's confidence, optimism, and energy.

14

· ·

Parenting Parents
Building Faculty Skill

It is all well and good for me to propose that educators become more parental vis à vis parents; it is another thing altogether to expect teachers to jump at the chance to think of themselves in this way. It is fine for me to recommend the clarifying and proclaiming of core values, conditions for membership, and guidelines for partnership; it is something else again for teachers to cope during the several years it takes for these to become well established in a school community. In fact, as I have acknowledged, this effort can, at first, increase the possibility of conflict with students and, more worrisomely for teachers, the possibility of conflict with parents, and teachers often have a hard time even imagining how to assume a more parental posture toward parents. This is quite understandable. Teachers not only specialize in relating to youth rather than adults, they receive virtually no useful training in how to communicate with parents, let alone how to manage conflict with them. The assumption has always been that they will somehow acquire the necessary skills on their own, and most teachers do so, or at least they acquire sufficient skills to get by.

But not sufficient skills to feel truly secure. In thirty years of working in schools I have met very few teachers who approach parents with anything like the confidence they bring to their teaching (except for some veteran practitioners dealing with much younger parents). I have, however, met large numbers who feel anxious and worried, often disproportionately so. Even gifted teachers, acknowledged classroom wizards, widely respected and liked, come to parent conferences, as one described herself to me, "not fully apprehensive, exactly, but potentially apprehensive." Teachers deserve concrete, practical help about ways to be appropriately parental with parents in face-to-face situations—that is, ways to improve communication and the relationship and to prevent, reduce, and resolve misunderstandings and conflicts.

Perspective

Effective professional development in this area should begin with perspective before turning to particular methods. It should encourage educators to approach the whole topic of parent communication with three assumptions in mind: parents are sincere and anxious and unconfident; problems are inevitable and often valuable; the ideal role for the teacher is to be a "pretty good problem solver"—not perfect, just pretty good. When parents bring concerns to the school these are generally honest, even when exaggerated or entirely wrong. Earl Oremus, head of Marburn Academy in Columbus, Ohio, reminds his teachers that no matter how negative a parent's way of communicating, "the source of the complaint is usually noble: a genuine concern for the child."[1] Sincerity is no guarantee of accuracy; a father's assessment of a situation may be wildly incorrect, which can make it hard to remember that he means well, especially if his tone is hostile, negative, or demanding, but the core impulse to support and protect his child is perfectly normal.

If sincerity is no guarantee of parents' accuracy, it is also no indicator of their confidence, no matter how assertive they may seem. In my experience it is wise to assume that parents are insecure about their parenting, that somewhere underneath most questions they ask—and most complaints and criticisms they make—lies a measure of anxiety and some lack of confidence about their own ability to shape their child's growing up. (This won't always be true, but it will be true often enough to make it the most useful default assumption.) Hence, they are likely to be anxious even about the experience of coming in for a routine conference. I will never forget attending my first conference when my older son was in kindergarten. I had already taught high school and preschool, was a newly trained child psychologist and a consultant to teachers, but I realized, as I sat on a tiny child's chair in the classroom waiting for the meeting to begin, that my palms were sweaty. I had no particular reason to worry, but I also didn't know what I would hear. I was much more than "potentially apprehensive"; I was wired.

Not all parents come to school as anxious as this, but many do; even the aggressively critical are just as likely to be anxious and unconfident about their own parenting. This is often obscured because, as noted, many more parents now tend to present themselves as entitled, even demanding consumers whose tax or tuition dollars are purchasing a service, even an outcome. Not infrequently, the parents who are most insistent and assertive are attributing to the school an issue that actually has roots at home. Displacement of this kind is by no means easy to address, in part because it does not invalidate the parents' views (their complaint about a school issue, for example, may be exaggerated and yet contain a kernel of truth), but it is all the more reason for educators to remind themselves that their first assumption about parents should be, "They're sincere, anxious, and unconfident."

Given these realities, educators need to anticipate the likelihood of periodic difficult encounters with parents and, where possible, see these as opportunities. Earl Oremus tells his staff that from time to time each will inevitably get a "blast" from an angry or upset parent. He urges them to remember, "We can't avoid problems, no matter how good we are or no matter how hard we try. Life is not perfect, and neither are the humans who live it." Every school, for example, has a small core of impossible parents who are a constant thorn in the side of teachers and administrators, who monopolize a disproportionate amount of time, and who seem immune to even the most skilled intervention. And almost every school has conscientious teachers who often seem to adopt a posture I have come to think of as the "perfectionistic victim"—a readiness to experience themselves in their dealings with difficult parents as simultaneously misunderstood and mistreated yet at fault and inadequate. They can feel and function better if they adopt a different stance, the "pretty good problem solver" I mentioned earlier. In this posture, they don't expect their performance, either in the classroom or with parents, to be flawless, and even in the face of sharp attack they don't retreat into self-criticism, helplessness, and resentment. They try to remember and acknowledge parents' sincerity and anxiety. This provides a basis for joining with concerned parents rather than struggling against them, no matter how little they may share the parents' viewpoint. Even when parents' concern is unfounded, it creates an opportunity to learn something useful about the context of a student's life and, often, to be helpful to the parents (and their child) by reassuring them or reframing the issue.

This perspective invites teachers to focus on their strengths rather than their vulnerabilities. It is an excellent way for them to be more appropriately authoritative when they interact with parents. In my work with schools I often take the faculty through an exercise in which they construct their own "competence catalog," an inventory of their collective knowledge base about how to have fruitful conversations with parents and how to manage difficult situations. I have found that most staffs already include internal experts who have developed artful ways to cope with challenging parents. They can take the lead in a general sharing of these approaches, a list that aids not only new teachers but veterans, who often need periodic refreshers to remind them of their competence and reinforce for them that they know more about this topic than they may think.

Building upon this perspective and these assumptions, practical training for teachers, though it may touch on many themes, must cover two key aspects for communicating well with parents: listening and telling. These have always been basic to good home-school communication and most of the suggestions I offer are not novel. They are, however, more important than ever, given the number of uncertain, unconfident, consumerist parents teachers must deal with, and they are also easy to forget, especially in the heat of a conversation between an anxious teacher and an anxious parent. I will outline essentials that I have found to be helpful, but cannot do them full justice. The printed page can suggest things to say or do, but cannot capture the tone of voice, facial expression, or—most important—the larger context of relationship within which a conversation occurs, all of which affect how points are presented and received.

Active Listening

For most educators, the primary worry is how to deliver messages to parents, not how to hear parents' messages. But hearing is the place to begin. Listening to parents is vital for gaining information, for conveying interest and empathy, and for building and sustaining cooperative relationships. Plus, the principles of good listening lead naturally into the principles of good telling when it is the teacher's turn to talk.

By "good listening" I mean "active listening." For a time in the 1970s active listening was all the rage in some psychotherapy circles. Popularized by the psychologist Carl Rogers,[2] it consists of paying close attention to what people tell you and to their feelings about what they're telling you, and periodically checking and clarifying to be sure you've understood them by restating what you've heard. This checking and clarifying is empathic—it aims to comprehend things from the other person's point of view, not your own. It avoids, at one extreme, cold objectivity, and, at the other, exaggerated sympathy. Rogers wanted a psychotherapy client to feel sincerely *heard,* to know that the therapist appreciated in a real way both the client's problem and the client as a person.

In schools, a deep, therapeutic level of empathy is not necessary, but communication always improves when parents feel heard—when they feel the teacher understands and cares about what they have to say and how they feel. Earl Oremus suggests that teachers acknowledge that a parent's concern is legitimate. "This doesn't mean that you have to agree with the parent's characterization of the problem," he adds, "it just means you verbally acknowledge that it is sensible for them to be concerned given their current understanding of the circumstances. It often helps to say something like: 'I can see why you are concerned. I would be, too, if I thought such and such were true for my child.'"[3]

Among other benefits, this kind of active listening helps to avoid misunderstandings, as the listener periodically checks to be sure of understanding what the speaker has said. It also inclines people to open up and to say more than they otherwise would because they see the listener's genuine interest and they feel respected and acknowledged. And this in turn reduces the potential for conflict; if you disagree with people but are obviously trying hard to understand them, it is harder for them to fight with you.

In active listening a teacher invites parents to share their views, thoughts, or questions, encourages them to enlarge upon these with examples, and periodically restates the key points they make, testing to be sure she has understood correctly. Thus, in a conference, she might ask parents what they see in their child at home, whether they have any questions about the student at school, and so on. If they voice a concern ("We've always been told that our son is gifted, and he studies hard, but he never gets an A in your class"), the teacher doesn't immediately defend or explain her grades, but instead invites the parents to elaborate ("Tell me more about that"), focusses on the student's behavior ("When you say he's working very hard, can you tell me what you mean?"), and tries to understand the meaning of the problem to the parents ("What is it about this that most concerns you?"). As the picture emerges, the teacher tries to summarize the parents' issue, which may be she is unfair ("It sounds like you really think I'm not giving him the marks he deserves"), or that their son isn't really gifted, after all ("This has left you wondering whether he's as bright as you've been told"), or that their son is intensely grade-conscious and might become depressed ("So you're concerned that his reaction could develop into a serious psychological problem"). It is important to remember that in clarifying parents' concerns, the teacher is not *telling* them what they think or feel but *asking* them, trying out a summary to see whether it matches how they understand things and what the problem means to them.

An important feature of active listening that can be especially useful to teachers is not to take literally—at least not at first—any emotionally laden communication, whether it is a charged question, a small complaint, or a full blast. Whenever parents raise any issue or use any tone that is surprising, challenging, or upsetting, the wise course is not to respond without first understanding what stimulated their question, comment, or accusation. Once this is understood, answering is much easier, the potential for conflict is reduced, and the conversation is more likely to stay focussed on the student's needs. When I think of active listening, I always remember this anecdote, told to me by a second-grade teacher:

> There was an urgent request from Betsy's mother to call at once. When I reached her, she immediately demanded, in this accusatory voice, "Why are you teaching Egypt that way?" Like she was a prosecutor. My heart sank. "Oh my God," I thought. "She's an Egyptologist. She knows much more about Egypt than I do. She thinks I'm incompetent." I was petrified. As it turned out, she knew nothing about teaching Egypt. In the carpool on the way home Betsy had said something about not remembering the names of the pharaohs. Her

mother just wanted me to make sure Betsy wasn't missing anything. I never would have known this if I hadn't
screwed my courage up and asked her to tell me about
her concern.

There are many ways to answer an accusatory "Why are you
teaching Egypt that way?" They range from "How dare you question
my teaching" all the way to "Please don't be mad at me; I've worked
very hard on the Egypt unit." Teachers might fantasize about the former, but they often fall into the latter, which is like scattering blood
near a shark: it invites attack. An ideal first response is to say to the
parent, as this teacher did, some version of "Tell me more."

When I offer these suggestions to teachers, they often register
two hesitations. The first is that engaging parents in this empathic
way is just asking for trouble, especially when it comes to inviting
critical parents to elaborate on their concern. "If somebody starts
killing me, why should I try to help them?" a high school teacher
once asked, to laughter and applause from his colleagues. This can
indeed seem suicidal, until you get used to doing it. It takes practice, to be sure, but it is a wonderful way of defusing conflict. It immediately shifts the dynamic in the conversation. Imagine a parent
who has said something disparaging or found fault, explicitly or im-
plicitly with a teacher. The teacher naturally feels an impulse
toward self-defense. The parent very likely anticipates this and is
ready to intensify the criticism. If the teacher, instead of resisting,
asks to learn more, this takes some of the wind out of the parent's
sails and shows a calm confidence and a genuine interest that, if
anything, raises the teacher's stature. The second hesitation is that
active listening means agreeing, that it will imply to parents that a
teacher agrees with their diagnosis or desire when this is not the
case. Not so. Listening does not mean agreeing. It means being sure
one has understood the other side from their point of view. A
teacher who has listened in this way is free to be equally clear. In
fact, it is vital to do so.

Talking Straight

For most educators, the primary concern in dealing with parents is how to deliver messages, especially when they are unwelcome or the parent is not a good listener. The key is to be simple and direct and, when the news is bad, candid and concerned.

Simplicity and directness begin with the Rule of Three. In a conference, and especially in any meeting about a specific problem a student has encountered or caused, parents are unlikely to remember more than three points clearly. Even if they don't have the sweaty palms I did in my son's kindergarten, they are likely to be feeling enough stress to impair their concentration and memory. This puts a premium on organization and on topic sentences, which are not always natural skills for teachers.

Some of the most gifted classroom practitioners I meet are not adept at summarizing a student's performance succinctly. Many, especially elementary faculty who still teach in a true developmental, child-centered way, are inclined to discuss their curriculum and a student's progress in an eclectic style that is, like child development itself, organic: it digresses, repeats, leaps ahead, and so on.

Many parents today need a more structured, focussed presentation. This might begin, "I have three key things I want to emphasize about Jane: she's a very hard worker; she's doing quite well in most subjects; but she is having some trouble with math," followed by data and examples for each of the three points. As straightforward as this may sound, I have not found it to be common. Many teachers are inclined to launch into the first topic ("I just want to tell you what a hard worker Jane is"), and after discussing this, proceed to the second. This can result in running out of time for the third—especially if it is a touchy one.

When it comes to touchy topics, most teachers say that they always start with the good news about a student before turning to problem areas because this sets a better tone for the discussion (and, although they don't say so, because it also postpones the possibility of—and reduces the time for—parental upsets). Beginning with a student's strengths surely makes good sense, but I have found it works best to include the bad news headline in the topic sentence: "Billy is a leader among his peers; he does extremely well in the subjects he likes, but he dislikes science and he puts very little effort into it." This gives the parents a framework for what they're going to hear, and provides a kind of up-front reminder to them and the teacher that there is an important area of concern that shouldn't be avoided.

No matter how discouraging the information that has to be communicated to parents, simplicity and directness call for being clear and concrete, for not getting lost in abstractions and generalizations. One of the most common ways that teacher-parent communication goes awry is when teachers do have bad news to present to parents about a student, are afraid of doing so, and try to minimize or sugarcoat the unwelcome data. Near-nuns and near-monks who are at least potentially apprehensive don't want to make anyone feel bad or risk conflict with other adults. They not only put the problem topic last on the agenda, they resort to generalizations that, they hope, will convey their concern without provoking distress or attack. Unfortunately, this not only fails to inform parents accurately, it leaves them doubting the teacher's connection to their child. This is a cardinal sin.

Above all else, parents need to know that their child's teachers know their child. Otherwise, they are likely to doubt what teachers tell them, and rightly so. Whenever a school staff member gave my wife and me good news about either of our sons but didn't seem to know him, I discounted the report. Whenever someone gave us bad news but clearly did know our son, I took what I heard seriously and, however concerned I was, I also felt hope: here was somebody I could trust. The way teachers confirm that they know a student is by being specific; confidence, like God, is in the details. Thus a kindergarten teacher, instead of telling parents, "Your daughter shows some evidence of aggressive tendencies," would be better-advised to say, "She has provoked a fight almost every day for the past three weeks." Instead of, "Your son has a problem with authority," she might say, "He refuses most of our requests and makes a sharp grimace like this [demonstrating] whenever we ask him to do something." Being specific requires courage, but it projects a teacher's authority, compels parents' attention, and confirms that the teacher knows the student.

Shaping Collaboration

Implicit in the foregoing is that in face-to-face encounters with parents, educators need to shape the discussion in a more planful way than many are used to. Shaping means managing the time and the flow of the conversation. Typically, parent-teacher conferences are relatively short, often no more than twenty minutes. They occur on the teacher's turf and the teacher should structure them (educators who don't treat their time as valuable are inviting parents to do the same). The teacher can say, "We only have twenty minutes and I'm eager to hear what you might want to tell or ask me, and I have three things I want to be sure to go over with you." Even if the meeting involves a major issue, includes a number of participants, and is scheduled for an hour, structure is important; someone from the school should begin by stating the purpose of the meeting and noting its time limit.

Managing the discussion means not just starting clearly but ending clearly. Teachers consistently report they have a hard time ending conversations with parents. What's needed is to keep an eye on the clock and be ready to deliver a five-minute warning ("We only have five minutes left and I still have one key item to cover"). If time is running out and there is clearly much more to discuss, I generally recommend scheduling another session, rather than extending the current one, which only delays the next set of parents waiting in line and adds to the teacher's anxiety and distraction. This is also a way to send a tacit message that the teacher's time is important, which can help parents stay on topic in future conferences. At the close of the meeting, it is ideal for the teacher to restate the key themes that have been addressed, both those brought up by parents and the three presented by the teacher. It is also important to underscore areas where teacher and parents have different views or outright disagreements, and what, if anything, has been adopted as a next step in addressing these.

Troubleshooting

When I'm working with a school's faculty and we reach this point in the workshop, a teacher will sometimes ask a version of the "yes, but" question: "Yes, this all sounds great, but what do I do after I've done all this and the parents are still upset or still won't listen?" There is no silver bullet. Problems are inevitable despite the most skillful efforts. Parents are not always grateful when given straight but unwelcome information about their son or daughter. They tend to take such news personally (it would be odd if they didn't) and, depending on the situation and the personalities involved, they can become angry, hurt, or scared. This can interfere with their ability to hear accurately even the most concrete facts (all the more reason for the Rule of Three) and can lead to tense conversations. But it is not a reason to avoid being simple, direct, candid, and concerned. In the long run, and in the interest of solving the student's problem, it is much more important to earn parents' respect than their affection. Purchasing the latter at the price of the former not only leaves the teacher feeling like a sell-out, it does a real disservice to the student and to the parents. It repeats the very error that parents make when, trying to befriend their children, they avoid setting limits on them or letting them learn from the consequences of a mistake. Being direct with parents models for them the kind of authoritative approach they need to take with their children.

Fortunately, even in difficult encounters it is not always necessary to make the choice between being liked and being respected.

In my experience, parents respond better to even the most hard-to-take news about their child if the teacher shows concern and worry. Tone is crucial. "Jim is on the verge of being expelled" can be said in a warning tone that conveys "you better shape him up—and what's wrong with you, anyway?" or with a kind of earnest distress that conveys "I'm really worried that something very bad could happen to him." In fact, one can often make the most unwelcome observations ("she doesn't seem to have a single friend in the class" or "he may have to repeat sixth grade unless things improve") if one begins them with "I'm worried that—" or "I'm concerned that—" or "I'm puzzled that—." Of course, sometimes a no-nonsense warning is needed—if, say, Jim's misbehavior is extreme and his parents have been minimizing it even as it has escalated. But even in these situations, a combination of candor and concern can improve the prospects of a good outcome.

Needless to say, this doesn't mean parroting the sample phrases suggested in this chapter—I include them for illustration and suggestion, not as something to be memorized and applied in a rote, formulaic way. Teachers need to adapt them to fit their own particular strengths and styles. Any of the measures I have recommended will fail when used as a gimmick rather than as an expression of a genuine desire to work together with parents to solve a problem on a student's behalf.

And even the most genuine and sympathetic presentation won't always work, of course. There are unavoidably times when teacher and parent cannot agree. The teacher has followed every suggestion, has listened actively and fully understood the parents' viewpoint—but does not share it. Parents, for their part, cannot accept the teacher's assessment. In these instances it doesn't help to force a false closure. Often, the best thing to do is to register the disagreement. ("We both agree that Sally is underachieving, but you're convinced it's because she's bored in my class and I'm convinced she's afraid to try.") Teachers tell me all the time that they have great difficulty restraining themselves from proposing to alter their approach in such situations, even if they are absolutely certain of their own diagnosis and prescription. The prospect of parents' dismay or disapproval activates teachers' closet omnipotence (and makes them feel guilty), so they volunteer some additional or different intervention even when they feel it is unnecessary or unwarranted.

It can be useful to offer intermediate solutions (time to wait and see what develops, a follow-up conference in a month, a consultation from another teacher or the principal, and so on). But if these don't truly make sense to the teacher, I think it's better to conclude by saying simply, "I guess we see it differently." If the parents' reply is, "So what are you going to do about it?" and the honest answer is, essentially, "Nothing," there is only one approach left.

An impasse can sometimes be resolved by finding out from parents what they wish and what they fear. That is, what it is they want the teacher to do and what it is they are afraid of if this doesn't happen. From one point of view, this is another way of finding out the meaning of the problem to them. If asked sincerely ("What is it you wish I would do?"), it can change the whole dynamic of the disagreement, in the same way that inviting parents to say more about a blast they've just given a teacher does. The parent has to shift from blaming and criticizing to asking for something. If the follow-up question is also asked sincerely ("What are you afraid of [worried about] if I can't do that?"), it can not just break a standoff but touch a parent's vulnerability, sometimes turning anger to tears. If this doesn't work, the parents will probably want to see the principal to press their case. The teacher can only give the principal a heads-up that things have reached an impasse and the parents are unsatisfied and likely to look upstairs for a solution.

In this regard, these days more parents than ever do threaten to go over the teacher's head to get their way, and more actually try. The numbers of both are not large, but they are certainly growing. Just as it is hard to tell a nervous person to relax, it is hard to advise teachers not to worry about these threats and trespasses. Their worry may be unavoidable, but as a practical matter, the only useful response to such a threat is to invite the parent to go right ahead and call the principal—and then make sure to warn the principal. As for parents who go right to the top without trying to reach an accord with the teacher, a good principal will rarely intervene without first making sure the parents have actually had the full conversation with the teacher—and when satisfied that this is so, the principal will still actively consult and include the teacher in the response to parents.

There are also many more parents now who want instant responses to their concerns and who try to use e-mail to conduct discussions with teachers about their children, and who ambush teachers on the telephone, or in the parking lot, on the soccer sidelines, even at the supermarket. Teachers don't want to seem rude or withholding, yet often feel intruded upon and unprepared and reluctant to respond in detail, especially in public. In all these situations, it is almost always best to suggest and to insist on, politely but firmly, a scheduled face-to-face conference. E-mail is a terrible medium for exchanges about emotionally charged issues between people who don't know each other well; there is no such thing as virtual active listening. Here, as with the other ambushes, the teacher can say, "I'd love to talk with you about this, so please call me to set up a time to meet," or, "I'd be happy to discuss this with you but I can't do it now. Let's plan a time to talk at school." Teachers can find this easier to do if the school has published guidelines to this effect.

Protecting the Investment

I hope it's clear by now that parenting parents mainly asks for more of what authoritative teachers have always offered, that it is neither complicated nor condescending, neither dismissive nor intrusive. It involves a sincere effort to collaborate with parents on behalf of students, one conducted on the school's terms but attuned to parents' interests, one in which the teacher provides nurture (active listening), structure (the Rule of Three and the shaping of the conversation), and latitude (honestly facing the real-life facts and consequences of students' performance and behavior) to parents. It respects parents' responsibility, and it models for them the essentials they need to provide their children. Best of all, it is simple.

Simple, but not necessarily easy. Some of the measures I recommend are counterintuitive; they call for a patience that is hard for some educators and a directness that is hard for others. Formal training can foster some skills in these areas; sustaining these skills, and by extension protecting the school's investment in purpose and conduct, requires continuing mutual support. Teachers, as they implement and defend a school's values and norms, as they anticipate and encounter blasts, surprises, and challenges from parents, and as they address parents' anxiety, need to be able to turn to one another for advice, for sympathy, to ventilate frustration—and to keep learning.

Communicating with parents, like communicating with students, improves best not with practice alone but with practice and collegial reflection. Thus, before a parent meeting that promises to be especially difficult, it can really help to consult with a colleague, anticipating what the parents might say and what one wants to convey, recalling past approaches that have worked with similar parents, brainstorming ways to handle a worst-case scenario, and so on. After the meeting, though the natural impulse may be to forget it as fast as possible, the better response is to debrief it, reflecting on what went well, what didn't, and asking, "What can I learn?" Teachers' lives are already busy; they can't devote lots of time to this learning. But sharing and nurturing their collective ability to parent parents is an excellent way to reduce stress and improve outcomes all around: for students, for parents, and for themselves.

15

Paradox, Realism, and Hope

In this book I have gathered evidence that the marked declines in students' behavior and values that so trouble schools stem from marked declines in parents' competence and confidence—specifically, in their provision of three essentials of psychosocial development: nurture, structure, and latitude. These declines, along with those in parents' own behavior at school, derive from, among other factors, economic and cultural trends in American life that, although deeply rooted, have intensified, spawning both insecurity and a radical individualism that are toxic to families and to child development. All this, I have asserted, requires a more realistic, broader notion of school accountability, an acknowledgment that students' performance and behavior are shaped more, in Csikszentmihalyi's phrase, by "the experiences, habits, values, and ideas they acquire from the environment in which they live"—especially the families in which they live—than by what happens in school.[1] Nevertheless, there are real measures schools can take to strengthen their impact, preserve their institutional integrity, and fulfill their developmental mission: clarifying purpose and conduct, redefining the home-school partnership, and helping faculty to assume a more authoritative, parental stance with parents. I have outlined specific steps that can help schools implement these changes.

When I make this case to educators, it strikes some as paradoxical. Not long ago, for example, after I had presented it to a group
of principals, one fixed me with a thoughtful look. "You've shown
us that schools aren't as powerful as we thought and that the tide is
running against us—and then you've urged us to be bolder and
assert ourselves." He paused. "I like it." He paused again, longer.
"But you're asking us to become countercultural in a way. And what
if the tide just keeps getting stronger?"

What indeed? The steps I recommend do, in essence, require
schools to resist strong currents in American life, a role they have
rarely played. Historically, they have always reflected society more
than they have shaped it. And although they can't thrive if they
don't assert their essential institutional priorities, this assertion, by
itself, may not suffice. What schools really need most is what their
students really need most—and it lies beyond the control of both:
they need parents to choose children, to rebalance their lives more
in favor of family and child development. Needless to say, signs of
movement in this direction are scarce. On the contrary, parents are
at best ambivalent about family engagement rather than ready to
increase their commitment at home. So, at the very least, we should
not expect the crisis in childrearing to abate soon. We should anticipate that too many parents will continue to minimize their responsibility for meeting the emotional needs of their children, that those
who do accept this responsibility will continue to find it difficult to
fulfill, and that schools will continue to face the challenges that
have increasingly marked their dealings with students and parents.

An unhappy prospect, but one that must be faced. Its implication, however, and the ultimate message of this book, is not that educators should give up; it is rather that they should hold on, that
they must be simultaneously realistic and hopeful. If the impact of
schooling cannot be as powerful as we might wish, schools are not
helpless. If the need to strengthen their impact has never been

greater, there are at least some clear ways to accomplish it. And even if the tide continues to run against them, teachers and administrators—indeed, everyone involved in the enterprise of schooling—need not despair. Rather, they must reconsider what constitutes real progress against the tide and what makes the swimming worthwhile. This is the only way to sustain high levels of competence and effort—and to nourish hope.

Staying Real

The relevant paradigm for me is the classroom: educators need to do for themselves what they do for students—balance high expectations against practical realities. Anyone who has ever taught knows that teachers often do their best work with what is not their best-performing class. In fact, if we think of teaching in terms of the value it adds to student achievement, the best work is often done with the less gifted or more disadvantaged pupils who are challenging to teach and who make gains in small, inconsistent increments. A good teacher has high expectations for all students and works assiduously to help all of them reach the benchmark, but never actually knows whether a given group will do so. But the teacher always knows the baseline from which the group began. He doesn't give up on his standards or his students, but he knows that progress is best measured by where they end up with respect to the baseline and in light of the effort it took them—and him—to get there, not just where they end up with respect to the benchmark or to students in other classes. He also knows that his students are more likely to persevere and succeed if he doesn't just concentrate on overcoming their weaknesses but consciously builds on their strengths, as well.

In the same way, if the developmental functioning of the family continues to be undermined by the trends and forces reviewed in

Part One, the challenge to educators may intensify, and even if their effort and competence in clarifying purpose and conduct and re-defining partnership are all first-rate, students' performance and behavior and the behavior of their parents may fail to improve as expected. Nevertheless, the effort and competence will still have been first-rate. And in that case the real question will be not whether the school has achieved the success it originally envisioned but whether it has achieved more than it otherwise would have. And just as with students, perseverance and performance are likely to be better if those involved in the project build on their strengths in addition to learning from their mistakes.

This perspective may seem too minimalist or pessimistic to inspire the commitment and hard work our schools need if they are to master the challenges before them. It certainly doesn't match the grandiosity of No Child Left Behind. To situate schooling in its larger context, as I have done in this book, can be discouraging, especially to those who prefer to see its influence as limitless. But this contextual perspective is also liberating. It tempers naive expectations and offers relief for the rampant demoralization, the frustration, and futility endemic among educators.

At every level, from the classroom through the district office, one can find people working longer and harder and often better, but feeling chronically thwarted, inadequate, and criticized. Unable to rapidly accelerate the pace of student achievement or rapidly reduce the excesses in student and parent behavior no matter what they do, convinced the problem must lie in school, they often end up blaming one another.

Their collective distress is inevitable, so long as the crisis in childrearing is oversimplified as a crisis in schooling and educators are held responsible for solving it. However well-intentioned, such a mission keeps everyone from seeing the strengths of schools. It obscures not only the effort teachers and administrators invest but the competence they exercise. It keeps them (and all of us) from appreciating their legitimate achievements, from realizing that although American education may need lots of improving, the real surprise about our schools, *given what they are up against,* is not how bad so many of them are, but how good.

Nurturing Hope

This perspective has a second benefit: it nurtures hope. It is not always optimistic, but it is hopeful, which is much more important. I first learned the distinction between optimism and hope from Vaclav Havel, the Czech playwright and president, thanks to a school principal, Andy Odoardi. As I was completing the last chapter of my earlier book, Andy asked me to speak to a group of principals about maintaining morale while leading reform. He gave me a short article of Havel's called "Never Hope Against Hope," which points out that hope is not a state of the world but a state of mind, an "orientation of the spirit," that it springs from commitment, not certainty, and that one need not be optimistic about an outcome to be hopeful about one's goals.

That insight was so simple and powerful that I rewrote the last chapter of that book around it. In the years since, as I have worked with educators from hundreds of schools who have been struggling to cope with the problems this book has explored even as they were striving to implement all the instructional mandates thrust upon them, its relevance has continued to grow for me. I repeat it here in this last chapter:

> Hope in this deep and powerful sense is not the same as joy when things are going well, or willingness to invest in enterprises that are obviously headed for early success, but rather an ability to work for something to succeed. Hope is definitely not the same thing as optimism. It's not the conviction that something will turn out well, but

the certainty that something makes sense, regardless of how it turns out. It is this hope, above all, that gives us strength to live and to continually try new things, even in conditions that seem . . . hopeless.[2]

Few of us are truly comforted by being told that something is easy when we find it hard. Minimizing the complexity of problems and exaggerating the promise of solutions may invite early optimism and energy but leads inevitably to demoralization and despair. It obscures conscientious effort and genuine progress. We can never find real hope in ignoring real life. We can only find it in committing ourselves to things that make sense.

When Christopher Jencks and his colleagues concluded that schooling's contribution to children's adult lives was small, the evidence, which many in education found depressing, did not lead them to dismiss the importance of improving schools. It suggested rather that, instead of trying to assess schools solely in terms of their ultimate effect on students' life outcomes, we should judge them in terms of their immediate impact on students and teachers, which can be very large. "Some schools are dull, depressing, even terrifying places, while others are lively, comfortable, and reassuring," Jencks pointed out. "If we think of school life as an end in itself rather than a means to some other end, such differences are enormously important." There was, he insisted, a strong case for improving the quality of children's and teachers' lives for its own sake.[3]

I think of this when I watch a gifted teacher's face as she interacts with her class, or when I ask teachers what they treasure about their work and hear them describe the joy they experience when they really connect with students. At these moments it is unmistakably clear that students—and teachers—are better off just because of the experience itself. And at these moments I realize what writing this book has reconfirmed for me: there is nothing closer to the core of a civilization than the raising of the young; it is the noblest of tasks. It has doubtless never been easy, but it has surely never been more complex and there has never been so much of it left up to the school. If we are to give it its due, we must celebrate not just the positive outcomes that result from skillful endeavor but the very commitment to children that keeps dedicated teachers, in the face of unprecedented challenge, trying their best and hoping for the best. Our children deserve no less. We can ask no more.

Appendix

· ·

Practical Parent Education

I t is a rare school that doesn't offer at least periodic programs to help parents in their childrearing. Evening lectures by psychologists and psychiatrists, guidance counselors, and pediatricians are now common in all kinds of schools. I noted in Chapter Eleven my view that the content of the programs has improved but their impact has not; educators are hard-pressed to point to visible results.

To recap, the first difficulty is attendance: audiences are shrinking and those who do attend are generally the parents who are already doing a good job with their children from the school's point of view, not those who in the eyes of the school really need to change their parenting practices. The second issue is readiness: more parents today need help with the most basic aspects of parenting, not just higher-level issues, and this makes it hard to address all their needs in the time available. But the chief obstacle stems from the very nature of parenting: for the most part it cannot be carried out planfully as the application of expert advice.

Although parent programs should definitely be continued, they should be seen primarily as supporting positive parents, calming their anxiety and encouraging them to keep up their efforts. (This is often dismissed as "preaching to the choir," but choirs don't continue singing well without periodic encouragement and guidance.) These programs will rarely attract the parents who need them most, and even if they do, will rarely change their behavior. As a result, these programs should turn away from idealized, technique-oriented approaches to parent guidance and emphasize instead manageable, practical steps that parents can implement to improve nurture, structure, and latitude. The following sections elaborate on the limitations of the standard approaches and outline ways to present those manageable, practical steps.

Trillin's First Law: Technique Won't Save You

There is no shortage of advice for parents. The self-help shelves of bookstores are glutted with titles offering guidance about ways to prevent problems and accelerate development in children. There is, unfortunately, a pernicious paradox in this tide of counsel: it erodes the very strength and assurance it aims to build. Much of it is misguided and simplistic and rests on the false assumption that parenting can become the application of expert strategies disconnected from who we are and how we live. The path to more effective childrearing begins by turning away from the notion of parenting-as-expertise. It starts with a principle I came to reluctantly years ago but have found strongly confirmed in recent years, and which I now think of as Trillin's First Law of Parenting: *Technique won't save you.*

Childrearing, once seen largely as a matter of natural competence rooted in intuition and experience, is now presented by the current advice writers much more as a matter of deliberate strategy and tactics, a change Elkind describes as moving from "how do" to "how to." Pediatricians and psychologists used to emphasize children's progression through a sequence of developmental stages and encouraged parents to rely on their intuitive understanding as they responded to a child's unfolding tendencies and needs.[1] Knowing the how-do would help parents develop their own how-to. Today, however, the emphasis is on tips and techniques. Too often, the techniques are not based on solid psychological research and tend to promote a one-size-fits-all list of tactics, as though the same methods were suited to children of any age or disposition.[2]

Without question, parents need some techniques to raise their children—none could survive a day without some sort of planned maneuver—and some of the advice books include some sensible tactics. But the idea that childrearing can be *based* on tactics and *built upon* professional expertise ends up disabling rather than empowering parents. It increases anxiety instead of reducing it, stimulating parents to be ever more perfectionistic and vigilant in avoiding errors. And most important, it ignores the vital impact of context and relationship in family life.

What really determines a child's response to a parent's intervention is its meaning to the child, which is determined largely by the patterns that characterize their relationship. A son will perceive a particular piece of discipline by his mother one way if he feels unhesitatingly that she is deeply, actively committed to him, another if she doesn't. In the same way, the mother's response to her son's behavior depends on what it means to her, which is affected by everything from whether it's been a bad day or the spouses have been fighting to whether the behavior reminds her of herself as a child.

This brings us to Calvin Trillin, the journalist and humorist. After years of preaching "technique won't save you" to parents, I was delighted to read *Family Man*, his reflection on raising his daughters. Early on, he remarks that he has always found childrearing advice to be futile, because even when parents earnestly seek it, they aren't actually likely to follow it. For most parents, he writes, "the process of rearing children is so all-encompassing that there isn't any way to adhere to any policy that doesn't coincide with their natural way of doing things. Getting advice on the best way to bring up children is like getting advice on the best way to breathe; sooner or later, you're probably going to forget it and go back to your old in-and-out."[3] Trillin is onto something really important here.

As I have already suggested, parenting is instant and reflexive, made up almost entirely of interchanges that are spontaneous and immediate. Parents can try to be considerate and planful when they are reflecting on it in the abstract, but almost never in the midst of their actual engagement with children. Then they are dealing whole person to whole person, a situation in which relationship, context, personality, and history often overwhelm rationality.

This doesn't mean that parents can't modify their behavior or improve their handling of children, but that they can't transform themselves and can't simply apply, in any authentic, reliable, consistent way, a set of methods, maneuvers, tactics, and gimmicks that are not natural to them. It also means that trying to rely primarily on technique disables parents' natural authority. Though how-to parenting books, for example, seem to be full of constructive solutions, they tend to concentrate mostly on parental shortcomings; they keep parents intimidated and focussed on avoiding mistakes. They make them alternately hesitate too much and press too hard, and leave them vulnerable to endless second-guessing. They increase the very anxiety they aim to reduce and thus complicate the delivery of the developmental basics that really do help children.

Other factors also limit the value of giving parents advice, but the implications for schools' efforts at parent education should already be clear. Offering parents lots of technique programs or giving them long lists of books to read is not only unlikely to improve their childrearing, it also, ironically, risks the very thing schools want least: encouraging parents to imagine that they can be successful without truly engaging with their children. No technique can let us separate the way we parent from the way we live. Parents' care and teaching are inseparable—their children are learning from them literally all the time, even when parents aren't formally instructing them.[4] Indeed, parents have been designed by nature to teach their children in this way and the most important scientific advice for parents is that "they need to be allowed the time and energy to exercise their natural ability to help [children] learn."[5] Everything parents do sends children messages and gives them data from which to form impressions and draw conclusions. This, again, is why context and relationship are crucial to childrearing.

Among the parents I meet at school programs, more and more seem to be struggling, fundamentally, with the tension between their own personal fulfillment and their children's development that I described in Chapter Nine. They are hungry for methods to solve current problems that are really symptoms of more basic issues (trying to get by on quality time, or feeling too guilty to set limits and say no, or being unable to let a teenager face the consequences of a bad decision, and so on). Not only does a tips-and-techniques approach not resolve these deeper dilemmas, it perpetuates them; it provides a kind of cover for disinvesting in children. It helps parents, as described in Chapter Eight, define down children's needs for security and contact. It also allows parents to kid themselves, to imagine that applying the right methods at the right moment can substitute for a fundamental engagement with children. But only genuine engagement can confirm for children in ways beyond words that their parents care enough to give the very best—of themselves—to one another and to their children.

Educators see the necessity for more direct parenting and home-making by parents, but don't feel they can press parents to reshape their lives. After all, it is not the school's business to tell parents how to live and teachers and principals know that many parents can't exert much control over their work schedules. Schools can, however, help parents by presenting programs that encourage them to make small, doable increases in nurture, structure, and latitude.

Nurture: More and Mr. Rogers

The place to begin is where development does, with nurture. Parents can start by raising the "nurture ratio" in the household, that is, by reversing the decline of direct parenting and abandoning the myths of quality time and family efficiency. The short form of what is likely to benefit most children is "more and Mr. Rogers"—more time overall and more of it that includes the virtues Mr. Rogers embodied.

Nurture doesn't require rare skill, but it does require being present, being available to and engaged with a child. A sufficient and relatively predictable amount of time—freely given, not frantically squeezed—brings many gains that help a child feel not just loved but cared for. It allows for the fact that the needs of children are unpredictable, nonrational, and can't be scripted; it permits teaching and modeling; it avoids the disabling pressure to make every moment positive; it enhances relationships with children and makes children more responsive to discipline; and it puts money in the bank for the times when a parent must provide structure and set limits.

An overall sufficiency of time permits a mother and father to know their child better and thus to improve their attunement. When a parent and child see each other relatively little and on an inconsistent basis, each has a harder time learning to "read" the other. It is more difficult for them to establish patterns of communication, spoken and unspoken, that let them come to take each other for granted in positive ways, to be confident about how the other will react.

Better attunement and a more nurturant emotional link between parent and child facilitate not just nurture but the provision of structure and latitude. Just as guilt about not being with children enough inhibits parents' willingness to provide structure, confidence that they have spent time makes it easier for them to hold the line when they need to. It makes a deposit in the relationship account, so to speak, a balance on which parents can then draw when they must forbid a pleasure or insist on an obligation. And since well-nurtured children are on the whole less willing to risk their parents' displeasure and more likely to obey, investing in nurture makes the limits-and-discipline part of childrearing easier.

A decent balance in the relationship bank also helps latitude. Giving children sufficient freedom to learn from experience depends on—and contributes to—confidence in both parent and child. It is easier for a father to let a daughter learn from safe mistakes and do her own age-appropriate problem-solving when he has some confi-

dence in her. This is true whether she is a nine-year-old going off
to overnight camp or a fourteen-year-old who has a personality
clash with her math teacher. When the father has spent enough
time with his daughter to really know her, it is in most instances
easier for him to be more confident about her. In most circumstances a well-nurtured child is herself more likely to be confident
and willing to tackle a challenge, and to be resilient and able to persist in the face of adversity, which in turn will strengthen the parent's confidence in her, and so on.

If one basic minimum is increasing the quantity of contact, the
other is shifting its quality. The simplest way to summarize the re-
direction is to say that most children could benefit from more
Mr. Rogers in their lives. By this I mean more time spent with parents that is not primarily about production and performance, competition and achievement. Too many children have far too much
of that already. The time I'm recommending is not aimed at accelerating skills, but at *being with* children, enjoying them, listening to
them, telling stories to them, playing games they want to play,
teaching by example and occasionally by precept when a moment
presents itself, but not in a primary, formal way.

Mr. Rogers was surely interested in your growth and the expansion
of your skills, and he liked to show you things, but his focus was not
on making you be better, or indeed on making you produce or achieve
anything. He wanted to be with you, and when he was with you,
he was "consistent, patient, respectful, and pleasingly repetitive," as
one writer described him. In this connection, I think of a nursery
school director who told Arlie Russell Hochschild why she liked
classroom aides hired from Mexico, Guatemala, and the Philippines.
"[They] know how to love a child better than the middle-class white
parents. They are more relaxed, patient, and joyful. They enjoy the
kids more. These professional parents are pressured for time and anxious to develop their kids' talents. I tell the parents that they can
really learn how to love from the Latinas and the Filipinas."[6] Programs for parents would do best to help them introduce more of

these qualities into their childrearing, to ease up rather than gear up, to listen rather than instruct, to enjoy rather than achieve.

Secondary school teachers may wonder how this kind of talk would be relevant to their students' parents. Teenagers, after all, are not demanding, "Nurture me more; spend more time with me," and they're certainly not into Mr. Rogers. But none of us, as I have said, ever outgrow the need for nurture, even though we seek and receive it in different ways as we move through the life cycle. As children grow up and move into the world of school and peers, then reach puberty and move toward adulthood, they not only take with them the lessons of their early nurture, they need their parents to remain available—not always as actively engaged as before, but still present. They need to rely on a bedrock sense of being loved and supported even as they try to separate themselves and become more independent. They still turn to mom and dad for all sorts of reassurance, guidance, testing, and problem solving. They may do so with a chip on one shoulder, or in the mode of a help-rejecting complainer ("I need your assistance; nothing you suggest is right"). Their mood shifts may be mercurial. They may tell parents to stay away, but they don't mean far away. Like all of us, they are comforted and more confident when they know that their parents are available, responsive, and in touch.

Structure: Trillin's Second law

Improving the provision of structure does not require parents to transform themselves into hard-nosed disciplinarians or nit-picking fanatics. It asks them to establish and enforce the core values that are to guide their children's behavior and conduct, to be as clear as they can about the key outlines of the box within which they want the children to grow up—not to fill the box with detailed lists, but to be clear about its boundaries. For me, the simplest way to approach this is through what, at the risk of overdoing it, I would call

Trillin's Second Law: *lenient on small things, strict on big ones; differences in style but not in values.*

Trillin recalls a study he once read that compared parents in New York's Chinatown with white middle-class parents in Massachusetts. The researchers found the Chinese parents to be more permissive in many respects, especially about small matters, such as whether a child left his room untidy, or neglected minor household chores, or stayed up past his bedtime. But they were quite strict about issues that were very important to them, such as "fighting with or tormenting or belittling a sibling [in which case] the Chinatown parents were murder. They simply wouldn't stand for it."[7] Trillin observes that marriages that last a long time "are often unions of people with different tastes and similar values" and adds, "It isn't difficult to adjust to any difference, as long as it's a difference that rests on taste or style or personality. . . . Adjusting to differences in values would be another matter. After the girls were grown, Alice [his wife] decided that, in retrospect, we did have a child-rearing policy, similar to the policy used by Chinatown parents in that study I'd read about: we were lenient about small matters and strict about large ones. We never had to talk about which were which."[8]

This offers a doubly excellent template for structure in raising children. First, it concentrates on key priorities, not a laundry list of tasks and rules. What matters is not so much which particular issues parents find most important but that they communicate a common message about those issues—in other words, that they define their core values, the nonnegotiables that define membership in their family, and that they consistently emphasize these. This provides a framework for children's behavior and helps them acquire the more general sense of the importance of a framework, even if, when they are eventually raising children of their own, they adopt one that differs from their parents'. Second, it addresses the most common questions that arise whenever parents are advised to improve structure and limits: "What if my spouse and I have different styles of dealing with our kids? What if we don't agree on the values we want to instill in them?" My answer, like Trillin's, is that the first is not a problem but the second is.

Differences in parenting style are not just common, they are almost inevitable and reflect many factors, including gender and personality, among others. They cause static in the parental relationship and can spark occasional friction, but when this occurs within a larger context that is sufficiently clear and harmonious about core values, it doesn't damage children. In fact, it permits them to see that many differences between parents are of a safe, containable kind, and so creates a model for tolerance and negotiation that will stand them in good stead when they become parents themselves.

Of course, not every couple agrees so readily about the large matters as Calvin and Alice Trillin apparently did. In my experience, when a mother and father have very different values and thus handle structure (and, often, nurture and latitude) very differently from each other, children's development can be seriously compromised because it lacks the core consistency that makes life predictable and meaningful. Value differences lead to lots of miscommunication and misunderstanding and to children playing one parent off against the other.

Trying to resolve value conflicts also presents serious difficulties to the parents, because values are so personal and so deeply felt and are not easily amenable to rational analysis and persuasion. Nonetheless, when parents disagree about the large matters, nothing is more important than to try to overcome—or at least reduce—their division. This kind of talking usually needs more than just a heart-to-heart and it certainly needs more than attending a program at school. It typically requires a skilled third party such as a psychotherapist, who can both mediate the discussions and offer an informed perspective on the couple's issues.

For those who do share values in common and who seek a place to improve the structure they provide for their children, there is an effective place to begin: by not selling out. If parents find themselves consistently—not occasionally, but repeatedly—giving in on a limit that is truly important to them, backing away from a commitment that genuinely matters to them, they should ask themselves why, and consider how they might begin to hold the line. The chances are that their cowardice is making them feel guilty and that they wish they could assert themselves in a meaningful way. The longer they wait, the harder it will be. If their child is used to their giving in, they will probably need to provide advance notice of their change of heart instead of just springing it full-blown. (In this case they might announce something like "We haven't been insisting on X because we know that you'll dislike it, but it is really important to us and we want you to know we're going to start insisting on it, as of now.")

One issue about which parents have strong feelings but often sell out is TV. This is a place where they could, if they chose, help their children's personal, social, and academic development by controlling what and when children watch. In a more general vein, research has suggested three areas where parents can very helpfully assert themselves and frame a box for their children, areas that become more important as adolescence looms: knowing where the kids are, how they spend their money, and who their friends are.[9]

This finding from a well-known study made immediate sense to me when I first encountered it, because these conditions were nonnegotiables for my parents when I was growing up. They rarely refused me permission to go out with my friends on a weekend night, for example, but they always had to know where I was going to be. When I started out as a psychologist I took it for granted that most parents knew where their teens went, with whom, and what they spent their money on. I soon realized how naive I had been, that a great many parents had no idea about these things. As with almost every facet of parenting, it is very difficult, if not fruitless, to wait until a child reaches adolescence to begin insisting on them. And it is entirely fruitless for parents to announce conditions they don't intend to monitor and enforce. When parents mean what they say, children almost always know and it almost always affects their behavior.

Needless to say, there is no way to set firm limits like these without causing at least periodic bad feeling and friction. This is not just inevitable, it is useful. For young people to develop a strong sense of identity they need parents to be adults to them. This does not mean being cruel or harsh or unkind. It means acknowledging that children need to be socialized and accepting responsibility for that task. There is no way to do this and keep children perpetually happy with themselves and their parents. If youth are to become upright adults, they must learn, as Elkind says, that deeds are tied to motives and consequences.[10] Teaching this lesson requires parents to tolerate children's anger and dislike; holding the line on important issues rarely makes one popular. But the ultimate point of parenting is not to have children *like* us all the time, but to have them *be like* us when they are raising their own children. And when parents do try to set limits but can't bear having children be upset, they create an impossible situation, conveying, in essence, a paradoxical message: "You must do what I say and not have negative feelings toward me even though I have upset you." Parents certainly have a right to limit how children express their dislike, but not to expect that children not feel natural disappointment or resentment. What they need to do is let their children "get glad again."

The phrase is my mother's. Sometimes, when she just seemed impossibly rigid, when my sister and brother and I thought she was wildly unfair and told her so, she would say, "Well, I guess you'll just have to get glad again," and walk off. Instead of arguing further (so that we could convince her or make her feel sorry for us and give in) she just stopped negotiating. She wasn't upset, she didn't yell. She said it matter-of-factly and left the room. It was, I suppose, her version of "Because your goddamn father says so." It made me furious—temporarily. I used to think to myself, "I'll teach her. I won't get glad again. Not ever." But of course I always did. Children always do. But even if they didn't, there still isn't much else a parent can say after explaining the reasons for a decision and repeating them a time or two. As long as the decision is consistent, in a broad, general way, with established family practices and core values, it is unlikely to harm the children. Even if they hate it they will be able to make sense out of it. And as long as parents can remember that children's dislike is temporary and can let them get glad again, they can be truer to themselves and give their children a framework for growing up and for being parents themselves.

Latitude

The key to helping parents improve latitude is to help them moderate the résumé-building and the self-esteem paradox explored in Chapter Seven. Achievement, resilience, and self-esteem do not result, as many parents have come to believe, from an early, sustained focus on performance, winning, and praise but much more from an emphasis on effort, perseverance, and facing up to meaningful challenges. When parents try to fast-track their children, to arrange a life of constant success and vigilant avoidance of negative experiences, they often end up hindering the very outcomes they seek. What children truly need are the freedom and the encouragement to tackle age-appropriate obstacles on their own, and to learn from the results of their efforts, whatever these may be. They need, in short, greater latitude, more support for their autonomy. As with nurture and structure, small steps in this area can make a meaningful difference, but here the primary task is itself paradoxical: more latitude means less intervention.

Children of all ages benefit when parents do not lock them into an overscheduled and overachieving mode, signing them up for too many activities and pressing them too hard to be competitively

successful—pursuing, from early on, reputation rather than pleasure, as Postman says. The emphasis, especially in the early years,
should be on enjoyment and exploration, on fun and skill-building,
not on cutthroat competition and burnishing a résumé. Few children benefit from participating in more than one or two out-of-
school activities at any given time. One should be the limit if it
involves a heavy time commitment, and in adolescence, if students
take advantage of school-based teams and activities, there is even
less justification for major out-of-school involvements. (Remember
that the question is not whether young people can tolerate multiple commitments, but whether this is good for them. Some children
do truly thrive in multiple simultaneous pursuits at high levels, but
they are rare.) As for competition, there is no need to ignore its natural expression in children or to sterilize youth sports. Everyone
likes to win, and the motivation to win can encourage skill development. The key is to keep this emphasis within bounds, to avoid
Vince Lombardi-ism, and not to conduct six-year-old soccer with
pre-Olympic intensity.

If "less is more" represents one way to improve latitude, another
would be "Don't Just Do Something, Stand There." I first heard this
phrase from a mentor of mine in my early days as a psychologist,
who used it as a warning against depriving teenagers of latitude. Too
many parents, he noted, intervene too hastily to solve their teens'
problems, many of which they are actually helpless to fix, and many
of which the teens would best solve on their own. In this view, parents should listen first, and then, if needed, help with problem solving, preferably by encouraging the young person to participate in
the solution, wherever appropriate. This approach involves three
simple steps: don't always take a child's problem literally, hear the
child out, and give the child a chance to do the problem-solving,
or at least to participate in it.

The first of these seems to be harder and harder for parents. A
thirteen-year-old son may come home from school morose and tear-
ful and announce, "No one likes me. I don't have any friends." A

sixteen-year-old daughter may come home complaining that the varsity basketball coach is unfair and putting lesser players ahead of her. In each case, parents can be sure that something has happened, but don't know what. If they ask, they will hear the stories—from the perspectives of the teens. It is vital not to assume that these versions are fully accurate and then spring into action. For one thing, all children see their lives through a very subjective personal lens. If parents take the daughter literally and call the coach to complain about her unfairness, they will be doing so without having heard the coach's side of the story. More important, many of the problems children encounter don't need intervention, they need attention. Quite often, even as older adolescents, children just need to tell parents the dilemma, they need to recite it, relive it, rework it, vent their frustrations about it, voice their worries about it. They don't always need actual advice.

This eases a great burden and minimizes the chances of making things worse. Frequently, especially as children get older, the problems they present are ones parents can't fix. (How can a father or mother go about making friends for a thirteen-year-old who feels no one likes him?) Not having to be the omniscient, omnipotent fixer is a great relief. It can free a parent to be more empathic. Moreover, it lessens the risk of compounding the distress. Hastening to give advice can actually add to children's frustration. Lots of quarrels start out with a child presenting a dilemma, a parent suggesting a course of action, the child rejecting this, the parent insisting, and so on. Often, advice is something we parents offer mainly to relieve our own anxiety and helplessness. (Fathers, in my experience, tend to shift more rapidly into a problem-solving mode and are more prone than mothers to premature suggestion.)

Much more helpful to children of all ages is to start by standing there—that is, by attending to the child and engaging actively, but as a listener and explorer first and only then, if necessary, as a fixer. In one way or another, the key first message to convey is, "Tell me more; keep talking." The telling itself is a key part of the relief the child experiences; it immediately makes her less alone with the problem, especially one that is serious and difficult. And happily, the mere telling is often enough. Whether the child is a teen who has had a falling out with a group of friends or a toddler who has broken a favorite toy, it is remarkable how quickly she can recover once her burden and the feelings that come with it are aired.

In the course of hearing the child's story, there comes at least one choice point, a moment where a parent must decide whether to intervene and if so, how. This is rarely a conscious choice, but it could be. If there were a magical way to stop the action temporarily and think through the options, we could ask ourselves, among other questions, Does this problem, however intensely the child experiences it, need to be solved right away? Does it represent an opportunity to learn, safely, an important lesson? Would the child benefit from struggling with it? (This would be especially important if it involved a bad decision or misbehavior.) In the moment, unable to freeze the frame, we don't pause to ask ourselves all these questions, we just react. This is unavoidable. There is, however, a good, straightforward, learnable way to preserve latitude. It is to ask some version of, "What do you think you might do about this?" Inviting the child to present his plan if he has one (and to think about a plan if he hasn't) encourages autonomy and problem-solving. If the solution he proposes seems unwise and his parents have a better possibility, or he has no idea what to do and they do have one, they should certainly offer theirs.

This approach requires patience, to be sure, but the patience of a gardener, not the patience of a saint or the ministrations of a therapist.[11] Often, children seek help about problems that are direct and obvious or for which parents have a ready solution; they should offer it. At times, young people just want to be told what to do or how to act, not to figure it out for themselves; parents should tell them. And there are times when they have gotten themselves into trouble and parents can't resist bailing them out; they should do so. It is a *consistent pattern* of solving and telling and bailing out that limits latitude in a negative way. Similarly, there is no benefit in trying to be therapeutic with one's children, exploring all the subtleties of their thoughts and feelings about every issue they encounter. They can be driven to distraction (and to silence) by parents who need to know the nuances of their every reaction to every problem. Being available when they do need us and being able to tune in and listen when a big issue occurs is usually sufficient.

Talking Straight

These steps are by no means the only effective ones parents might take—the complete list would be very long—but they already test the "technique won't save you" principle. Schools need to offer programs that stay real about parenting. In Chapter Fourteen, I noted the importance of teachers' talking straight and being candid in conferences with parents. Talking straight is also important in parent education programs. This means many things. One is starting early. Virtually everything that helps parents manage an adolescent needs to begin prior to adolescence. It doesn't work, for example, to suddenly start providing structure when a child turns thirteen. This doesn't suggest that high schools abandon all efforts at parent education, but it does argue for a school district's concentrating its efforts on parents of preschool and elementary students.

Talking straight means reminding parents that the most powerful, enduring lessons they teach are through the example they set, not the sermons they preach and the counsel they offer. Care and teaching, as noted earlier, are inseparable. The latter occurs automatically in the course of the former. The deepest way for parents to think about influencing children is to consider what they are modeling.

Finally, talking straight means respecting resilience. Implicit in useful programs for parents is confidence in the growth potential of children who receive good-enough childrearing. Nurture, structure, and latitude all support a child's natural coping ability. They help children develop their own strengths and confidence, including their ability to learn and grow, to reach out and find help when they need it, to tolerate adversity when they must, to learn from life, and to rebound from disappointment. Even when life events, family losses, and other difficulties conspire against them, children can often adapt well if the three developmental essentials are in place. Schools can best help parents by encouraging them to resist the addiction to technique and attend in small but consistent ways to nurture, structure, and latitude. The parents who do so are certain to make a positive difference in their children's lives.

Notes

Introduction

1. Elkind, 1994, p. 8.
2. Comer, 1997, p. 89.
3. Commission on Children at Risk, 2003, p. 10.

Chapter 1

1. Gewertz, 2001, p. 1.
2. D'Auria, 1995, p. 152.
3. National Commission on the Role of the Schools and the Community in Improving Adolescent Health, 1990, p. 3.
4. Commission on Children at Risk, 2003, pp. 5, 68–75.
5. Yankelovich, 1999, pp. 32–34, citing various sources; Farkas, 1997.
6. Vaishnav, 2000, p. A1; Edds, 2003, p. A3.

Chapter 2

1. For more on the concept of mastery, see MacTurk and Morgan, 1995.
2. Popenoe, 1996, p. 12.
3. Most researchers have identified two principal dimensions of parenting, one having to do with support, warmth, affection, responsiveness, and encouragement, the other with control, supervision,

and limit setting (Amato and Booth, 1997, p. 17). These two include what I identify here as a third, latitude, which refers to parents' support for and tolerance of children's freedom to learn from experience and to express themselves (see Coopersmith, 1967).

4. Furstenberg and Hughes, 1997, p. 43.

5. Kagan, 1984, p. 253.

6. Popenoe, 1996, p. 14.

7. Kaye, 1983.

8. Taylor, 2002, pp. 39–40. On the concept of infant-mother attachment as an evolved biobehavioral system, see Bowlby, 1953, and Ainsworth, Blehar, Waters, and Wall, 1978.

9. Bruner, 1983, p. 86, citing Kaye, 1983.

10. Stern, 1987.

11. Kagan, 1984, p. 108.

12. Taylor, 2002, p. 40.

13. Shonkoff and Phillips, 2000, p. 29. See also Rothbaum and others, 2000.

14. Kagan, 1998, pp. 115, 113.

15. Rathbun, DiVirgilio, and Waldfogel, 1958; Winick, Meyer, and Harris, 1975.

16. Shonkoff and Phillips, 2000, pp. 5, 90.

17. Goleman, 1995, pp. 81–82; Shoda, Mischel, and Peake, 1990.

18. Damon, 1995, p. 74.

19. Bednar, Wells, and Peterson, 1989, p. 278. See also Baumeister, Campbell, Krueger, and Vohs, 2003.

20. National Public Radio, 2003.

21. Bednar, Wells, and Peterson, 1989, p. 266.

22. Kagan, 1998, p. 92.

23. Goleman, 1995, p. 80.

24. Winnicott, 1992; Winnicott and Winnicott, 1982.

25. Kagan, 1984, p. 252.

26. When I speak of what is good for or best for children I mean *American* children, unless otherwise specified.

Chapter 3

1. Baumrind, 1991, p. 62. See also Baumrind 1971, 1978, 1982, 1989.

2. Steinberg, 1996, pp. 118–120.

3. Steinberg, 1996, pp. 109–110; Kagan, 1984, pp. 205, 260–262; Arcus, 1991.

4. Steinberg, 1996, p. 108; Amato and Booth, 1997, p. 17.

5. Taylor, 2002, pp. 121–123. So, too, with the neurobiology of sexuality. In males the brain circuitry that promotes sexual behavior is located close to the circuitry that promotes aggression, whereas for women the sexuality circuits are intertwined with those that affect maternal nurturing.

6. Popenoe, 1996, p. 140. For more on these male and female differences see Lamb, Pleck, Charnov, and Levine, 1987.

7. Maccoby, 1998, p. 262.

8. Youniss and Smollar, 1985, pp. 89–91; Maccoby, 1998, p. 271.

9. Popenoe, 1996, pp. 143–144; Maccoby, 1998, p. 267.

10. Maccoby, 1998, pp. 274–275, 283–284.

11. Maccoby, 1998, p. 257; Amato and Booth, 1997, p. 20; Goldstein, 1982, pp. 843–848; Coley, 2001, p. 749.

12. Taylor, 2002, p. 226.

13. Steinberg, 1987, pp. 269–275.

14. Maccoby, 1998, p. 278; Popenoe, 1996, p. 142.

15. Popenoe, 1996, p. 159.

16. Koestner, Franz, and Weinberger, 1990, pp. 709–717; Popenoe, 1996, p. 149.

17. Amato, 1994, pp. 1031–1042. See also Snarey, 1993.

18. Baumrind, 1982, p. 44.

19. Putnam, 2000, p. 19.

20. Sampson, Raudenbush, and Earls, 1997, pp. 918–924.

21. Putnam has constructed a Social Capital Index of the fifty states, based on surveys that measure such things as people's expressed trust in their fellow citizens, the rates at which they join organizations, volunteer, vote, socialize with their friends, and so on. States that score high in these categories are the ones where children are better off, as measured by low rates of infant mortality, child abuse, teenage pregnancy, school dropout, crime, homicide, and suicide. They are also the states whose students score highest on standardized tests—even allowing for such factors as race, poverty, parent educational levels, school spending, class size, and so on (Putnam, 2000, pp. 296–302, citing Bronfenbrenner, Moen, and Garbarino, 1984).

22. Judith Rich Harris (1998) makes the radical argument that parents have virtually no impact on children's behavior except within the context of family relationships, that a child's personality and behavior in the rest of life are shaped by a combination of genetic tendencies and children's own peer socialization together. Rowe (1994) makes the same kind of claim and Pinker (2002) has vigorously supported it. Research evidence to the contrary, however, abounds. This is one area where evolutionary, sociobiological, and genetic theorists have, I think, gone overboard, relying on simplistic additive definitions of personality and simplistic blunt methods for measuring it. For thoughtful critiques of their view, see Gardner, 1998; Collins and others, 2000; Maccoby, 2000, 2002; and Menand, 2002. Many studies of both humans and animals confirm the direct and decisive impact of parents on their offspring, including Conger, Cui, Bryant, and Elder, 2000; Schiff, Duyme, Dumaret, and Tomkiewitz, 1982; Kagan, 1994; and Cowan and Cowan, 2002. See also Sroufe, 2002; Suomi, 1997, 2002; Anisman, Zaharia, Meaney, and Merali, 1998; Caldji and others, 1998; and Liu and others, 1997.

23. Dodge, Coie, Pettit, and Price, 1990; see also Coie, Dodge, and Kupersmidt, 1990, and Coie and others, 1995.

24. See Ogbur, 2003; Steinberg, 1996, pp. 132–136, and Belluck, 2000, p. 1.

25. Tocqueville, [1835] 2001.

26. Bronfenbrenner, 1972, pp. 99–100.

27. Elkind, 1998, p. 241.

28. See Parke and Bhavnagri, 1989; Devereux, 1970; Dishion, Patterson, Stoolmiller, and Skinner, 1991; Fuligni and Eccles, 1993; Mounts and Steinberg, 1995; Collins and others, 2000, pp. 227–228.

Chapter 4

1. Coontz, 1992.

2. This and the preceding paragraph draw heavily on Hernandez, 1993, pp. 99–105 and 417–418; on Coontz, 1992, pp. 25 and 39; and on Cherlin, 1992, p. 25.

3. Popenoe, 1996, pp. 23, 38–39.

4. Postman, 1994, p. 67.

5. Reich, 2001, p. 174.

6. I recommend particularly three of Elkind's books, 1981, 1994, and 1998.

7. Lugaila, 1998; Halpern, Fernandez, and Clark, 2000; Vandivere, Moore, and Zaslow, 2000.

8. Hewlitt and West, 1998, p. 49; Hernandez, 1993, pp. 423–424.

9. Hochschild, 2003, p. 1.

10. McLanahan and Sandefur, 1994, pp. 2, 45; Hernandez, 1993, pp. 420–421; Dawson, 1991, pp. 573, 578; Sheline, Skipper, and Broadhead, 1994; Hanson, 1999; McNeal, 1999; Sandefur, McLanahan, and Wojtkiewicz, 1992. Students who misbehave violently in school are eleven times more likely to come from a fatherless, single-mother home.

11. Dawson, 1991; Stanton, Tian, Oci, and Silva, 1994; Remez, 1992; Zill and Schoenborn, 1990; Popenoe, 1996, pp. 57–58, citing a list of relevant studies. Father-absent boys are more likely to show as

adults an endocrine profile of lowered testosterone and raised cortisol, which is common among anxious subordinates in male primate groups. They are also more likely to be seen as deficient in basic social skills (Taylor, 2002, p. 194; Tucker and others, 1997; Flinn and England, 1997).

12. See McLanahan and Sandefur, 1994, for a thorough—and sobering—review of the research on the impact on children of growing up without married parents.

13. There is abundant evidence, drawn not just from the U.S. but from a number of countries, that stepfathers are, as one research team found, "massively over-represented as perpetrators of both sexual and physical abuse." See Daly and Wilson, 1987, pp. 228–230, and 1999, pp. 30–32, 50; Russell, 1984, pp. 15–22.

14. Based on Elkind, 1994.

15. Taylor, 2002, pp. 54–57; Repetti, Taylor, and Seeman, 2002.

16. Elkind, 1994, pp. 38, 119, 146.

Chapter 5

1. Shorter, 1977.

2. Elkind, 1994, pp. 41–42, 48–49.

3. Swidler, 1980, p. 136.

4. Popenoe, 1996, p. 24, citing Yankelovich survey.

5. Kagan, 1984, p. 245.

6. Putnam, 2000, p. 100.

7. Bowlby, 1953, p. 16.

8. Hewlitt and West, 1998, pp. 48–49.

9. Hochschild, 1997, p. 6; Hewlitt, 1992, p. 91.

10. Fuchs, 1988, p. 111; Reich, 2001, p. 119.

11. Ehrle, Adams, and Tout, 2001.

12. Hochschild, 1997, p. 10, citing several sources.

13. Hewlitt, 1992, p. 81.

14. There are also researchers (Barnett and Hyde, 2001; Baruch, Barnett, and Rivers, 1987) who argue that children not only

survive day care and dual-career parenting readily but that these offer positive benefits: working can improve the well-being of mothers who would otherwise feel unfulfilled and make them good role models for their daughters. My clinical experience leaves me unsure about these assertions, and unsure that claimed benefits outweigh the costs of depriving *very young* children of substantial, regular, traditional parental care. But even if they do ultimately prove to be correct, they endorse the postmodern value of autonomy. There is no way to argue that dual careers and nonparental child care promote togetherness and child-centeredness in the family.

15. National Institute of Child Health and Human Development, Early Child Care Research Network, 1999.

16. Brooks-Gunn, Han, and Waldfogel, 2002.

17. National Institute of Child Health and Human Development, Early Child Care Research Network, 2003; Sylva and others, 2003.

18. Elkind, 1994, p. 56

19. Elkind, 1994, p. 56.

20. Hochschild, 1997, p. 224; Ziegler and Lang, 1991, p. 122; Capizzano, Tout, and Adams, 2000; Fox and Newman, 1997, p. 6; Farkas, 1997; Schor, 1992, pp. 12–13.

21. Richardson and others, 1989 (see also Zill, 1983, and Vandell and Corasaniti, 1988); Resnick and others, 1997; Heymann and Earle, 1996.

22. Presentation on parenting at The Human Relations Service, Nov. 17, 2001. See Brazelton, 1994.

23. Putnam, 2000, p. 212, citing data from the Department of Transportation.

24. Csikszentmihalyi and Schmidt, 1998, p. 11; Csikszentmihalyi, Rathunde, and Whalen, 1993.

25. Hochschild, 1997, p. 212.

26. Hochschild, 1997, pp. 51, 215, 218.

27. Howe, 1994, p. 10.

28. Martin, 1999, p. 130.

29. Gray, 1995, p. 51.

Chapter 6

1. Elkind, 1994, p. 59.

2. Elkind, 1998, pp. 20–22.

3. Elkind, 1994, p. 145.

4. Elkind, 1998, p. 111; Postman, 1994, p. 4.

5. Steinberg, 1996, p. 167.

6. See Pappano, 2001, p. A6; LaFerla, 2000, pp. 1, 10; Anderman, 2000, p. D-2.

7. Blum and Rinehart, 1997; National Center on Addiction and Substance Abuse, 1999, p. 5; Jarrell, 2000, Section 9, p. 1; Purdum, 2000, 4, p. 1; Rich, 2001, p. 80.

8. Goodman and Goodman, 1999.

9. Roberts, Foehr, Rideout, and Brodie, 1999; Whitman, 1998, p. 33. Other studies find different levels of media and TV activity among children, but all are high. See also Jordan and Sullivan, 1997, and TV Turnoff Network (www.tvturnoff.org).

10. Singer and Singer, 1976, pp. 74–80; U.S. Surgeon General's Report, 1972; Burton, Calonico, and McSeveney, 1979, pp. 164–170.

11. Minority students are especially affected. Sixty-nine percent of black and 50 percent of Latino children watch at least four hours of TV per day, versus only 36 percent of white children. Jackson, 2001, p. A23; Roberts, Foehr, Rideout, and Brodie, 1999, p. 41.

12. Whitman, 1998, p. 32.

13. Kunkel, 2000.

14. Yankelovich, 1999, pp. 32–34, citing various sources; Farkas, 1997; Jordan and Sullivan, 1997, and TV Turnoff Network (www.tvturnoff.org); Putnam, 2000, p. 223; Roberts, Foehr, Rideout, and Brodie, 1999.

15. Postman, 1994, pp. 72, 86.

16. Postman, 1994, pp. 85–86.

17. Mitchell, Finkelhor, and Wolak, 2001, pp. 3011–3014.

18. Zirkel, 2001b, pp. 717–718.

19. Stoll (1999, p. 88) is actually quoting another writer's attack on television, but presents the citation as equally relevant to the Internet. See also Bray, 2002.

20. D. Evans, 2002, p. 37.

Chapter 7

1. Kraus, [1971] 1998.

2. Bruer, 1999, p. 62.

3. Bruer, 1999, pp. 86–87; Ridley, 2000, pp. 231–232.

4. Notable examples include the work of Theodore Sizer, 1992, and Howard Gardner, 1993.

5. Students who seek such accommodations come disproportionately from well-off suburbs, and in a group of top-notch private schools the rate of such students was four times the national average, suggesting that many of the families were "upper-income game players" (Zirkel, 2001a, p. 639).

6. Gross, 1998, pp. 37–38.

7. Postman, 1994, pp. 4, 129–130.

8. Powers, 2001, p. A32; Gehring, 2001, pp. 6–7; National Alliance for Youth Sports (http://www.nays.org/). See also Edds, 2003, p. A3.

9. Wong, 2001.

10. Luthar and Becker, 2002.

11. Straight, 2001, pp. 13–14.

12. Kantrowitz and Wingert, 2001, p. 52.

13. Kluger, 2001, p. 50.

14. Powers, 2001, p. A32; National Alliance for Youth Sports, 2001.

15. Kohn, 1999; Mueller and Dweck, 1998.

Chapter 8

1. Putnam, 2000, p. 258–259.

2. Fukuyama, 1999, pp. 5–6, 12, 25.

3. Wallulis, 1998, pp. 2–3.

4. Hochschild, 2001, pp. 62–63.

5. For a good start on this literature, see Reich, 2001, and Hochschild, 1997—this chapter draws heavily on both—and also Fukuyama, 1999; Putnam, 2000; Frank, 1999; Schor, 1992; Hewlitt, 1992; and Hewlitt and West, 1998.

6. Schor, 1992, pp. 2, 29; Reich, 2001, p. 112; Uchitelle, 1999, p. BU 4; Walsh, 2000, p. 28; Armour, 1997, p. 1; Putnam, 2000, p. 213; Lawlor, 1997, p. 10; McDowell, 1999, p. 16; Ward, 1997, p. 12F; Lauria, 1999, p. E1.

7. Schor's findings on overwork sparked challenges about how much actual work people are doing, but the evidence is overwhelming that they spend much more time *being at work*, which inevitably means less time being with the family. See Frank (1999, p. 50) for additional references.

8. Reich, 2001, pp. 5–6, 17, 93–94; Frank, 1999, p. 33.

9. Reich, 2001, p. 7, emphasis in original.

10. Reich, 2001, pp. 83–85, 98–103.

11. Wallulis, 1998, p. 7.

12. McGinn, 2003, p. 58.

13. Reich, 2001, p. 156.

14. Reich, 2001, p. 5; Shellenbarger, 1998, p. B-1; Hochschild, 1997, pp. 199–200.

15. Schor, 1992, pp. 22–23.

16. Schor, 1992, p. 112; see also p. 127.

17. Tocqueville, [1835] 2001, p. 211.

18. Veblen, [1899] 1994, p. 74.

19. Schor, 1992, pp. 3, 107, 110–111; Frank, 1999, pp. 14–32.

20. Schor, 1992, p. 120; Brickman and Campbell, 1971. For decades pollsters have asked Americans how much money they would need to fulfill their dreams. The answer has generally been, in essence, "twice what I make now"—no matter how much that is ("The Boomer Balancing Act," 1996).

21. Myers, 2000, p. 61, citing a range of studies. See also Schor, 1992, p. 115; Diener, Suh, Lucas, and Smith, 1999.

22. See Hochschild, 1997, pp. 11, 25, 28, 33, 249.

23. Kanter, 1989, p. 271.

24. Hewlitt, 1992, pp. 93–97.

25. Hochschild, 1997, pp. 45–50, 74–75, 199.

26. Hewlitt, 1992; A. A. Brooks, 1989.

27. Hewlitt, 1992, p. 108.

28. Hochschild, 2003, p. 29.

29. Hewlitt and West, 1998, p. 28.

30. Hochschild, 1997, p. 228.

Chapter 9

1. See Fukuyama, 1999, p. 14. This chapter draws heavily on Fukuyama and on Putnam, 2000.

2. This paragraph draws heavily on Kagan, 1984, pp. 242–245.

3. Putnam, 2000.

4. Popenoe, 1996, p. 118.

5. Schwartz, 2000, p. 85.

6. Fukuyama, 1999, pp. 88–89.

7. Yankelovich, 1999, p. 32.

8. The concept of creative destruction was developed by the economist Joseph Schumpeter (1950); see Fukuyama, 1999, pp. 5–6, 8.

9. Diamond, 1999, p. 18.

10. Fukuyama, 1999, pp. 5–6.

11. Fukuyama, 1999, p. 13.

12. Fukuyama, 1999, p. 102; Akerlof, Yellen, and Katz, 1996.

13. For a discussion of this, see Fukuyama, 1999, pp. 102–104.

14. Hewlitt, 1992, pp. 134–135, citing Yankelovich, 1981, p. 91. For a skewering of the recovery and self-help fads, see Kaminer, 1992.

15. Fukuyama, 1999, pp. 14–15.

16. Hewlitt, 1992, p. 122, citing Guttman, 1987, p. 198.

17. Flanagan, 2002, pp. 113–114.

18. Wolfe, 1999, pp. 110–111.

19. Wolfe, 1999, pp. 113–114.

20. D. Brooks, 2000, pp. 227–228. This paragraph also draws on Whitman, 1998, p. 88.

Chapter 10

1. Dryfoos, 1998, makes the case for "full-service schools."

2. For an overview of current SPED issues, see Berman, Davis, Koufman-Frederick, and Urion, 2001.

3. For critiques of the design and misuse of the high-stakes tests, see Elmore, 2002; Haney, 2002; and Ohanian, 2003. Gerald Bracey has also highlighted testing fallacies in his regular monthly Research column in *Phi Delta Kappan*.

4. The law's provisions are by now well known. Students must pass specific tests to graduate and schools whose scores do not show annual progress are threatened with all sorts of sanctions, such as having to pay for tutoring students who fail the test, or having to pay to transport students to other schools. Ultimately the principal and teachers can be dismissed or the school closed. The law is not just draconian but loopy. For example, school districts can be punished by having funds withheld if they don't hire a full complement of qualified, certified teachers, as though there are enough of these teachers available and districts have simply been refusing to hire them.

5. R. Evans, 1999.

6. Csikszentmihalyi, 1995, p. 107.

7. Belfield and Levin, 2002.

8. Coleman, 1966. See also Coleman, 1987a, 1987b, and Coleman and others, 1974.

9. Jencks and others, 1972, pp. 255–256.

10. Holt, [1964] 1995; Silberman, 1970; Kozol, 1990.

11. Edmonds, 1979, p. 23.

12. Rosenthal and Jacobson, 2003.

13. Barton and Coley, 1992.

14. Gallagher, 1998.

15. Robinson and Brandon, 1994.

16. Gardner, 2000. Zip Code is many ways a proxy for a community's social capital, which as noted, correlates highly with student scores (and behavior).

17. Armor, 2003, pp. 32–33.

18. See in this regard Frymier, 1992.

19. Barton and Coley, 1992, p. 4.

20. Howe, 1993, p. 32.

Chapter 11

1. For an overview of these kinds of programs, see Elias and others, 1997.

2. For contrasting views of character education, see Kohn, 1998; Lickona, 1991; and Ryan and Bohlin, 1999.

3. See Elias and others, 1997. Two programs that have built strong followings among teachers are Open Circle (www.open-circle.org; Seigle, 2001) and the Responsive Classroom (Northeast Foundation for Children; www.responsiveclassroom.org).

4. R. Evans, 1996, pp. 206–209.

5. Glickman, 1993, pp. 8.

Chapter 12

1. One of the most respected is the National Network of Partnership Schools based at Johns Hopkins University. See also Epstein, 2002.

2. Finn, 1998, p. 23.

3. Nord, Brimhall, and West, 1998; Nord and West, 2001; Zill and Nord, 1994.

Chapter 13

1. R. Evans, 1996. See especially chapters 2 and 10.

2. R. Evans, 1996, pp. 21–26; Gould, 1991, p. 66.

3. R. Evans, 1996, chapter 6.

Chapter 14

1. Oremus, 2003.

2. Rogers, 1972.

3. Oremus, 2003.

Chapter 15

1. Csikszentmihalyi, 1995, p. 107.

2. Havel, 1993, p. 68.

3. Jencks and others, 1972, p. 256.

Appendix

1. Elkind, 1998, pp. 11–12, 248. Benjamin Spock's *Baby and Child Care* (1968) was the exemplar of this approach. See also Selma Fraiberg's *The Magic Years* (1959).

2. Elkind, 1998, pp. 14, 248.

3. Trillin, 1998, pp. 5–6.

4. Gopnik, Meltzoff, and Kuhl, 1999, p. 202.

5. Gopnik, Meltzoff, and Kuhl, 1999, p. 200.

6. Hochschild, 2003, p. 191.

7. Trillin, 1998, p. 8.

8. Trillin, 1998, pp. 49, 60.

9. Buchanan, Maccoby, and Dornbusch, 1992.

10. Elkind, 1998, pp. 243, 250.

11. White, 1966, p. 409.

References

Ainsworth, M., Blehar, M. C., Waters, E., and Wall, S. *Patterns of Attachment*. Hillsdale, N.J.: Erlbaum, 1978.

Akerlof, G., Yellen, J., and Katz, M. "An Analysis of Out-of-Wedlock Childbearing in the United States." *Quarterly Journal of Economics*, 1996, *111*, 277–317.

Amato, P. R. "Father-Child Relations, Mother-Child Relations, and Offspring Psychological Well-Being in Early Adulthood." *Journal of Marriage and the Family*, 1994, *56*, 1031–1042.

Amato, P. R., and Booth, A. *A Generation at Risk*. Cambridge, Mass.: Harvard University Press, 1997.

Anderman, J. "Lolitas with a Beat." *Boston Globe*, Jan. 23, 2000, pp. D-1, D-2.

Anisman, H., Zaharia, M. D., Meaney, M. J., and Merali, Z. "Do Early-Life Events Permanently Alter Behavioral and Hormonal Responses to Stressors?" *International Journal of Developmental Neuroscience*, 1998, *16*, 149–164.

Arcus, D. "The Experiential Modification of Temperamental Bias in Inhibited and Uninhibited Children." Unpublished doctoral dissertation, Harvard University, 1991.

Armor, D. J. "Environmental Effects on IQ: from the Family or from Schools?" *Education Week*, Nov. 19, 2003, pp. 32–33.

Armour, S. "Latest Victim of Downsizing Is the Lunch." *USA Today*, Nov. 21, 1997, p. 1.

Barnett, R. C., and Hyde, J. S. "Women, Men, Work, and Family." *American Psychologist*, 2001, *56*(10), 781–796.

Barton, E., and Coley, R. J. *America's Smallest School: The Family*. Princeton, N.J.: Educational Testing Service Policy Information Center, 1992. Available online: http://www.ets.org/research/pic/pir.html. Access date: Nov. 14, 2003.

Baruch, G., Barnett, R., and Rivers, C. *Lifeprints: New Patterns of Love and Work for Today's Women*. New York: Signet, 1987.

Baumeister, R. F., Campbell, J. D., Krueger, J. I., and Vohs, K. D. "Does High Self-Esteem Cause Better Performance, Interpersonal Success, Happiness or Healthier Lifestyles?" *Psychological Science in the Public Interest*, 2003, *4*, 1-44.

Baumrind, D. "Current Patterns of Parental Authority." *Developmental Psychology Monographs*, 1971, *41*(1), Part 2.

Baumrind, D. "Parental Disciplinary Patterns and Social Competence in Children." *Youth and Society*, 1978, *9*, 3.

Baumrind, D. "Are Androgynous Individuals More Effective Persons and Parents?" *Child Development*, 1982, *53*, 44–75.

Baumrind, D. "Rearing Competent Children." In W. Damon (ed.), *Child Development Today and Tomorrow*. San Francisco: Jossey-Bass, 1989.

Baumrind, D. "The Influence of Parenting Style on Adolescent Competence and Substance Use." *Journal of Early Adolescence*, 1991, *11*(1), 56–95.

Bednar, R. L., Wells, M. G., and Peterson, S. R. *Self-Esteem: Paradoxes and Innovations in Clinical Theory and Practice*. Washington, D.C.: American Psychological Association, 1989.

Belfield, C. R., and Levin, H. M. "Does the Supreme Court Ruling on Vouchers in Cleveland Really Matter for Education Reform?" National Center for the Study of Privatization in Education, Occasional Paper No. 50. New York: Teachers College, Columbia University, 2002.

Belluck, P. "Reason Is Sought for Lag by Blacks in School Achievement." *New York Times*, July 4, 2000, p. 1.

Berman, S., Davis, P., Koufman-Frederick, A., and Urion, D. "The Rising Costs of Special Education in Massachusetts: Causes and Effects." In C. E. Finn Jr., A. J. Rotherham, and C. R. Hokanson (eds.), *Rethinking Special Education for a New Century*. Washington, D.C.: Thomas B. Fordham Foundation and the Progressive Policy Institute, 2001.

Blum, R. W., and Rinehart, M. *Reducing the Risk: Connections That Make a Difference in the Lives of Youth*. Minneapolis: Division of General Pediatrics & Adolescent Health, University of Minnesota Adolescent Health Program, 1997.

"The Boomer Balancing Act: Baby Boomers Talk About Life and the American Dream." *Roper Starch Worldwide*, Aug. 1996, pp. 38–41.

Bowlby, J. *Child Care and the Growth of Love*. New York: Pelican, 1953.

Bray, H. "$37 M Buys Experiment in Schools." *Boston Globe*, Sept. 22, 2002, p. D1.

Brazelton, T. B. *Touchpoints: Your Child's Emotional and Behavioral Development.* Boulder, Colo.: Perseus, 1994.

Brickman, P., and Campbell, D. T. "Hedonic Relativism and Planning the Good Society." In M. H. Appley (ed.), *Adaptation-Level Theory.* New York: Academic Press, 1971.

Bronfenbrenner, U. *Two Worlds of Childhood, U.S. and U.S.S.R.* New York: Simon & Schuster, 1972.

Bronfenbrenner, U., Moen, P. and Garbarino, J. "Child, Family, and Community." In Ross D. Parke (ed.), *Review of Child Development Research.* Vol. 7. Chicago: University of Chicago Press, 1984.

Brooks, A. A. *Children of Fast-Track Parents.* New York: Viking, 1989.

Brooks, D. *Bobos in Paradise.* New York: Simon & Schuster, 2000.

Brooks-Gunn, J., Han, W., and Waldfogel, J. "Maternal Employment and Child Cognitive Outcomes in the First Three Years of Life: The NICHD Study of Early Child Care." *Child Development,* 2002, *73*(4), 1052–1072.

Bruer, J. T. *The Myth of the First Three Years of Life.* New York: Free Press, 1999.

Bruner, J. "State of the Child." *New York Review of Books,* Oct. 1983, *27,* 84–89.

Buchanan, C., Maccoby, E., and Dornbusch, S. "Adolescents and Their Families After Divorce: Three Residential Arrangements Compared." *Journal of Research on Adolescence,* 1992, *2,* 261–291.

Burton, S. G., Calonico, J. M., and McSeveney, D. R. "Effects of Preschool Television Watching on First-Grade Children." *Journal of Communication,* Summer 1979, pp. 164–170.

Caldji, C., Tannenbaum, B., Sharma, S., Francis, D., Plotsky, M., and Meaney, M. J. "Maternal Care During Infancy Regulates the Development of Neural Systems Mediating the Expression of Fearfulness in the Rat." *Proceedings of the National Academy of Science,* 1998, *95,* 5335–5340.

Capizzano, J., Tout, K., and Adams G. "Child Care Patterns of School-Age Children with Employed Mothers." Occasional Paper Number 41. Washington, D.C.: Urban Institute, 2000.

Cherlin, A. J. *Marriage, Divorce, and Remarriage.* Cambridge, Mass.: Harvard University Press, 1992.

Child Trends Databank. ADHA Indicators. Available online: http://www.childtrendsdatabank.org/indicators/76ADHD.cfm. Access date: Oct. 21, 2003.

Coie, J. D., Dodge, K. A., and Kupersmidt, J. B. "Peer Group Behavior and Social Status." In S. R. Asher and J. D. Coie (eds.), *Peer Rejection in Childhood.* New York: Cambridge University Press, 1990.

Coie, J. D., Terry, R., Lenox, K. F., Lochman, J. E., and Hyman, C. "Peer Rejection and Aggression as Predictors of Stable Risk Across Adolescence." *Development and Psychopathology*, 1995, 7, 697–713.

Coleman, J. S. *Equality of Educational Opportunity*. Washington, D.C.: U.S. Government Printing Office, 1966.

Coleman, J. S. "Families and Schools." *Educational Researcher*, 1987a, Aug.-Sept., pp. 36–37.

Coleman, J. S. *Public and Private High Schools: The Impact of Community*. New York: Basic Books, 1987b.

Coleman, J. S., and others. *Youth: Transition to Adulthood*. Report of the President's Science Advisory Committee Panel on Youth. Chicago: University of Chicago Press, 1974.

Coley, R. L. "(In)visible Men: Emerging Research on Low-Income, Unmarried, and Minority Fathers." *American Psychologist*, 2001, 56(9), 743–753.

Collins, W. A., Maccoby, E. E., Steinberg, L., Hetherington, E. M., and Bornstein, M. H. "The Case for Nature *and* Nurture." *American Psychologist*, 2000, 55(2), 218–232.

Comer, J. *Waiting for a Miracle*. New York: Dutton, 1997.

Commission on Children at Risk. *Hardwired to Connect: The New Scientific Case for Authoritative Communities*. New York: Institute for American Values, 2003.

Conger, R., Cui, M., Bryant, C., and Elder, G. "Competence in Early Romantic Relationships: A Developmental Perspective on Family Influences." *Journal of Personality and Social Psychology*, 2000, 79, 224–237.

Coontz, S. *The Way We Never Were*. New York: Basic Books, 1992.

Coopersmith, S. *The Antecedents of Self-Esteem*. San Francisco: Freeman, 1967.

Cowan, A., and Cowan, C. P. "What an Intervention Design Reveals About How Parents Affect Their Children's Academic Achievement and Social Competence." In J. Borkowski, D. Landesman-Ramey, and S. Bristol (eds.), *Parenting and the Child's World: Multiple Influences on Intellectual and Social-Emotional Development*. Mahwah, N.J.: Erlbaum, 2002.

Csikszentmihalyi, M. "Education for the Twenty-first Century." *Daedalus*, 1995, 124(4), 107–114.

Csikszentmihalyi, M., Rathunde, K., and Whalen, S. *Talented Teenagers: The Roots of Success and Failure*. New York: Cambridge University Press, 1993.

Csikszentmihalyi, M., and Schmidt, J. A. "Stress and Resilience in Adolescence: An Evolutionary Perspective." In K. Borman and B. Schneider (eds.) *The Adolescent Years: Social Influences and Educational Challenges*. Ninety-

Seventh Yearbook of the National Society for the Study of Education. Chicago: University of Chicago Press, 1998.

Daly, M., and Wilson, M. "Risk of Maltreatment of Children Living with Stepparents." In R. Gelles and J. Lancaster (eds.), *Child Abuse and Neglect: Biosocial Dimensions*. New York: Aldine de Gruyter, 1987.

Daly, M., and Wilson, M. *The Truth About Cinderella*. New Haven, Conn.: Yale University Press, 1999.

Damon, W. *Greater Expectations*. New York: Free Press, 1995.

D'Auria, J. "Tremors We Should Not Ignore." *Daedalus*, 1995, *124*(4), 149–152.

Dawson, D. A. "Family Structure and Children's Health and Well-Being: Data from the 1988 National Health Interview Survey on Child Health." *Journal of Marriage and the Family*, 1991, *53*(3), 573–584.

Devereux, E. C. "The Role of Peer Group Experiences in Moral Development." In J. P. Hill (ed.), *Minnesota Symposia on Child Psychology*, 1970, *4*, 94–140.

Diamond, J. *Guns, Germs, and Steel*. New York: Norton, 1999.

Diener, E., Suh, S. M., Lucas, R. E., and Smith, H. L. "Subjective Well-Being: Three Decades of Progress." *Psychological Bulletin*, 1999, *125*, 276–302.

Dishion, T., Patterson, G., Stoolmiller, M., and Skinner, M. "Family, School, and Behavioral Antecedents to Early Adolescent Involvement with Antisocial Peers." *Developmental Psychology*, 1991, *27*, 172–180.

Dodge, K. A., Coie, J. D., Pettit, G. S., and Price, J. M. "Peer Status and Aggression in Boys' Groups: Developmental and Contextual Analyses." *Child Development*, 1990, *61*(5), 1289–1309.

Dryfoos, J. G. *Full-Service Schools: A Revolution in Health and Social Services for Children, Youth, and Families*. San Francisco: Jossey-Bass, 1998.

Early Child Care Research Network, National Institute of Child Health and Human Development. "Child Care and Mother-Child Interaction in the First 3 Years of Life." *Developmental Psychology*, 1999, *35*(6), 1399–1413.

Early Child Care Research Network, National Institute of Child Health and Human Development. "Does Amount of Time Spent in Child Care Predict Socioemotional Adjustment During the Transition to Kindergarten?" *Child Development*, 2003, *74*(4), 976–1005.

Edds, K. "On Deck, at Bat and, Increasingly, in Court." *Washington Post*, June 6, 2003, p. A3.

Edmonds, R. "Effective Schools for the Urban Poor." *Educational Leadership*, Oct. 1979, pp. 15–24.

Ehrle, J., Adams, G., and Tout, K. *Who's Caring for Our Youngest Children? Child Care Patterns of Infants and Toddlers*. Washington, D.C.: Urban Institute, 2001. Available online: http://newfederalism.urban.org/html/op42/occa42.html. Access date: Oct. 21, 2003.

Elias, M., Zins, J., Weissberg, R., Frey, K., Greenberg, M., Haynes, N., Kessler, R., Schwab-Stone, M., and Shriver, T. *Promoting Social and Emotional Learning*. Alexandria, Va.: Association for Supervision and Curriculum Development, 1997.

Elkind, D. *The Hurried Child*. Reading, Mass.: Addison-Wesley, 1981.

Elkind, D. *Ties That Stress*. Cambridge, Mass.: Harvard University Press, 1994.

Elkind, D. *All Grown Up and No Place to Go*. Reading, Mass.: Addison-Wesley, 1998.

Elmore, R. F. "Testing Trap." *Harvard Magazine*, Sept.-Oct., 2002, pp. 35–97.

Epstein, J. L. *School, Family, and Community Partnerships: Preparing Educators and Improving Schools*. Boulder, Colo.: Westview Press, 2002.

Evans, D. "Technological Progress: An Oxymoron?" *Education Week*, Nov. 6, 2002, p. 37.

Evans, R. *The Human Side of School Change*. San Francisco: Jossey-Bass, 1996.

Evans, R. "The Great Accountability Fallacy." *Education Week*, Feb. 3, 1999, 52, 35.

Farkas, S., with Johnson, J. *Kids These Days: What Americans Really Think About the Next Generation*. New York: Public Agenda, 1997.

Finn, J. D. "Parental Engagement That Makes a Difference." *Educational Leadership*, 1998, 55(8), 20–24.

Flanagan, C. "Leaving It to the Professionals." *Atlantic Monthly*, Mar. 2002, pp. 110–116.

Flinn, M. V., and England, B. G. "Social Economics of Child Glucocorticoid Stress Responses and Health." *American Journal of Physical Anthropology*, 1997, 102, 33–53.

Fox, J. A., and Newman, S. A. "After-School Crime or After-School Programs: Tuning In to the Prime Time for Violent Juvenile Crime and Implications for National Policy." Report to the U.S. Attorney General. Washington, D.C.: Department of Justice, 1997.

Fraiberg, S. *The Magic Years*. New York: Scribners, 1959.

Frank, R. H. *Luxury Fever*. New York: Free Press, 1999.

Frank, R. H. "Why Living in a Rich Society Makes Us Feel Poor." *New York Times Magazine*, Oct. 15, 2000, pp. 62–64.

Frymier, J. *Growing Up Is Risky Business, and Schools Are Not to Blame*. Bloomington, Ind.: Phi Delta Kappa, 1992.

Fuchs, V. *Women's Quest for Economic Equality*. Cambridge, Mass.: Harvard University Press, 1988.

Fukuyama, F. *The Great Disruption*. New York: Free Press, 1999.

Fuligni, A., and Eccles, J. "Perceived Parent-Child Relationships and Early Adolescents' Orientation Toward Peers." *Developmental Psychology*, 1993, *29*, 622–632.

Furstenberg, F., Jr., and Hughes, M. E. "The Influence of Neighborhoods on Children's Development: A Theoretical Perspective and a Research Agenda." In J. Brooks-Gunn, G. J. Duncan, and J. L. Aber (eds.), *Neighborhood Poverty*, Vol. 2. New York: Russell Sage Foundation, 1997.

Gallagher, J. "Education, Alone, Is a Weak Treatment." *Education Week*, July 8, 1998, pp. 43, 60.

Gardner, H. *Frames of Mind*. New York: Basic Books, 1993.

Gardner, H. "Do Parents Count?" *New York Review of Books*, Nov. 5, 1998, pp. 19–22.

Gardner, H. "Paroxysms of Choice." *New York Review of Books*, Oct. 19, 2000, pp. 44–49.

Gehring, J. "More Schools Calling Foul on Unsportsmanlike Behavior." *Education Week*, Oct. 17, 2001, pp. 6–7.

Gewertz, C. "'Freak Dancing' Craze Generates Friction, Fears." *Education Week*, Feb. 28, 2001, pp. 1, 16.

Glickman, C. D. *Renewing America's Schools: A Guide for School-Based Action*. San Francisco: Jossey-Bass, 1993.

Goldstein, H. S. "Fathers' Absence and Cognitive Development of 12-17 Year-Olds. *Psychological Reports*, 1982, *51*, 843–848.

Goleman, D. *Emotional Intelligence*. New York: Bantam, 1995.

Goodman, R. D., and Goodman, B. "The Lost Children of Rockdale County." *Frontline* # 1804. Washington, D.C.: Public Broadcasting System, 1999. Available online: http://www.pbs.org/wgbh/pages/frontline/shows/georgia/. Access date: Oct. 21, 2003.

Gopnik, A., Meltzoff, A. N., and Kuhl, K. *The Scientist in the Crib: Minds, Brains, and How Children Learn*. New York: Morrow, 1999.

Gould, S. J. *Bully for Brontosaurus*. New York: Norton, 1991.

Gray, F. du Plessix. "Starving Children." *The New Yorker*, Oct. 26, 1995, p. 51.

Gross, J. "Stress on Wall Street? Try the Eighth Grade." *New York Times*, Oct. 5, 1998, Metro Section, pp. 37–38.

Guttman, D. *Reclaimed Power: Toward a New Psychology of Men and Women in Later Life*. New York: Basic Books, 1987.

Halpern, A., Fernandez, L., and Clark, R. "Snapshots of America's Families: Children's Environment and Behavior." Washington, D.C.: Urban Institute, 2000. Available online: http://newfederalism.urban.org/nsaf/children_c1.html. Access date: Oct. 21, 2003.

Haney, W. "Ensuring Failure." *Education Week*, July 10, 2002, pp. 56, 58.

Hanson, T. L. "Does Parental Conflict Explain Why Divorce Is Negatively Associated with Child Welfare?" *Social Forces*, 1999, *77*, 1283–1316.

Harris, J. R. *The Nurture Assumption: Why Children Turn Out the Way They Do*. New York: Simon & Schuster, 1998.

Havel, V. "Never Hope Against Hope." *Esquire*, Oct. 1993, p. 68.

Hernandez, D. J. *America's Children*. New York: Russell Sage Foundation, 1993.

Hewlitt, S. A. *When the Bough Breaks*. New York: HarperCollins, 1992.

Hewlitt, S. A., and West, C. *The War Against Parents*. Boston: Houghton Mifflin, 1998.

Heymann, J., and Earle, A. "Family Policy for School Age Children: The Case of Parental Evening Work." Harvard University: Malcolm Wiener Center for Social Policy and the John F. Kennedy School of Government, Apr., 1996, H-96-2.

Hochschild, A. R. "A Generation Without Public Passion." *Atlantic Monthly*, Feb. 2001, pp. 62–63.

Hochschild, A. R. *The Time Bind: When Work Becomes Home and Home Becomes Work*. New York: Henry Holt, 1997.

Hochschild, A. R. *The Commercialization of Intimate Life: Notes from Home and Work*. Berkeley: University of California Press, 2003.

Holt, J. *How Children Fail*. Boulder, Colo.: Perseus, 1995. (Originally published in 1964.)

Howe, H., II. *Thinking About Our Kids*. New York: Free Press, 1993.

Howe, H., II. "Families, Communities, and Children." *Harvard Graduate School of Education Alumni Bulletin*, 1994, 38(2), 10.

Jackson, D. "Help a Student—Turn Off the TV." *Boston Globe*, Apr. 13, 2001, p. A23.

Jarrell, A. "The Face of Teenage Sex Grows Younger." *New York Times*, Apr. 2, 2000, Section 9, pp. 1, 8.

Jencks, C., Smith, M., Aciand, H., Bane, M. J., Cohen, D., Gintis, H., Heyns, B., and Michelson, S. *Inequality: A Reassessment of the Effect of Family and Schooling in America*. New York: Basic Books, 1972.

Jordan, A. B., and Sullivan, J. L. *Children's Educational Television Regulations and the Local Broadcaster: Impact and Implementation*. Philadelphia: Annenberg Public Policy Center of The University of Pennsylvania.

Available online: http://www.appcpenn.org/02_reports_releases/report_
1997.htm. Access date: Dec. 12, 2003.

Kagan, J. *The Nature of the Child*. New York: Basic Books, 1984.

Kagan, J. *Galen's Prophecy*. New York: Basic Books, 1994.

Kagan, J. *Three Seductive Ideas*. Cambridge, Mass.: Harvard University Press,
1998.

Kaminer, W. *I'm Dysfunctional, You're Dysfunctional: The Recovery Movement
and Other Self-Help Fashions*. Reading, Mass.: Addison-Wesley, 1992.

Kanter, R. M. *When Giants Learn to Dance: Mastering the Challenges of Strategy,
Management, and Careers in the 1990s*. New York: Simon & Schuster,
1989.

Kantrowitz, B., and Wingert, P. "The Parent Trap." *Newsweek*, Jan. 29, 2001,
pp. 48–53.

Kaye, K. *The Mental and Social Life of Babies: How Parents Create Persons*.
Chicago: University of Chicago Press, 1983.

Kluger, J., with Park, A. "The Quest for a Superkid." *Time*, Apr. 30, 2001,
pp. 50–55.

Koestner, R., Franz, C., and Weinberger, J. "The Family Origins of Empathic
Concern: A Twenty-Six Year Longitudinal Study." *Journal of Personality
and Social Psychology*, 1990, 58(4), 709–717.

Kohn, A. "How Not to Teach Values." In A. Kohn, *What to Look for in a Classroom*. San Francisco: Jossey-Bass, 1998.

Kohn, A. *Punished by Rewards: The Trouble with Gold Stars, Incentive Plans, A's,
Praise, and Other Bribes*. Boston: Houghton Mifflin, 1999.

Kozol, J. *Death at an Early Age*. New York: New American Library, 1990.
(Originally published in 1967.)

Kraus, R. *Leo the Late Bloomer*. New York: HarperCollins, 1998. (Originally
published in 1971.)

Kunkel, D. *Sex on TV: A Biennial Report to the Kaiser Family Foundation*, 2000.
Available online: http://www.kff.org/content/2001/3087. Access date:
Oct. 21, 2003.

LaFerla, R. "Teenage Shoppers (Purses by Brinks)." *New York Times*, Sept. 10,
2000, Section 9, pp. 1, 10.

Lamb, M. E., Pleck, J. H., Charnov, E. L., and Levine, J. A. "Characteristics of
Maternal and Paternal Behavior and Involvement." In J. B. Lancaster,
J. Altman, A. S. Rossi, and L. R. Sherrod (eds.), *Parenting Across the
Lifespan*. New York: Aldine de Gruyter, 1987.

Lauria, J. "Americans Labor Longer Than Workers in Any Industrial Nation,
Study Says." *Boston Globe*, Sept. 5, 1999, p. E1.

Lawlor, J. "Minding the Children While on the Road." *New York Times*, July 12, 1997, Business Section, p. 10.

Lickona, T. *Educating for Character: How Our Schools Can Teach Respect and Responsibility*. New York: Bantam, 1991.

Liu, D., Diorio, J., Tannenbaum, B., Caldji, C., Francis, D., Freedman, A., Sharma, S., Pearson, D., Plotsky, P. M., and Meaney, M. J. "Maternal Care, Hippocampal Glucocorticoid Receptors and Hypothalamic-Pituitary-Adrenal Responses to Stress." *Science*, 1997, *277*, 1659–1662.

Lugaila, T. "Marital Status and Living Arrangements: March 1998 (Update)." Current Population Reports P20–514. Washington, D.C.: U.S. Bureau of the Census, 1998.

Luthar, S. S., and Becker, B. E. "Privileged but Pressured? A Study of Affluent Youth." *Child Development*, 2002, *73*(5), 1593–1610.

Maccoby, E. E. *The Two Sexes*. Cambridge, Mass.: Harvard University Press, 1998.

Maccoby, E. E. "Parenting and Its Effects on Children: On Reading and Misreading Behavior Genetics." In J. T. Spence (ed.), *Annual Review of Psychology, 2000*. Palo Alto, Calif.: Annual Reviews, 2000.

Maccoby, E. E. "Parenting Effects: Issues and Controversies." In J. Borkowski, D. Landesman-Ramey, and S. Bristol (eds.), *Parenting and the Child's World: Multiple Influences on Intellectual and Social-Emotional Development*. Mahwah, N.J.: Erlbaum, 2002.

MacTurk, R., and Morgan, G. (eds.). *Mastery Motivation: Origins, Conceptualizations, and Applications: Advances in Applied Developmental Psychology*, Vol. 12. Norwood, N.J.: Ablex, 1995.

Martin, J. *Miss Manners' Guide to Domestic Tranquility*. New York: Crown, 1999.

McDowell, E. "The Many Amenities of Corporate Retreats." *New York Times*, Sept. 12, 1999, Business Section, p. 16.

McGinn, D. "The CEO's Challenge." *Newsweek*, Apr. 28, 2003, pp. 50–58.

McLanahan, S., and Sandefur, G. *Growing Up with a Single Parent*. Cambridge, Mass.: Harvard University Press, 1994.

McNeal, R. "Parental Involvement as Social Capital: Differential Effectiveness on Science, Achievement, Truancy, and Dropping Out." *Social Forces*, 1999, *78*, 117–144.

Menand, L. "What Comes Naturally." *The New Yorker*, Nov. 25, 2002, pp. 96–101.

Mitchell, K. J., Finkelhor, D., and Wolak, J. "Risk Factors for and Impact of Online Sexual Solicitation of Youth." *Journal of the American Medical Association*, June 20, 2001, *285*, 3011–3014.

Mounts, N., and Steinberg, L. "An Ecological Analysis of Peer Influence on Adolescent Grade Point Average and Drug Use." *Developmental Psychology,* 1995, *31,* 915–922.

Mueller, C. M., and Dweck, C. S. "Praise for Intelligence Can Undermine Children's Motivation and Performance." *Journal of Personality and Social Psychology,* 1998, *75*(1), 33–52.

Myers, D. G. "The Funds, Friends, and Faith of Happy People." *American Psychologist,* 2000, *55*(1), 56–67.

National Center on Addiction and Substance Abuse. *Dangerous Liaisons: Substance Abuse and Sex.* New York: National Center on Addiction and Substance Abuse, 1999.

National Commission on the Role of the Schools and the Community in Improving Adolescent Health. *Code Blue: Uniting for Healthier Youth.* Washington, D.C.: National Association of State Boards of Education and American Medical Association, 1990.

National Public Radio. "Fred 'Mister' Rogers Dies of Cancer." *Morning Edition,* Feb. 27, 2003.

Nord, C. W., Brimhall, D., and, West, J. "Fathers' Involvement in Their Children's Schools." U.S. Department of Education, National Center for Education Statistics, 1998. Available online: http://nces.ed.gov/pubs98/fathers/. Access date: Oct. 21, 2003.

Nord, C. W., and West, J. "Fathers' and Mothers' Involvement in Their Children's Schools by Family Type and Resident Status." U.S. Department of Education, National Center for Education Statistics, 2001. Available online: http://nces.ed.gov/pubs2001/2001032.pdf. Access date: Oct. 21, 2003.

Ogbu, J. U. *Black Students in an Affluent Suburb.* Mahwah, N.J.: Erlbaum, 2003.

Ohanian, S. "Capitalism, Calculus, and Conscience." *Phi Delta Kappan,* 2003, 84(10), 736–747.

Oremus, E. "Guidelines for Teachers and Administrators: Resolving Parents' Problems." Columbus, Ohio: Marburn Academy, 2003.

Pappano, L. "Back to School Shocking." *Boston Globe,* Aug. 27, 2001, pp. A1, A6.

Parke, R., and Bhavnagri, N. P. "Parents as Managers of Children's Peer Relationships." In D. Belle (ed.), *Children's Social Networks and Social Support.* New York: Wiley, 1989.

Pinker, S. *The Blank Slate.* New York: Viking, 2002.

Popenoe, D. *Life Without Father.* Cambridge, Mass.: Harvard University Press, 1996.

Postman, N. *The Disappearance of Childhood*. New York: Vintage, 1994.

Powers, J. "Trying to Check Hockey Parents." *Boston Globe*, Feb. 9, 2001, pp. A1, A32.

Purdum, T. S. "Behind the Wheel and Driving the Nation's Culture." *New York Times*, Sept. 17, 2000, Section 4, p. 1.

Putnam, R. *Bowling Alone*. New York: Simon & Schuster, 2000.

Rathbun, C., DiVirgilio, L., and Waldfogel, S. "A Restitutive Process in Children Following Radical Separation from Family and Culture." *American Journal of Orthopsychiatry*, 1958, *28*, 408–415.

Reich, R. *The Future of Success*. New York: Knopf, 2001.

Remez, L. "Children Who Don't Live with Both Parents Face Behavior Problems." *Family Planning Perspectives*, 1992, *24*, 41–43.

Repetti, R., Taylor, S. E., and Seeman, T. E. "Risky Families: Family Social Environments and the Mental and Physical Health of Offspring." *Psychological Bulletin*, 2002, *128*, 2.

Resnick, P. B., Blum, R., Bauman, K., Harris, K., Jones, J., Tabor, J., Beuhring, T., Sieving, R., Shew, M., Ireland, M., Bearinger, L., and Udry, J. R. "Protecting Adolescents from Harm." *Journal of the American Medical Association*, Sept. 1997, 823–832.

Rich, F. "Naked Capitalists: There's No Business Like Porn Business." *New York Times Magazine*, May 20, 2001, pp. 50–92.

Richardson, J., Dwyer, K., McGuigan, K., Hansen, W., Dent, C., Johnson, C. A., Sussman, S., Brannon, B., and Glay, B. "Substance Use Among Eighth-Grade Students Who Take Care of Themselves After School." *Pediatrics*, 1989, *84*, 556–566.

Ridley, M. *Genome: The Autobiography of a Species in 23 Chapters*. New York: HarperCollins, 2000.

Roberts, D. F., Foehr, U. G., Rideout, V. J., and Brodie, M. *Kids and Media @ the New Millennium: A Kaiser Family Foundation Report*, 1999. Available online: http://www.kff.org/content/1999/1535/KidsReport%20FINAL.pdf. Access date: Oct. 23, 2003.

Robinson, G. E., and Brandon, D. P. *NAEP Test Scores: Should They Be Used to Compare and Rank State Educational Quality?* Arlington, Va.: Educational Research Service, 1994.

Rogers, C. *On Becoming a Person: A Therapist's View of Psychotherapy*. Boston: Houghton Mifflin, 1972.

Rosenthal, R., and Jacobson, L. *Pygmalion in the Classroom*. New York: Rinehart & Winston, 1968.

Rothbaum, F., Weisz, J., Pott, M., Miyake, K., and Morelli, G. "Attachment and Culture: Security in the United States and Japan." *American Psychologist,* 2000, *55,* 10, 1093–1104.

Rowe, D. *The Limits of Family Influence: Genes, Experience, and Behavior.* New York: Guilford Press, 1994.

Russell, D. "The Prevalence and Seriousness of Incestuous Abuse: Stepfathers vs. Biological Fathers." *Child Abuse and Neglect,* 1984, *8,* 15–22.

Ryan, K., and Bohlin, K. E. *Building Character in Our Schools.* San Francisco: Jossey-Bass, 1999.

Sampson, R., Raudenbush, S. W., and Earls, F. "Neighborhoods and Violent Crime: A Multilevel Study of Collective Efficacy. *Science,* 1997, *277,* 918–924.

Sandefur, G. D., McLanahan, S., and Wojtkiewicz, R. A. "The Effects of Parental Marital Status During Adolescence on High School Graduation." *Social Forces,* 1992, *71*(1), 103–121.

Schiff, M., Duyme, M., Dumaret, A., and Tomkiewitz, S. "How Much Could We Boost Scholastic Achievement and IQ Scores? A Direct Answer from a French Adoption Study." *Cognition,* 1982, *12,* 165–196.

Schor, J. B. *The Overworked American.* New York: Basic Books, 1992.

Schumpeter, J. A. *Capitalism, Socialism and Democracy.* New York: Harper Brothers, 1950.

Schwartz, B. "Self-Determination: The Tyranny of Freedom." *American Psychologist,* 2000, *55*(1), 79–88.

Seigle, P. "Reach Out to Schools: A Social Competency Program." In J. Cohen (ed.), *Caring Classrooms/Intelligent Schools.* New York: Teachers College Press, 2001.

Sheline, J. L., Skipper, B. J., and Broadhead, W. E. "Risk Factors for Violent Behavior in Elementary School Boys: Have You Hugged Your Child Today?" *American Journal of Public Health,* 1994, *84,* 661–663.

Shellenbarger, S. "More Executives Cite Need for Family Time as Reason for Quitting." *Wall Street Journal,* Mar. 11, 1998, p. B-1.

Shoda, Y., Mischel, W., and Peake, K. "Predicting Adolescent Cognitive and Self-Regulatory Competencies from Preschool Delay of Gratification." *Developmental Psychology,* 1990, *26*(6), 978–986.

Shonkoff, J. P., and Phillips, D. A. (eds.). *From Neurons to Neighborhoods: The Science of Early Childhood Development.* Washington, D.C.: National Research Council Institute of Medicine, 2000.

Shorter, E. *The Making of the Modern Family.* New York: Basic Books, 1977.

Silberman, C. *Crisis in the Classroom: The Remaking of American Education.*
New York: Random House, 1970.

Singer, J., and Singer, D. "Can TV Stimulate Imaginative Play?" *Journal of Communication,* Summer 1976, pp. 74–80.

Sizer, T. R. *Horace's Compromise.* Boston: Houghton Mifflin, 1992.

Snarey, J. *How Fathers Care for the Next Generation.* Cambridge, Mass.: Harvard University Press, 1993.

Spock, B. *Baby and Child Care.* (rev. ed.) New York: Hawthorne Books, 1968.

Sroufe, L. A. "From Infant Attachment to Promotion of Adolescent Autonomy: Prospective, Longitudinal Data on the Role of Parents in Development." In J. Borkowski, D. Landesman-Ramey, and S. Bristol (eds.), *Parenting and the Child's World: Multiple Influences on Intellectual and Social-Emotional Development.* Mahwah, N.J.: Erlbaum, 2002.

Stanton, W., Tian, R., Oci, S., and Silva, A. "Sociodemographic Characteristics of Adolescent Smokers." *International Journal of the Addictions,* 1994, 7, 913–925.

Steinberg, L. "Susceptibility of Adolescents to Antisocial Peer Pressure." *Child Development,* 1987, 58, 269–275.

Steinberg, L. *Beyond the Classroom.* New York: Simon & Schuster, 1996.

Stern, D. *The Interpersonal World of the Infant.* New York: Basic Books, 1987.

Stoll, C. *High-Tech Heretic.* New York: Anchor, 1999.

Straight, S. "A Generation Unscathed." *Los Angeles Times,* Aug. 12, 2001, pp. 13–34.

Suomi, S. J. "Long-term Effects of Different Early Rearing Experiences on Social, Emotional, and Physiological Development in Nonhuman Primates." In M. S. Kesheven and R. M. Murra (eds.), *Neurodevelopmental Models of Adult Psychopathology.* Cambridge, England: Cambridge University Press, 1997.

Suomi, S. J. "Parents, Peers, and the Process of Socialization in Primates." In J. Borkowski, D. Landesman-Ramey, and S. Bristol (eds.), *Parenting and the Child's World: Multiple Influences on Intellectual and Social-Emotional Development.* Mahwah, N.J.: Erlbaum, 2002.

Swidler, A. "Love and Adulthood in American Culture." In N. J. Smelser and E. H. Erikson (eds.), *Themes of Work and Love in Adulthood.* Cambridge, Mass.: Harvard University Press, 1980.

Sylva, K., Melhuish, E., Sammons, P., Siraj-Blatchford, I., Taggart, B., and Elliot, K. "The Effective Provision of Pre-School Education (EPPE) Project: Findings from the Pre-School Period." University of London Institute of

Education, 2003. Available online: http://www.ioe.ac.uk/cdl/eppe/index.htm. Access date: Oct. 21, 2003.

Taylor, S. E. *The Tending Instinct*. New York: Henry Holt, 2002.

Tocqueville, A. de. *Democracy in America*. (R. D. Hefner, ed.) New York: Signet (Penguin Putnam), 2001. (Originally published 1835.)

Trillin, C. *Family Man*. New York: Farrar, Straus, & Giroux, 1998.

Tucker, J. S., Friedman, H. S., Schwartz, J. E., Criqui, M. H., Tomlinson-Keasey, C., Wingard, D. L., and Martin, L. R. "Parental Divorce: Effects on Individual Behavior and Longevity." *Journal of Personality and Social Psychology*, 1997, *73*, 381–391.

Uchitelle, L. "At the Desk, Off the Clock and Below Statistical Radar." *New York Times*, July 18, 1999, p. B-4.

U.S. Surgeon General. "Television and Growing Up: The Impact of Televised Violence." Appendix 3. *Report of the U.S. Surgeon General*. Washington, D.C.: Government Printing Office, 1972.

Vaishnav, A. "Classroom to Courtroom." *Boston Globe*, July 21, 2000, pp. A1, C13.

Vandell, D. G., and Corasaniti, M. A. "The Relation Between Third-Graders' After-School Care and Social, Academic, and Emotional Function." *Child Development*, 1988, *59*, 868–875.

Vandivere, S., Moore, K. A., and Zaslow, M. "1999 Snapshots of America's Families II: Children's Family Environment." Washington, D.C.: Urban Institute, 2000. Available online: http://newfederalism.urban.org/nsaf/family-environ.html. Access date: Oct. 21, 2003.

Veblen, T. *The Theory of the Leisure Class*. New York: Penguin, 1994. (Originally published in 1899.)

Wallulis, J. *The New Insecurity: The End of the Standard Job and Family*. Albany: State University of New York Press, 1998.

Walsh, M. W. "As Overtime Rises, Fatigue Becomes Labor Issue." *New York Times*, Sept. 17, 2000, pp. 1, 28.

Ward, B. "Working Harder to Obtain the Same Vacation." *New York Times*, May 11, 1997, p. 12F.

White, R. *Lives in Progress*. New York: Holt, Rinehart, & Winston, 1966.

Whitman, D. *The Optimism Gap*. New York: Walker, 1998.

Winick, M., Meyer, K. K., and Harris, R. C. "Malnutrition and Environmental Enrichment by Early Adoption." *Science*, 1975, *190*, 1173–1175.

Winnicott, D. *The Child, the Family, and the Outside World*. Boulder, Colo.: Perseus, 1992.

Winnicott, D., and Winnicott, C. *Playing and Reality*. London: Routledge, 1982.

Wolfe, A. *One Nation, After All*. New York: Penguin, 1999.

Wong, E. "New Rules for Soccer Parents: 1) No Yelling. 2) No Hitting Ref." *New York Times*, May 6, 2001, pp. 1, 30.

Yankelovich, D. *New Rules: Searching for Self-Fulfillment in a World Turned Upside Down*. New York: Random House, 1981.

Yankelovich, D. "Public Opinion and the Youth of America." In S. Halperin (ed.), *The Forgotten Half Revisited*. Washington, D.C.: American Youth Policy Forum, 1999.

Youniss, J., and Smollar, J. *Adolescent Relations with Mothers, Fathers, and Friends*. Chicago: University of Chicago Press, 1985.

Ziegler, E. F., and Lang, M. E. *Child Care Choice: Balancing the Need of Children, Families and Society*. New York: Free Press, 1991.

Zill, N. *American Children: Happy, Healthy, Insecure*. New York: Doubleday Anchor, 1983.

Zill, N., and Nord, C. W. *Running in Place: How American Families Are Faring in a Changing Economy and Individualistic Society*. Washington, D.C.: Child Trends, 1994.

Zill, N., and Schoenborn, C. *Development, Learning, and Emotional Problems: Health of Our Nation's Children 1988*. Washington, D.C.: National Center for Health Statistics, Nov. 16, 1990. Available online: http://www.cdc.gov/nchs/data/ad/ad190.pdf. Access date: Nov. 1, 2003.

Zirkel, P. A. "Sorting Out Which Students Have Learning Disabilities." *Phi Delta Kappan*, 2001a, 82(9), 639–940.

Zirkel, P. A. "A Web of Disruption?" *Phi Delta Kappan*, 2001b, 82(8), 717–718.

Acknowledgments

This book took a long time, shifting from and then returning to its original destination as an effort to help schools cope with changes around them that are unplanned, unprecedented, and under-acknowledged. En route, it took a number of unexpected turns—turns that ultimately helped me learn a great deal about the state of children, families, and schools in America but that left me in need of periodic confirmation and correction. I was lucky to receive both. Whatever the book's flaws, which remain mine, it is immeasurably better for the generous, constructive criticism of colleagues and friends who read it in various stages: Leslie Bedford, Jane Bryan-Jones, Hardy Jones, Mark Kline, Bryn Roberts, Keith Shahan, Frank Upham, Jeane Whitehouse, and Allan Wyatt. Skip McKoy and Haskel Cohen did double duty, reading it twice. So did Norman Colb, who, as usual, offered provocative conceptual help at key moments. My perspective on families and child development owes much to years of collaboration with Arnold Kerzner and the staff at The Human Relations Service. Hilary Powers greatly improved the clarity of the final text. Lesley Iura at Jossey-Bass provided both reality checks and encouragement throughout. Paula Evans read all the major drafts and endured my preoccupation with each. To all, my great thanks.

Index

A

Academic achievement: of children in single-parent and stepfamilies, 62; effects of television on, 89; and expectations, 154; father's role in, 47; and parent involvement, 182; parents' anxiety about, 100–103; parents' response to poor, 13; and peer pressure, 54

Academic excellence, 166

Acceptance, 22, 32

Accountability, 150–153

Active listening, 211–214, 245–246

Activities: of adolescents, 70; over-scheduling of, 104–105, 108, 243–244; quality versus quantity, 78–79

Adaptability, 36

Administrators: intervention in parent-teacher conferences, 221; lawsuit training for, 12–13; parents seeking advice from, 14–15, 178; primary responsibility of, 172; resistance reduction strategies of, 200–204; staff communication strategies for, 201–203; strength perspective of, 204–205; and turnaround of low-performing school, 182; views of, 156

Adolescents: activities of, 70; with disengaged parents, 41; and expansion of structure, 27; friction between parents and, 84–87, 242; importance of nurture to, 238; listening to, 245–246; of 1950s versus today, 66; parents' view of, 85–86; personal spending of, 86–87, 241; responsibilities of, 70; separation of adults from, 86; sexually transmitted disease among, 88; unsupervised time of, 70, 87; workload of, 102

Advising systems, 198

Advisory council, 180, 181, 184

Affiliation, 20

African Americans: attitudes of, 54; in 1950s America, 59; television viewing time of, 256n.11

Aggression: of children in day care, 73; at sports events, 105, 109; on Web sites, 93–94

Alaska, 7

Alimony, 133

American Medical Association, 5

America's Smallest School: The Family (Barton, P. & Coley, R.), 154

Antisocial behavior, 8–9

Anxiety, of parents: about children's competence, 100–111; about work, 118–119; effects of, 103–105

Anxiety, of teachers, 207–208

Arkansas, 7

Asian Americans, 54

Attachment: and change, 193; infants versus adults, 19–20; in nuclear versus fragile families, 63. *See also specific types of attachment*

Attendance: at parent education programs, 161, 231; at parent-teacher conferences, 186–187

Attention deficit disorder, 10, 62, 94, 103

Attention span, 10, 94

Attitude: of African American students, 54; effects of television on, 89–90; of parents toward school, 6

Attunement, 24–25

Authentic instruction, 152

Authoritarian parents, 40–41. *See also* Controlling parents

Authoritative parents: benefits of, 43; involvement of, 187; overview of, 42; and peer pressure, 54–55; of shy children, 42; and unilateral authority, 83

Authority: lack of trust in, 130, 131; lack of unilateral, 82–83; in nuclear versus fragile families, 63; parents' reliance on mutual, 83–84; and school purpose and conduct, 174–175; unilateral versus mutual, 83

Autonomy: as basis of fragile family, 64; as complement to affiliation, 20; example of parents' building of, 33; need for, 20; of toddlers, 20. *See also* Latitude

B

Baby Boom parents, 113–114

Barton, P., 154, 158

Baumrind, D., 39

Bedtime, 14–15, 67

Behavior: decline in appropriate, 5–6; effects of television on, 90; parents' response to, 11–12, 13–14; and rejection by peers, 53; school's response to, 160–161. *See also* Conduct

Behavior disorder, 10, 29

Bell, T., 150

Bennis, W., 118

Bereavement, 193–194

Books, parenting, 17–18, 34–35, 232

Boredom, 108

Boston, 168–169

Bowlby, J., 71

Boys: importance of fathers for, 47; independence of, 20

Brain development, 98–99, 149

Brazelton, T. B., 78

Brooks, D., 138, 140

Bush, G., 151

C

Cafeteria, 7

California, 7

Cars, 120

Ceremonies, 86

Change, 192–195, 200–201. *See also* Resistance; School reform

Character education, 163–164

Charter schools, 182

Cheating, 8, 11

Child abuse, 52, 63, 254n.13

Child care. *See* Day care

Child development. *See* Development

Child support, 133

Childrearing. *See* Parenting

Children: constant happiness of, 242–243; in families with bad marriages, 68; listening to, 245–246; parents problem solving for, 244–247; parents' response to complaints of, 14, 180

Chinatown, 239

Civil rights movement, 132

Classroom modifications, 147–148

Classroom placement, 14, 101–103

Clinton, W., 151

Clothing, inappropriate, 13, 86

Clubs, 88

Coaches, 105
Coalition of Essential Schools, 169
Code of conduct, 172–173
Coherence, 174–175
Coleman, J., 153, 154, 158
Coley, R., 154, 158
Collectivism, 21
College admissions, 101–102, 155
College prep courses, 103
Colorado, 7
Comer, J., 166
Commercials, 89
Commission on Children at Risk, 5
Communication: of administrators
    to teachers, 201–203; for parent
    education, 173–174; parents' styles
    of, 45–46; of school's values, 183.
    See also Parent communication
Communities: and friend selection,
    53–54; importance of, 50–52; and
    test scores, 155
Compensation. See Salaries
Competence: emphasis on, 97–100;
    parents' anxiety about, 100–111
Competition: and drinking and drug
    use, 105; effects of, 110–111;
    emphasis on, 97–100, 244; parents'
    anxiety about, 100–111; in sports,
    104–105
Computers, 93, 94
Concentration, 10, 94
Conduct, 170–175, 183–184. See also
    Behavior
Confidence: function of nurture in,
    22; function of structure in, 27–28;
    importance of, 236–237; of parents,
    208–209; raising, 30; and reciproc-
    ity, 22
Consequences: avoidance of, 97,
    106–107; benefits of, 109–110;
    lack of, 84; and self-esteem, 97; in
    sports, 109–110
Consistency, 240
Conspicuous consumption, 119–120
Consumerism, 116–121

Controlling parents, 33–34. See also
    Authoritarian parents
Conyers, Georgia, 88
Coontz, S., 58
Cooperative skills, 9
Cortisol, 65
Courtesy, 84, 130
Creative destruction, 131
Csikszentmihalyi, M., 153, 223
Culture: and adaptability, 36; and
    coherence of school, 175; freedom
    in, 128; and independence, 20–21;
    and latitude, 35–36; and nurture,
    35–36; and peer pressure, 54; and
    roles of mothers and fathers, 45;
    and structure, 27, 35–36
Curriculum, expansion of, 147
Cutting classes, 106

D

Dancing, 4
D.A.R.E. (Drug Abuse Resistance
    Education), 163
D'Auria, J., 5
Day care: effects of, 73–74; extended
    hours in, 75; number of children
    in, 72–73; perceived benefits of,
    254–255n.14; quality of, 73–74;
    staff turnover rates in, 74; time
    spent in, 73
Delayed gratification, 28, 85
Democracy, 119
Dependence, 18–21
Depression, 65
Development: elements of healthy,
    21; importance of early years in,
    25–26; latitude's role in, 31–34;
    need for independence, 18–21;
    in nuclear versus fragile families,
    63; nurture's role in, 21–26;
    parenting books' advice on, 34–35;
    structure's role in, 26–30
Differentiation, 85
Dinners, 70, 79–80
Direct parenting, 70–72

Directness, 215–217, 218, 247–248

Disappointment: benefits of, 32, 109–110; need for, 242–243

Discipline, parental: of authoritarian parents, 40–41; of controlling parent, 33–34; of mothers versus fathers, 46–47; and parents' guilt, 95–96; of permissive parents, 41; and self-esteem, 30; tone of voice during, 77–78; variance in, 35–36. *See also* Expectations

Discipline, school: communicating expectations about, 170–174; current strategies for, 160

Disengagement, of parents, 34, 41

Disruptive technology, 91–92

Diversity, 175

Divorce: current rates of, 61–62; efforts to deter, 139; in 1950s America, 58

Drinking: examples of, 11–12; of latchkey children, 75; parents' response to, 11–12; and peer pressure, 54; and stress, 105; and unsupervised time, 87

Drug use: of latchkey children, 75; and peer pressure, 54; preventive programs for, 163; and stress, 105; and unsupervised time, 87

du Plessix Gray, F., 79

E

Economy, 115–116, 130–131

Edmunds, R., 154

Education: lack of student investment in, 10; parents' knowledge of, 180–181; school as small part of, 153. *See also* School

Effective schools movement, 154

Efficacy, 154

Elkind, D., 54, 61, 63–64, 66, 69, 74, 81, 242

Emotional intelligence, 164

Emotional Intelligence (Goleman, D.), 28

Empathy, 48

Employability, 118

Employment. *See* Work

Entrepreneurship, 117, 124

Estrogen, 44

Europe, 127

Evans, J., 166–167

Expectations: and academic achievement, 154; adhering to, 241–242; importance of, 28; lack of, 84; of marriage, 69; of parent education, 162; for respect, 171, 172. *See also* Discipline, parental; Structure

Extended day programs, 75

F

Failure, 31–32, 109–110

Family: Americans' desire for, 138; efforts to restore, 139; factors affecting today's, 69; factors missing from, 137; focus of, 69–70; influence of, 154–155; of 1950s America, 58–60, 71; nuclear versus permeable, 61; past assumptions of, 60; problems with, 62, 64; reversal with work, 123; risky, 64–65; sacrifices for, 70

Family, decline of: economic factors for, 115–126; historical perspective of, 57, 60–64; overview of, 113–115

Family meals, 70, 79–80

Family vacations, 13, 108

Fathers: benefits of, 44; communication style of, 46; discipline of, 46–47; of illegitimate children, 133; importance of, 47–48, 253–254n.10–11; involvement in parent-teacher conferences, 185–186; and latitude, 49; number of children without, 61, 136; and nurture, 48; parenting styles of, 44–50, 124; play of, 46; principle role of, 45, 136; rationalizations of, 125; and reaction to stress, 44; and structure, 49. *See also* Parents

Feminism, 122, 132–133, 137

Fenway High School, 168–169

Fighting. *See* School violence

Flanagan, C., 137

Flextime, 121

Florida, 7, 105

Fragile family, 61, 63–64

Freedom: and the breakup of society, 134–135; cost of, 135–136; extensiveness of, 129; history, 127, 128, 129; and liberation movements, 132–133; sacrificing, 138–140; and technological innovation, 130–131; and trust, 129–130; in various cultures, 128. *See also* Independence; Individualism; Latitude

Friction, between adolescents and parents, 84–87, 242

Friends: parents as, 95–96; parents' knowledge of, 241; selection of, 53–54

Frontline (television program), 88

Fukuyama, F., 130, 131

Functioning, unevenness in, 10

Funding, special education, 149

G

Games, children's, 104, 108–109

Gardner, H., 155

Gay and lesbian rights movement, 132

Gender, 20

Georgia, 88

Girls: importance of fathers for, 47–48; independence of, 20

Globalization, 117

Goal, of school, 166–167

Goals 2000 initiative, 151

Goleman, D., 28, 33, 164

Gould, S. J., 192

Governance, school, 179–181, 182

Government, 130

Grade grubbing, 101

Gratification, delayed, 28, 85

Green, J., 186–187, 189

Group association, 129

Guilt, 95–96, 125–126, 196

Guns, 7

H

Happiness: amount of money needed for, 258n.20; father's role in, 48; impossibility of constant, 242–243; and materialism, 119, 120–121

Harassment, 93–94

Havel, V., 227

Headmistresses of the East, 171

Health, 62

Hewlitt, S. A., 71, 73, 133–134, 135

High school, 3–4, 170

High-stakes testing. *See* Testing

Hochschild, A. R., 78, 114, 122–123, 125, 237

Holt, J., 153

Home making, 137

Home-school partnership. *See* School-parent partnership

Honesty. *See* Directness

Hope, 224–229

Hormones, 44, 65, 253–254n.11

Howe, H., 79, 158

Human potential movement, 133

The Hurried Child (Elkind, D.), 54

I

Identity development, 85, 242

Impulse control, 92

Inclusion, 147–148

Independence, 18–21. *See also* Freedom

Independent schools, 174, 182

Individualism, 20–21, 119, 127–129. *See also* Freedom

Individuation, 20–21

Industrial economy, 117, 130

Infants: attachment of, 19–20; brain development of, 98–99; learning of, 19; mother's reaction to, 23–24; premature, 148; time spend in day care by, 73

Information dissemination, 92–93

Information economy, 117, 131

Insecurity, 114

Integration, 85

Internet: anti-intellectual nature of, 94; and attention span, 94;

Internet, *continued*
  and information dissemination, 93;
  overview of, 91; parents' resistance
  to, 86; and sexual behavior, 93;
  speed of, 94. *See also* Web sites

J

Japan, 116
Jencks, C., 153, 154, 228
Job. *See* Work

K

Kagan, J., 25, 28, 32
Kaiser Family Foundation, 89
Kentucky, 7
Kettering, C., 120
Kindergarten, 100
Korean War, 26
Kozol, J., 153

L

Latchkey children, 74–75
Latino people, 256n.11
Latitude: and culture, 35–36; definition of, 97; example of managing,
  33–34; excess amounts of, 35;
  importance of, 31–33; improvement of, 243–247; link to nurture,
  237; loss of, 107–108; of mothers
  versus fathers, 49; overview of, 31;
  and parenting style, 40–43; and
  resilience, 32; variance in, 35–36.
  See also Autonomy; Freedom
Lawsuits: administrators' preparation
  for, 12–13; to avoid consequences,
  106–107; examples of, 11, 12
Learning: disabilities in, 147–149; of
  infants, 19; parent involvement in,
  187–189
Learning styles, 149
Listening, 211–214, 245–246
Lombardi, V., 110, 244
The Lost Children of Rockdale
  County (television program), 88
Love, 68
Low-performing school, 181–182

Loyalty, 117, 118
Luxury items, 120

M

Marburn Academy, 208
Marriage: current views of, 68–69;
  delays in, 61; and economy, 118;
  efforts to restore, 139; expectations
  of, 69; in 1950s America, 58, 60; in
  nuclear versus fragile families,
  63–64; past view of, 67–68; as a
  value, 68–69
Maryland, 7
Massachusetts, 105, 239
Materialism, 119–121
Maternal deprivation, 71
Maternity leave, 14
Mathematics, 47
McCarthyism, 59
Meaney, M., 23
Mental illness, 10, 62
Miller, Z., 99
Minnesota, 7
Mission statement, 165–166
Mississippi, 7
Money: of adolescents, 86–87, 241;
  amount needed to be happy,
  258n.20
Morale, 227–229
Mothers: benefits of, 44; communica-
  tion style of, 46; discipline of,
  46–47; involvement in parent-
  teacher conferences, 185–186; and
  latitude, 49; and nurture, 48; par-
  enting styles of, 44–50, 124; play
  of, 46; principle role of, 45, 136;
  rationalizations of, 125; reaction
  to infant, 23–24; and reaction to
  stress, 44; and structure, 49. *See also*
  Parents
Mothers, working. *See* Working
  mothers
Motto, 166
Mozart effect, 99
Mr. Rogers' Neighborhood (television
  show), 22

Music, 99, 104
Mutual authority, 83–84

N

A Nation at Risk, 150–151, 152, 154
National Alliance for Youth Sports,
    105, 109
National Organization for Women,
    137
Near-latchkey children, 75
Negotiation. *See* Mutual authority
New York City, 88, 239
New York Times, 88, 103
No Child Left Behind Act (2002),
    151, 154, 178, 226, 260n.4
Northern Ohio Soccer League, 105
Nostalgia trap, 58
Nuclear family, 61, 63–64, 65–66,
    70–71
Nurture: for acceptance, 22; for
    adolescents, 238; alternative views
    of, 25–26; and culture, 35–36;
    excess amounts of, 35; function of,
    22–23; importance of, 22; link to
    latitude, 237; link to structure, 95,
    236; of mothers versus fathers, 48;
    needed increase in, 235–238; ori-
    gins of, 23–24; overview, 21–22;
    and parenting style, 40–43; school's
    reaction to deficits in, 26; and
    stress, 23–24; time required for,
    71–72; variance in, 35–36

O

Odoardi, A., 227
Oral sex, 88
Oregon, 7
Oremus, E., 208, 209, 212
Organizational coherence, 174–175
Orientation programs, 174, 183
Overprotective parents, 34, 42
Oxytocin, 44

P

Parent communication: directness in,
    215–217, 218; in parent-teacher

conferences, 215–221; preparation
    for, 222; professional development
    in, 208–217; shaping of, 217–218;
    training for teachers in, 200, 207.
    See also Communication
Parent disengagement. *See* Disengage-
    ment, of parents
Parent education: attendance at, 161,
    231; communication strategies for,
    173–174; current methods of, 161;
    expectations of, 162; goal of, 231–
    232; obstacles to, 161–162, 231;
    parent involvement in, 183–184;
    parents' readiness for, 161–162, 231
Parent involvement: and academic
    achievement, 182; appropriate
    tasks in, 184–185; benefits of, 184–
    185; in children's lives, 187–189;
    current view of, 177–178, 181–182;
    management of, 181; needed
    amount of, 183; in parent educa-
    tion, 183–184; in parent-teacher
    conferences, 185–187; in school
    governance, 179–181, 182; in
    school life, 184–187; in turnaround
    of low-performing school, 182;
    types of, 179
Parent-child interaction: amount of
    time necessary for, 78; and attune-
    ment, 24–25; of children in day
    care, 73; low-quality, 76–77;
    between mother and infant, 23–24
Parenting: amount of time necessary
    for, 78; books on, 17–18, 34–35,
    232; choice of work over, 121–123;
    and cost of freedom, 135–136;
    dimensions of, 249–250n.3; and
    economy, 118; emphasis on tech-
    niques for, 232–235; essentials of,
    18; by example, 247; goal of, 242;
    lack of direct, 70–72; need for more
    nurture in, 235–238; in nuclear
    versus fragile families, 63–64;
    parents, 178–179, 221–222;
    requirements of, 37, 78; versus
    work, 123–125

Parenting styles, 39–40, 44–50, 124, 240. *See also specific styles*
Parents: advice seeking from, 14–15, 178; assumptions of, 208–209; attitude of, toward school, 6; as cause of decline in appropriate behavior, 5–6; conduct expectations for, 171–173; confidence of, 208–209; demand for respect by, 82; division of tasks between, 43; factors affecting, 15; freedom of, 70; friction between adolescents and, 84–87, 242; friend selection by, 53–54; as friends, 95–96; guilt of, 95–96, 125–126; as home makers, 137; ideal, 43–44, 50; inability to play, 15; influence of, 154–155, 252n.22; knowledge of education, 180–181; lack of support for school from, 6–7; parenting, 178–179, 221–222; preference for work, 121–123; problem solving for children, 244–247; reliance on mutual authority, 83–84; respect for school, 182; response to children's inappropriate behavior, 11–12, 13–14; sincerity of, 208; as suitable partners for teachers, 178; teachers' increased contact with, 198–199; teachers' perceptions of, 15, 160–161; view of adolescents, 85–86; worries about peer pressure, 52. *See also* Fathers; Mothers
Parent-school partnership. *See* School-parent partnership
Parent-teacher conferences: administrators' intervention in, 221; communication strategies for, 215–221; impromptu, 221; parent involvement in, 185–187; preparation for, 222; teachers' anxiety about, 207–208; time in, 217–218
Parochial schools, 182
Parties, 87
Pattern-seeking, 192

Peer pressure, 28, 52–55
Peers. *See* Friends
Pennsylvania, 7
Permeable family, 61, 70, 95
Permissive parents, 41
Perseverance, 32, 33, 94
Personality, 52–53
Plagiarism, 11
Play: benefits of, 108–109; children's games as, 104, 108–109; of mothers versus fathers, 46; parents' inability to, 15
Pop psychology, 133–134
Pornography, 8, 88
Postman, N., 92, 93, 104, 244
Poverty: and friend selection, 54; and materialism, 120; in 1950s America, 59; and social capital, 52; and test scores, 155
Pregnancy, 48, 59
Premarital sex, 133
Premature infants, 148
Presley, E., 4, 5
Preventive programs, 162–165
Principals. *See* Administrators
Private information, 92
Problem solving: for children, 244–247; father's role in, 47; importance of, 31–32; and self-esteem, 32; of teachers, 210
Professional development, 200, 207, 208–217
Protection, 45
Protestant tradition, 129
Public Broadcasting System, 88
Public information, 92
Puritans, 36, 129
Purpose, of school, 165–170, 174–175, 182–184
Putnam, R., 51
Pygmalion in the Classroom (Rosenthal, R.), 154

Q
Quality time, 75–80

R

Readiness. *See* School readiness
Reading, promotion of, 188
Recess, 100
Reciprocity, 22, 23, 24
Reform. *See* School reform
Reich, R., 117, 118
Rejection, peer, 53
Religious schools, 182
Report cards, 101, 198
Resilience, 32, 247–248
Resistance: overview of, 197–200;
    roots of, 191–196; strategies to
    reduce, 200–205. *See also* Change
Respect, 82, 171, 172, 182
Résumé building, 101
Risky family, 64–65
Rituals, 79
Rogers, C., 211
Rogers, F., 22, 30, 235–238
Rosenthal, R., 154

S

Salaries, 117, 118
Schedules, 79, 102, 104–105, 108
School: blaming of, 146; and deficits
    in nurture, 26; efforts of, 224–226;
    goal of, 166–167; importance of,
    156; increased responsibility of,
    144; influence of, 153–154, 155;
    overview of problems in, 6; parents'
    attitude toward, 6; parents' lack of
    support for, 6–7; parents' respect
    for, 182; as part of child's overall
    education, 153; of past, 145;
    purpose of, 165–170, 174–175,
    182–184; response to behavior,
    160–161; size of, 170; skipping of,
    106; strengths of, 204–205; and
    testing movement, 100; time spent
    in, 3. *See also* Education
School readiness, 9–10, 73
School reform: beginnings of, 159–
    160; and bereavement, 194; com-
    prehensiveness of, 158; history of,

150–151; multiple initiatives for,
    150; questions for, 149–150. *See
    also* Change
School violence, 7. *See also* Violence
School-parent partnership, 178
Schor, J., 119
Secure attachment, 23
Segregation, 59
SEL. *See* Social-emotional learning
    (SEL)
Self-absorption, 133
Self-care, 74–75
Self-esteem: and behavior disorder,
    29; and consequences, 97; and dis-
    cipline, 30; function of structure in,
    29–30; importance of, 29; and over-
    protective parents, 34; and problem
    solving, 32; raising, 30
Self-fulfillment, 129, 133
Sexual behavior: biology of, 251n.5;
    early onset of, 87–88; examples of,
    8; exposure to, 88, 89, 90, 93;
    father's importance in avoiding, 48;
    influences on, 87; parents' resis-
    tance to, 86, 89; and peer pressure,
    54; and sexual revolution, 132–
    133; and unsupervised time, 87
Sexual revolution, 132–133
Sexually transmitted disease, 88
Shame, 92, 93
Shaping, 217–218
Shopping, 120
Shy children, 42
Silberman, C., 153
Single parents, 61, 62–63
Skills acquisition, 92
Skipping school, 106
Smoking, 62, 75
Social awareness, 9
Social capital: benefits of, 51–52; defi-
    nition of, 51; and friend selection,
    53–54; function of, 127–128
Social Capital Index, 252n.21
Social competence, 27–28, 164
Social context, 50–51
Social-emotional learning (SEL), 164

Socioeconomic status, 52

Special education: challenges of, 148–149; funding for, 149; inclusion effort in, 147–148, 257n.5; strengths of, 205

Sports: versus children's games, 104; competition in, 104–105; consequences of, 109–110; oversheduling of, 104–105, 108

Sports events, 7, 13–14, 105, 109

Staff development. *See* Professional development

Standard of living, 118

Stepfamilies: and abuse, 254n.13; effects of, 62–63; number of children with, 61

Stern, D., 24

Strengths, school, 204–205

Stress: and alcohol and drug use, 105; created by teachers, 102; and nurture, 23–24; reactions of mothers versus fathers, 44; and risky families, 65

Structure: and culture, 27, 35–36; definition of, 26; and delayed gratification, 28–29, 85; excess amounts of, 35; expansion of, 27; function of, 27–29; importance, 26–27; link to nurture, 95, 236; loss of, 81, 84–87; of mothers versus fathers, 49; and parenting style, 40–43; and parents' guilt, 95–96; template for, 238–243; variance in, 35–36. *See also* Expectations

Summer camps, 103

Swidler, A., 68

Syphilis, 88

T

Taylor, S., 64–65

Teachers: anxiety about parent-teacher conferences, 207–208; characteristics of, 194–196; feelings toward fragile family, 65; guilt of, 196; impromptu conversations with, 221; maternity leave of, 14; parental contact with, 198–199; parents as suitable partners for, 178; parents seeking advice from, 14–15, 178; perceptions of parents by, 15, 160–161; problem solving of, 210; resistance issues of, 194–200; stress created by, 102; threats to go above heads of, 220–221; as victims, 210; views of, 156; Web sites to harass, 93–94

Technology, 91–94, 117, 130–131. *See also specific technology*

Teens. *See* Adolescents

Television: amount of time spent watching, 89, 256n.11; effects of, 89–90; efforts to eliminate, 188–189; exposure to sexual activity on, 88, 89, 90; number of, 90; parents' resistance to, 86, 89, 90–91

Temperament, 20, 25

Test scores, 155

Testing: modifications, 147, 257n.5; movement for, 99–100; and No Child Left Behind Act, 151, 260n.4

Testosterone, 44, 253–254n.11

Time: loss of, 108; necessary amount of, 78, 236; in parent-teacher conferences, 217–218; quality versus quantity, 75–80; required for nurture, 71–72; spent at work, 115–116; spent by adolescents, 70, 87; spent in day care, 73; spent watching television, 89

Tocqueville, A. de, 54, 119, 129

Toddlers, 20, 98–99

Tone, of voice, 77–78, 83, 219

Town School, 166–167

Training, legal, 12–13

Transcripts, 101

Trillin, C., 233, 238–239, 240

Trust, 129–130, 131

Turnover rates, day care, 74

Tutoring, 103

U

Unconditional positive regard, 21
Unilateral authority, 81–83
Urbanity, 69, 83

V

Vacations, 13, 108
Values contract, 171–172
Values, family: character education
   for, 163–164; and college admission, 155; function of, 127–128;
   of group association, 129; in
   nuclear versus fragile families, 63;
   preventive programs for, 163–165;
   prioritizing, 239–243; and purpose
   of school, 166; and reciprocity,
   23
Values, school, 182, 183
van der Bogert, R., 168
Veblen, T., 119–120
Verbal intelligence, 47
Veteran teachers, 194–195, 197
Violence: effects of television on, 90;
   of latchkey children, 75; in 1950s
   America, 58; and social capital, 51.
   See also School violence

Voice, tone of, 77–78, 83, 219
Volunteering. *See* Parent involvement

W

Washington, 7
Web sites, 93–94. *See also* Internet
West, C., 71
Winnetka, Illinois, 168
Winnicott, D., 35
Wolfe, A., 138
Women, working. *See* Working mothers
Women's movement, 71
Work: current view of, 121–122; ver-
   sus parenting, 123–125; parents'
   anxiety about, 118–119; parents'
   preference for, 121–123; past prin-
   ciples of, 116–117; predictability of,
   116–117, 118–119; reversal with
   family, 123; time spent at, 115–116,
   258n.7
Workaholism, 116, 122
Working mothers: and absence of
   home maker, 137; history of, 59;
   number of, 62, 72; and time for
   nurture, 72; views of, 122
World War II, 26

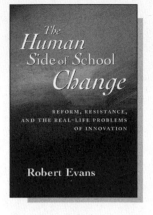

The Human Side of School Change
Reform, Resistance and the Real-Life Problems of Innovation
Robert Evans

Paperback/ 336 pages
ISBN: 0-7879-5611-2

"A unique, superb, and penetrating analysis of the human side of educational change. Evans knows the human realities of change and portrays them vividly in both individual and organizational terms. His discussion of hope and realism in the final chapter is a gem."
—Michael Fullan, dean, Faculty of Education, University of Toronto

"Evans has written a realistic yet hopeful book that sets a new standard for providing the leadership needed to implement school improvements. An engaging and much-needed update of the critical, but often overlooked, human side of change."
—Thomas J. Sergiovanni, Lillian Radford Professor of Education and senior fellow, Center for Educational Leadership, Trinity University

"School leaders will find this book realistic about the difficulties of change, rich in practical advice about school improvement, and useful in showing how to transcend the limits of their own experience to practice effective leadership."
—Thomas W. Payzant, superintendent, Boston Public Schools

In this insightful look at school reform, Robert Evans examines the real-life hurdles to implementing innovation and explains how the best-intended efforts can be stalled by educators who too often feel burdened and conflicted by the change process. *The Human Side of School Change* presents realistic advice on problem solving, communication, and staff motivation, offering a range of leadership strategies for building trust, confidence, capacity, and inspiration in schools. Evans provides a new model of leadership along with practical management strategies for building a framework of cooperation between leaders of change and the people they depend upon to implement it.

Robert Evans is a clinical and organizational psychologist and director of the Human Relations Service in Wellesley, Mass. A former high school and preschool teacher, he has consulted with hundreds of schools and districts throughout America and around the world and has worked extensively with teachers, administrators, school boards, and state education officials.

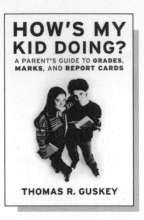

How's My Kid Doing?
A Parent's Guide to Grades, Marks, and Report Cards
Thomas R. Guskey

Paperback/ 176 pages
ISBN: 0-7879-6735-1

"The book is so eminently clear and sensible, it should be required reading for all educators and policymakers, not just parents. In jargon-free prose, Guskey strips away the murkiness surrounding grading and reporting, while never falling into oversimplification. There are many concrete suggestions for both writers and readers of reporting systems. A must for the faculty room as well as the family library."

—Grant Wiggins, president, Learning by Design

"Over the years, Tom Guskey is the teacher from whom I have learned the most about the principles of effective communication. He has consistently analyzed and articulated our communication options with immense clarity. He's done it again, this time for parents."

—Rick Stiggins, president, Assessment Training Institute

This book will help teachers talk with parents about their child's grades and report cards and give them the information they need to become better advocates and partners in their child's academic success. *How's My Kid Doing?* explains the advantages and shortcomings of different reporting methods, and offers strategies for teachers and parents working together to improve the system. It discusses plus and minus grades, grading on the curve, standards, and narrative evaluation. Thomas Guskey, the country's top expert on grading systems, provides concrete suggestions for improving school-home communications and shows how parents can help their children use report cards and other assessments as tools for improving their performance. He also reveals how newsletters, web pages, phone calls, open houses, and other school-home interactions can become effective means of better communication between teachers and parents.

Thomas R. Guskey is a professor of Educational Policy Studies and Evaluation at the University of Kentucky. He has taught at all school levels, worked as a school administrator in the Chicago Public Schools, and was the first director of the Center for the Improvement of Teaching and Learning, a national educational research center.

SUSAN MOORE JOHNSON
and
THE PROJECT ON THE NEXT GENERATION OF TEACHERS

FINDERS AND KEEPERS

*Helping New Teachers Survive and
Thrive in Our Schools*

Finders and Keepers
*Helping New Teachers Survive and
Thrive in Our Schools*
Susan Moore Johnson

Cloth/ 336 pages
ISBN: 0-7879-6925-7

*"Finders and Keepers brings new urgency and insight
to the questions "Who will teach our children?" and
"Will teachers stay in teaching?" At a time when expectations of teachers have never been higher or the challenges of teaching more daunting, Johnson and her
project team show how the choice to stay or leave is forged in the early months of becoming a teacher—through hiring practices, pay and other resources, relationships with students, colleagues or administrators, and opportunities for learning and leadership. This
book should compel attention from anyone concerned with the future of teaching."*
—Judith Warren Little, Carol Liu Professor in Education Policy,
University of California, Berkeley

This important and much-needed book is based on a longitudinal study of fifty
new teachers during their first years in the classroom. It highlights the cases
of ten, whose stories vividly illustrate the joys and disappointments of new teachers in today's schools. The book documents why they entered teaching, what they
encountered in their schools, and how they decided whether to stay or move on
to other schools or other lines of work. By tracking these teachers' eventual career
decisions, *Finders and Keepers* reveals what really matters to new teachers as they
set out to educate their students. The book uncovers the importance of the school
site and the crucial role that principals and experienced teachers play in the effective hiring and induction of the next generation of teachers.

Staffing the nation's schools presents both challenges and opportunities. For
teacher educators, district administrators, educational policymakers, teachers, principals, and staff development professionals, *Finders and Keepers* provides valuable
insights about how to better serve new teachers and the students they teach.

Susan Moore Johnson, a former high school teacher and administrator, is the
Pforzheimer Professor of Teaching and Learning at the Harvard Graduate School
of Education, where from 1993 to 1999 she served as academic dean. Johnson is a
member of the National Academy of Education and director of The Project on the
Next Generation of Teachers. She is the author of numerous articles and several
books, including *Teacher Unions in Schools* (Temple University Press), *Teachers at
Work* (Basic Books), and *Leading to Change* (Jossey-Bass).

Teaching with Fire
Poetry that Sustains the Courage to Teach
Sam M. Inrator and Megan Scribner

Cloth/ 256 pages
ISBN: 0-7879-6970-2

"Teaching with Fire *is a glorious collection of
the poetry that has restored the faith of teachers
in the highest, most transcendent values of their
work with children. . . . Those who want us to
believe that teaching is a technocratic and robotic
skill devoid of art or joy or beauty need to read
this powerful collection. So, for that matter, do
we all.*"

—Jonathan Kozol, author of
Amazing Grace and Savage Inequalities

Those of us who care about the young and their education must find ways to
remember what teaching and learning are really about. We must find ways to
keep our hearts alive as we serve our students. Poetry has the power to keep us vital
and focused on what really matters in life and in schooling.

Teaching with Fire is a wonderful collection of eighty-eight poems from well-
loved poets such as Walt Whitman, Langston Hughes, Billy Collins, Emily Dick-
inson, and Pablo Neruda. Each of these evocative poems is accompanied by a brief
story from a teacher explaining the significance of the poem in his or her life's
work. This beautiful book also includes an essay that describes how poetry can be
used to grow both personally and professionally.

Teaching with Fire was written in partnership with the Center for Teacher For-
mation and the Bill & Melinda Gates Foundation. Royalties will be used to fund
scholarship opportunities for teachers to grow and learn.

Sam M. Intrator is assistant professor of education and child study at Smith College. He is a former high school teacher and administrator and the son of two public school teachers. He is the editor of Stories of the Courage to Teach and author of
Tuned In and Fired Up: How Teaching Can Inspire Real Learning in the Classroom.

Megan Scribner is a freelance writer, editor, and program evaluator who has conducted research on what sustains and empowers the lives of teachers. She is the
mother of two children and PTA president of their elementary school in Takoma
Park, Maryland.